'Brilliant, timely and acutely aimed . . . a number of ingenious remedies' Robert Fox, *Evening Standard*

'Offers a compassionate but clear-eyed analysis. Its authors are unafraid to confront various bien-pensant shibboleths . . . an urgently topical and sensible guide to better future policy' Rupert Edis, *Literary Review*

'Betts and Collier offer innovative insights into how to more effectively meet the challenge, with an important new focus on international solidarity and refugee empowerment' Kofi Annan

'*Refuge* significantly raises the level of the current debate on asylum and migration. The book is full of ambitious proposals' Alessandro Casella, *Prospect*

'A rare and wonderful thing . . . Betts and Collier can look at the bigger picture. They may thereby have helped to improve millions of lives' David Goodhart, *Standpoint*

'Refugees and policy makers need practical answers to what is now a global crisis. This valuable book represents the kind of can-do thinking that we need to see' David Miliband, President and CEO of the International Rescue Committee

'Based on careful historical and economic analysis, *Refuge* proposes win-win-win improvements for the world's 20 million international refugees. *Refuge* is the seminal work on one of the world's most important problems' George Akerlof, Nobel Laureate in Economics 2001

'A brilliantly argued book . . . It's a call to action and it's absolutely needed' Sayeeda Warsi

'This book is both timely and radical. But it is also down-to-earth and practical. It is time to stop spouting the same old mantras about the existing refugee conventions and look at how we can best genuinely help refugees both now and in the future. Collier and Betts point the way' David Cameron

'A page-turner' Nomia Iqbal, BBC Asian Network

'Thank goodness for the wisdom, and humanity, of
Collier and Betts. They carefully map out a compelling plan
of action based on their observation that refugees bring with them
invaluable skills and resources. Every political leader, and every
citizen should read this book' Chris Anderson, Curator of TED

'A vital contribution to a discussion that should be at the top
of world leaders' agendas' *Kirkus Reviews*

'In the end, what's more important – doing good, or the
appearance of doing good? If we're as pure of heart as we like to
imagine, we'll seek out the policy that saves the most people, full stop.
And *Refuge* supplies an outstanding road map for getting us there'
The National Post

ABOUT THE AUTHORS

Paul Collier is the Professor of Economics and Public Policy at the
Blavatnik School of Government. His book, *The Bottom Billion*, won
the Lionel Gelber Prize, the Arthur Ross Prize awarded by the Council on
Foreign Relations, and the Corine Prize. Collier has served as Director of
the Research Department of the World Bank, and he is widely regarded
as one of the world's leading authorities on African development. His
other books include *The Plundered Planet* and *Exodus*.

Alexander Betts is Professor of Forced Migration and International
Affairs, and William Golding Senior Fellow in Politics at Brasenose
College, the University of Oxford. He served as Director of the Refugee
Studies Centre between 2014 and 2017. He has written for the *Guardian*, *New York Times* and *Foreign Affairs*. He has also given two TED
talks, which have garnered over three million views. He was named one
of *Foreign Policy*'s leading 100 global thinkers of 2016.

ALEXANDER BETTS AND PAUL COLLIER

Refuge

Transforming a Broken Refugee System

PENGUIN BOOKS

PENGUIN BOOKS

UK | USA | Canada | Ireland | Australia
India | New Zealand | South Africa

Penguin Books is part of the Penguin Random House group of companies
whose addresses can be found at global.penguinrandomhouse.com.

First published by Allen Lane 2017
Published in Penguin Books 2018
001

Set in 9.35/12.40 pt Sabon LT Std
Typeset by Jouve (UK), Milton Keynes
Printed in Great Britain by Clays Ltd, St Ives plc

A CIP catalogue record for this book is available from the British Library

ISBN: 978–0–141–98470–4

www.greenpenguin.co.uk

MIX
Paper from
responsible sources
FSC
www.fsc.org   FSC® C018179

Penguin Random House is committed to a
sustainable future for our business, our readers
and our planet. This book is made from Forest
Stewardship Council® certified paper.

Contents

List of Illustrations

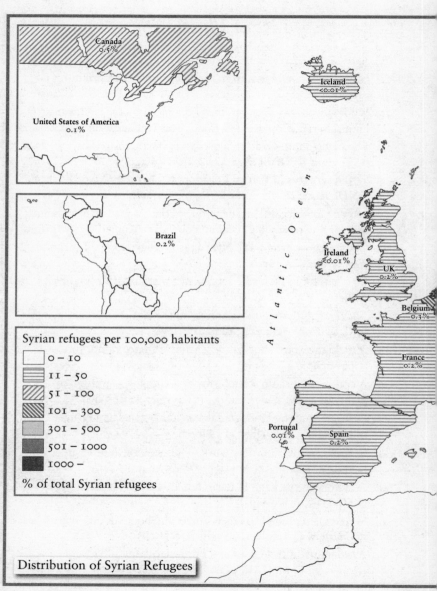

Canada
0.5%

Iceland
<0.01%

United States of America
0.1%

Brazil
0.2%

Ireland
<0.01%

UK
0.2%

Belgium
0.3%

France
0.2%

Atlantic Ocean

Portugal
0.01%

Spain
0.2%

Syrian refugees per 100,000 habitants

0 – 10
11 – 50
51 – 100
101 – 300
301 – 500
501 – 1000
1000 –

% of total Syrian refugees

Distribution of Syrian Refugees

Source: UNHCR

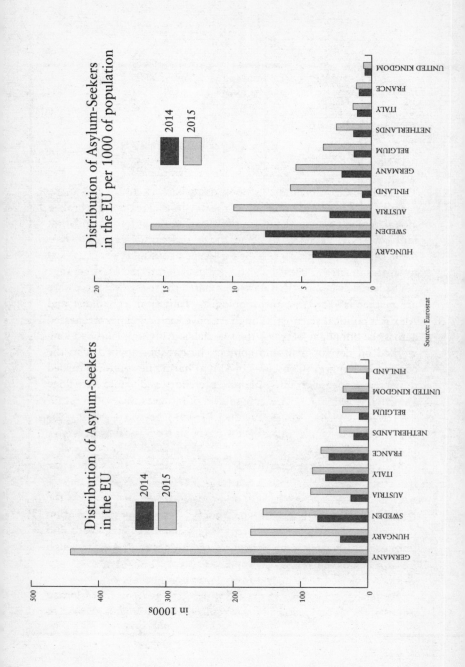

Distribution of Asylum-Seekers
in the EU

2014
2015

in 1000s

Distribution of Asylum-Seekers
in the EU per 1000 of population

2014
2015

Source: Eurostat

How We Came to Write This Book

The collaboration behind this book dates back to an invitation. By early 2015 Jordan was confronting the day-to-day reality of a broken global refugee system. Familiar with our work, a Jordanian think tank, WANA, asked us to come and brainstorm with the government. Neither of us was a Middle East expert: our main geographical interest is in Africa. We were also both outsiders to the narrow range of academic disciplines that have dominated the study of refugees: we are neither lawyers nor anthropologists. Paul is an economist and Alex is a political scientist, though we have each regularly trespassed across the boundary between the two fields. Although Paul had long worked on development and conflict, he had not applied it to the context of refugees. Conscious of 'do no harm', he routinely turned down requests to stray into unfamiliar territory and would have done so with this one. But to Alex the subject of refugees was not unfamiliar territory: it was his life's work. By 2015 he was directing the world's largest centre for refugee studies, at Oxford University. We became a team.

Arriving in Jordan that April, we found that with WANA we had landed on our feet. Its Director, Erica Harper, had all the knowledge of context that we lacked: and more, for her husband was the Director of UNHCR in Jordan. Andrew's impressive combination of vigour and intelligence was required: facing mounting needs and diminishing resources, his job was becoming impossible. Through Erica and Andrew we had ready access to the knowledge and networks we needed to remedy our own areas of ignorance.

We pitched an initially exploratory idea. The government of Jordan imposed the typical restrictions on refugees: they were not allowed to work. Jordan was also typical of many middle-income countries: not sufficiently poor to qualify for aid, but struggling to break beyond its current income level. We wondered whether the influx of refugees could be reconceived from being a burden to an opportunity for a new engagement with the international community. We floated the idea with NGOs, international organizations, and the government – all of whom were greatly frustrated by the dwindling levels of international support for refugees.

We visited Za'atari refugee camp, which reeked of lives on hold: a theme that will haunt this book. But in the course of our visit, serendipity lent a hand. With time to kill, our Jordanian official host suggested that we might care to see something entirely different of which the government was proud: just a brief detour. A mere fifteen minutes away, there it was: a different world. The King Hussain bin Talal Development Area (KHBTDA) had had £100m spent on it: a huge, well-equipped economic zone intended to attract business to this part of the country. The war across the border had intervened and it was only 10 per cent occupied: Jordanians didn't want to work there.

So, for four years, up to 83,000 refugees had sat in enforced idleness while fifteen minutes away a huge zone was empty for lack of workers. The combined intellectual resources of two Oxford professors managed to add two and two: with some appropriate international support, everyone could be better off. We soon realized that the idea could be extended around the country: there were zones and refugees all over the place. And was Jordan unique? Perhaps the same approach could work elsewhere. Of course, it was not a panacea: any conceivable initiative is going to face many practical impediments. But it was worth piloting in a few places. The Jordanian government was interested: it was time to move from an idea to a practical policy.

The typical lag between an academic idea and practical implementation is either years or eternity. But by the summer of 2015 the refugee situation was escalating into crisis: we needed a shortcut. We decided to write pieces that would be published quickly and read widely. By August we had the cover story of *The Spectator*, and by November a flagship piece in *Foreign Affairs*. They got noticed and, *faute de mieux*, their ideas were taken up. By January 2016 they were being pitched to the world's business leaders at Davos. By February, they were adopted officially at a conference in London jointly convened by the King of Jordan, David Cameron and the President of the World Bank. The so-called Jordan Compact launched a pilot project to create 200,000 jobs for Syrian refugees alongside Jordanian nationals, including in some of the economic zones. The success of that pilot now depends on the politicians.

But we wanted to broaden the scope of our reflection beyond Jordan. Behind the Jordan-related brainstorming lay a set of ideas for how to rethink a failing refugee system. Our approach is not simply to roll out the Jordanian pilot: all contexts are different. But there are broader ideas to carry forward: the argument that refuge is as much a development issue as a humanitarian issue, the focus on restoring refugees' autonomy through jobs and education, the emphasis on creating sustainable safe havens in the countries that host the majority of the world's refugees, the recognition of a role for business alongside government and civil society, and the desire to reconsider refugee assistance for a world utterly different from that for which the existing refugee system was originally designed.

Our original visit to Jordan coincided almost exactly with the start of the European 'refugee crisis'. That April, 700 people – mainly from refugee-producing countries – drowned crossing the Mediterranean, in what began a year of unprecedented refugee movements to Europe. The 1 million refugees to arrive in Europe during 2015 triggered an unheard-of demand for creative policy responses. And yet the more time elapsed, and the worse the crisis became, the greater the vacuum of policy ideas seemed to become.

By the end of 2015 there was almost unanimity that the existing refugee system was broken, and that a new approach was needed. But the vision was lacking. It was at that point that Laura Stickney from Penguin approached us with the idea for us to co-author a book on the refugee crisis to explain its origins and propose practical solutions. After some reflection – both of us already had significant writing commitments – we embraced the suggestion, recognizing it as an opportunity to outline our ideas in detail and contribute to the search for a more effective refugee system, fit for purpose in the twenty-first century.

Our goal has been to write for a generalist audience, to engage intelligent and interested members of the public keen to understand the origins of the 'refugee crisis' and to explore with us ideas for workable solutions. We also hope that a part of our readership will be policy-makers themselves. This work is not intended to be esoteric or idealistic; it aspires to be practical and realistic. It seeks to work with the constraints and opportunities of the contemporary world, and to channel them into a system that can provide refugees with autonomy and dignity, while meeting the concerns of host communities and the imperatives of democratic scrutiny.

All academic co-authors bring different starting points to a collaboration. We have been asked how two authors who have expressed different perspectives on aspects of migration came to agree on the book's core arguments. The answer is that we discussed, deliberated and debated. We reasoned through, based on the evidence, until we reached agreement. Both of us found this enriching and enlightening, and often ended up rethinking our original positions.

In writing the book we have tried to strike a balance between the responsibility to write thoughtfully and accurately on an issue that affects people's lives, and the urgency to engage. Most of the writing was done during the summer of 2016. We are especially grateful to our families, and above all Emily and Pauline – who also read and commented on several drafts – for their willingness to sacrifice a large part of our summer to writing.

We are also grateful to several of our colleagues, in Oxford and beyond, who have directly or indirectly shaped ideas in the book. These include Elizabeth Collett, Stefan Dercon, Matthew Gibney, James Milner, Naohiko Omata, and Olivier Sterck. More generally, Paul is grateful to colleagues at the Blavatnik School of Government and Alex to those at the Refugee Studies Centre and the Department of International Development. Finally, we'd like to thank James Pullen at the Wiley Agency for enabling us to place our ideas in the hands of our excellent publishers, and Laura Stickney at Penguin for her exceptional editing of the manuscript.

Introduction

We live in disturbed times. There are more people displaced than at any time since the Second World War. Most of these 65 million uprooted people remain within their own countries, but nearly a third – over 20 million – had no alternative but to cross a border. When they did, they became refugees.

They are fleeing mass violence in chronically fragile states like Syria, Afghanistan, and Somalia. Refugees are not like other migrants: they are not moving for gain but because they have no choice. They are seeking safety abroad. For the most part, refugees stay in the countries close to home. Almost 90 per cent of refugees are in havens in the developing world, and just ten of these countries host around 60 per cent of the world's refugees. Several of them – countries like Iran, Ethiopia, and Jordan – have been repeat hosts over decades. These havens are not atypically generous: they are simply located in a 'rough neighbourhood'.

Until recently, the world largely ignored the plight of refugees. The default response was for rich countries to wait for an emergency and then contribute money to the United Nations humanitarian system. This money was spent on establishing refugee camps providing food, clothing, and shelter until people could go home. These camps were always designed as if they were just for the short term. Invariably refugees lack the right to work or move freely; but being out of sight, they were out of mind. This might have made sense if refugees were able to go home relatively soon. But since the end of the Cold War, the average duration of exile has been over a decade and so the default response has been hopeless. Condemning millions of people to wasting their lives, this approach has contrived the rare folly of being both inhumane and expensive.

*

Then suddenly in April 2015 something changed. Something happened that was so alarming that the world woke up. There had been no overnight escalation in the number of refugees in the world. What changed was that, for the first time, refugees moved spontaneously in large numbers from the poorer regions of the world to the richest. With mass violence in Syria since 2011, some 10 million people had been displaced: 6 million within their own country and 4 million to neighbouring countries. Initially most had not moved further afield than Jordan, Lebanon, and Turkey. But since there are limited opportunities for Syrian refugees in those countries, the dynamic began to change.

For the first time in its history, Europe received a mass influx of refugees from outside of the European region. During the course of 2015, over a million asylum-seekers would come to Europe. The majority came from Syria but many also came from other fragile states like Afghanistan and Iraq, as well as a range of sub-Saharan African countries. At first, the primary route to Europe was the Central Mediterranean: people got in small boats in Libya and travelled across to the Italian island of Lampedusa. Then it became the Western Balkans: increasing numbers of Syrians crossed the Aegean Sea from Turkey to Greece and made their way on foot towards Germany.

From that April, when 700 people drowned crossing to Lampedusa, the media began to proclaim a 'global refugee crisis'. But in reality this was a European crisis. And it was a crisis of politics rather than a crisis of numbers. The response was muddled and incoherent; European politicians struggled desperately even to identify the real problem, let alone to find solutions to it. And this in turn led to tragedy and chaos across Europe. During that year, over 3,000 people, including many children, drowned while trying to reach Europe on rickety boats manned by gangs whose core business was migrant-smuggling.

Instead of cooperating on a coherent plan, European governments resorted to unilateral panic decisions, their policies being shaped more by the domestic politics of the moment than the search for collective solutions. Greece became the main reception country, its islands overwhelmed, though few refugees aimed to stay there: instead they moved north. Hungary built a razor wire fence to keep them out.

But Germany's response was quite different: from the summer of 2015 Chancellor Merkel effectively offered an open door. Unsurprisingly many more came, and not just from Syria. Perhaps Chancellor Merkel had expected other states to follow her lead. If so, the expectation was misplaced: not sharing Germany's unique history, they didn't. As hundreds of thousands came to Germany, the domestic political situation shifted radically. Within months of the open door, Chancellor Merkel had backtracked dramatically, returning thousands of people caught in transit, to Turkey. As public confidence in the asylum system – intended to distinguish 'refugees' from broader movements of people – collapsed, far-right parties gained growing support, and by early 2016 Europe had virtually closed its doors.

But while this catastrophe was absorbing political and media attention, the parallel tragedy was the neglect of the nearly 90 per cent of the world's refugees who remained in the developing world. The most vulnerable, with no means or desire to travel to Europe, remained in an utterly dysfunctional system. For every $135 of public money spent on an asylum-seeker in Europe, just $1 is spent on a refugee in the developing world.*[1] Fewer than one in ten of the 4 million Syrian refugees in Turkey, Lebanon, and Jordan receive *any* material support from the United Nations or its implementing partners. Moreover, most refugees around the world do not have the basic autonomy necessary to help themselves and their communities: they are not allowed to work. They are left dependent on a system that fails them.

When international agencies don't know what else to do they convene a conference. Despite a series of these high-level conferences convened by the United Nations there is still no clear strategy for the future of the global refugee system.

What, in the twenty-first century, should the world do about refugees? In this book, we seek to answer that question. To get there we start by diagnosis: why is the global refugee system not working today? From that base we suggest what needs to be done to build a system that works.

---

* Figures are in US dollars throughout.

THE PURPOSE OF REFUGE

Before that, though, we need to consider what refuge is for. There have been refugees for as long as there have been political communities. There is documentary evidence of people who needed to flee city-states in Ancient Greece or Rome in search of sanctuary. Since the creation of nation-states, often dated to 1648 and the Treaty of Westphalia, factors such as religious persecution, revolution, state formation, and conflict have occasionally left people needing to leave home in order to survive. At its core, refuge entails the principle that when people face serious harm at home, they should be allowed to flee and receive access to a safe haven, at least until they can go home or be permanently reintegrated elsewhere.

The modern refugee system was designed in the late 1940s. With the onset of the Cold War in 1948, the societies of Eastern Europe found themselves behind the Iron Curtain. Led by the USA, the concern of Western democracies was for opponents of the Communist regimes imposed on these societies by the Soviet Union. The purpose of the refugee system was that the people who were persecuted by these regimes should have the right to live elsewhere, and to be well cared for while a new home could be arranged. Through an international treaty now signed by 145 countries – the 1951 Convention on the Status of Refugees – and an international organization – the Office of the United Nations High Commissioner for Refugees (UNHCR) – governments committed to reciprocally allow people fleeing persecution onto their territories. Reflecting its intention, the legal definition of a refugee was someone who is outside her or his country of nationality and faces a 'well-founded fear of being persecuted for reasons of race, religion, nationality, membership of a particular social group or political opinion'. It was unambiguously a product of its time and place, explicitly temporary and at the time intended only to apply to people in Europe.

Time did not stand still. Refuge is as relevant today as it was in the late 1940s: the numbers speak for themselves. But both the causes of flight and the appropriate responses to flight have changed radically. Some refugees are indeed still fleeing persecution by their state. But the overwhelming majority are now fleeing disorder: the fallout from state breakdown. Some refugees still need temporary food and shelter and some need to be resettled permanently in a new country. But most need a haven where they can earn a living until they are able to return home once order has been restored.

The world has changed radically since 1948. As other global institutions designed in the late 1940s hit crisis, they were reformed. But, being out of sight, refugees never received the global attention needed for major change. The Convention and UNHCR are still there, ever less appropriate for modern needs. In the absence of root-and-branch reform, they have drifted into piecemeal adjustments.

In a classic instance of Eurocentrism, a convention explicitly focused on state persecution of individuals in postwar Europe was applied globally and permanently in 1967 without modification. Unsurprisingly, several of the countries that provide the main havens for refugees – notably those in the Middle East and Asia – have not signed it, believing it not to fit the realities of refuge in their regions. Elsewhere, its wording has since been tortured into reinterpretations stretched to fit new circumstances. With wide variation in legal interpretation, policy coherence has been lost. Court rulings have become eccentric: refugees in identical circumstances will be granted asylum in the courts of some nations but refused it in others; even within the same country, they will be granted asylum in some years but not others. Eccentricity is compounded by systematic omissions. For fifteen years, Somalis fleeing the ultimate state collapse did not qualify for asylum in some European countries because they had not been 'persecuted'. What began as coherent common rules for responding to persecution have evolved into chaotic and indefensible responses to the problem of mass flight from disorder.

Meanwhile, UNHCR found itself faced with refugee situations that had not been envisaged. A model intended for the temporary care of the persecuted was confronted with a mass flight from violence. In response to these emergencies UNHCR came up with a quick fix: camps. Designed for transience, by default they became permanent.

These legacy regimes bequeathed by the Cold War were the full extent of what was available to address the Syrian refugee situation that began in 2011. Their utter inadequacy was reflected in what ensued over the next four years. Unsurprisingly, the situation escalated into an unmanageable crisis.

Though a product of the Cold War, the Convention has noble aims, and some of its principles remain as relevant today. But arcane disputes about how words in a treaty can be reinterpreted to fit today's challenges miss the central point. The world of the twenty-first century must meet the needs of refugees. And this will be achieved not by pious adherence to the dictums of a bygone era, but by rising to the current challenge, just as our grandparents rose to the very different challenge that they faced. Left to lawyers alone, the limited global energy available for the reform of the refugee system will be dissipated, and so will the limited budgets. The way forward is not to reinterpret past wording, but to build a new system that works. We need an international agency that can guide this task of building anew. UNHCR is not currently equipped to be that agency, but it must become so.

There is a core to that new task in common with the one addressed in 1948. Put simply, refuge is about fulfilling a duty of rescue. Born out of our common humanity, it is based on the simple recognition that we have shared obligations towards our fellow human beings. Just as we cannot stand by and watch a stranger in our own community suffering, so too we have obligations towards distant strangers, when we are able to assist and it is not significantly costly to do so. The content of that obligation should involve meeting immediate needs and then returning people to normality as quickly as possible thereafter.

But during the current refugee crisis, we have lost sight of this underlying purpose. Refuge has become bound up with a broader, and distracting, discussion about the right to migrate. The policy and media focus has been on the 10 per cent who try to reach the developed world, rather than the 90 per cent who do not. 'Do refugees have a right to travel directly to Europe?' has been the main question within public debate. Yes, of course refugees have a right to migrate insofar as it is necessary in order to access a safe haven. But it is not an unqualified right to move. It becomes necessary only inasmuch as as we collectively fail to create a system that ensures refugees' needs are met in a coherent way. Refugees – as refugees – need and should be entitled to expect three things: rescue, autonomy, and an eventual route out of limbo. Currently, the majority of refugees are not getting any of them.

How can we provide these things sustainably and at scale? This is the critical question this book seeks to answer.

THE BROKEN SYSTEM

Even according to its own metrics, the refugee system is failing badly. The founding statute of UNHCR outlines two main roles: to provide protection to refugees and to find long-term solutions to their plight. Yet neither is being met.

Protection entails ensuring refugees get access to their core rights and needs in exile. But humanitarian assistance programmes around the world are desperately underfunded: even basic food rations are being cut year on year. In urban areas assistance is even more limited. Contrary to popular belief, most refugees are not in camps; over half now live in large cities like Nairobi, Johannesburg, and Beirut. The international community has still not adopted an adequate model for assistance outside camps. Despite the fancy international edifice of agencies, and the warm glow of media attention around them, *most* of the world's refugees receive virtually no material assistance at all from any of them.

This would not be such a problem but for the fact that there is almost universal non-compliance with the socio-economic rights specified in the Convention. Most host states place serious restrictions on the right to work; nor are these the only parts of the Convention that are ignored. From Australia to Kenya to Jordan to Hungary, governments turn away refugees at the border, or threaten to expel them, without even assessing their claims.

Solutions are generally used to imply a pathway out of intractable limbo. It is widely accepted that no refugee should have to remain indefinitely warehoused in a camp. Conventionally, there have been three recognized 'durable solutions' – repatriation when the conflict ends or there is political transition; resettlement to a third country; and local integration if the host country is prepared to offer a pathway to citizenship. Historically, different solutions have been preferred at different junctures. During the Cold War, the assumption was generally that refugees from the East would be permanently resettled in the West. After the Cold War, the focus shifted to creating the conditions to enable people to go home. Today, the route to durable solutions is largely blocked. In 2015, fewer than 2 per cent of the world's refugees received access to one of the durable solutions.

The international system has therefore become long-term humanitarian aid. A response designed for the short-term emergency phase of a crisis too often endures over the long term. Today over half of the world's refugees are in 'protracted refugee situations' and for them the average length of stay is over two decades. People are born into camps, grow up in camps, and become adults in camps. Without durable solutions, their lives become focused more on survival than hope.

Let's take the example of Amira, a Syrian refugee whose situation is typical of many. Amira is a woman with children, like around a quarter of the world's refugees. She can't go home, because her home has been destroyed – she comes from the city of Homs. She won't be resettled to a third country: less than 1 per cent of the world's refugees will be lucky enough to get that lottery ticket. So she has an impossible choice between three options.

She can do what just 9 per cent of Syrian refugees have done, and go and live in a camp. Assistance may be available but camps offer few prospects. They are in bleak, arid locations. In the now infamous Za'atari refugee camp, you can still hear the sound of mortars across the border late at night. Economic activity is restricted and, globally, over 80 per cent of refugees living in camps end up stuck there for at least five years. Alternatively, Amira could do what more than three quarters of Syrian refugees are currently doing, and live in an urban area in a neighbouring country. But assistance is limited, the formal right to work is usually restricted, and destitution is common. Most host countries refuse to consider permanent local integration. So she's got a third choice which an increasing number of Syrians are taking – trying to give her family some hope of a future by risking death to travel onwards to another country. And that's what we've seen in Europe.

Around the world, these three options represent the impossible choice with which we present refugees: long-term encampment, urban destitution, or perilous journeys. For refugees, these options *are* the global refugee regime. The twenty-first century can do better than this. What we need is not to return to the ideas of the late 1940s, but to harness the remarkable opportunities of globalization that did not exist at that time to meet the needs of our new situation. Host governments should not simply be browbeaten into compliance. They limit the choices available because they perceive refugees to be a security threat and an economic burden. And who can blame them when they take on such a large population and receive so little support from the international community?

THE NEED FOR A NEW APPROACH

The moment for a rethink is long overdue. Historically it has proven hard to transform the international system but there is one exception: moments of crisis. In 1971 the international monetary system underwent fundamental reform because governments reached a point at which the costs of the status quo were so great as to make continuity unconscionable. This is not the only example of change: at the end of the Cold War, global trade governance was radically reformed; with the emergence of climate change new institutions have been rapidly negotiated; faced with financial crisis, global leaders agreed in 2009 to replace the G8 with the G20 as the world's economic coordinator. We have now reached the refugee regime's '1971 moment'. The 2015 crisis has triggered recognition that the status quo is simply not in anyone's interests, and a new institutional architecture is needed.

Targeted persecution remains a real threat for a minority, but the overwhelming majority of refugees are fleeing a single cause: insecurity in fragile states. The relevant threats are to groups from violent areas rather than from states to targeted individuals.

Nor is the political situation like the late 1940s. The Cold War is long over: extremist religion has replaced extremist ideology, bringing completely different fears. Across much of Europe and the developed world, there has been a collapse in public support for asylum. Nor is this unique to the developed world; many host states in the developing world are finding it hard to sustain domestic political support for large-scale hosting.

Nor are the opportunities restricted to those of the late 1940s. New opportunities offer scope for solutions. Most refugees want to work and find ways of doing so, forgoing camps for urban areas even if it means relying on their own support networks. The globalized economy offers possibilities unimaginable seventy years ago. The internet can enable jobs, education, and money transfer to reach even the remotest communities. There are new actors: business, civil society, diaspora organizations, and refugee-led community organizations are all helping to meet refugees' needs. There are new techniques: from school choice to food banks to organ donations, creative models of institutional design are solving allocation problems.

Time has passed the refugee system by: it is now in a time-warp. But to address emerging challenges and seize potential opportunities, a new paradigm is urgently needed. The existing model is mired in collective action failure, and bereft of new thinking. The conferences convened to 'do something' about the refugee crisis – from the World Humanitarian Summit to the UN High-Level Meeting on Addressing Large Scale Movements of Refugees and Migrants – are ritual re-enactments that changed times have drained of real consequence. Not only is there a lack of practical new thinking, but the very institutions that should be generating it are clinging desperately on to the status quo.

One of the main themes in this book is the idea that refuge must be understood as not only a humanitarian issue but also one of development. Put simply, it is not just about indefinitely providing food, clothing, and shelter. It has to be about restoring people's autonomy through jobs and education, particularly in the countries in the developing world that repeatedly host the overwhelming majority of refugees. If this is done well, we argue, everyone stands to gain and refugees can be empowered to help themselves and contribute to their societies.

But there is no one-size-fits-all solution; different models will be effective for different countries. What works in Uganda will not be what works in Jordan. The key is to find models that simultaneously benefit host states and refugees, while enabling safe havens to remain politically viable. But we recognize that investing in autonomy in neighbouring countries is not sufficient. Although ideally refugees will eventually return home, sometimes they just won't be able to, at least not within a reasonable period. At that point, a pathway out of limbo – including through resettlement – remains imperative.

In this book we do three things. In Part I we take you back through the current refugee crisis, step by increasingly grim step, as a modern Greek tragedy unfolds. We show why, given the policies and institutions inherited from the late 1940s, this tragedy was inevitable.

In Part II we show that it does not have to be like this. An alternative approach is there for the building. We present four big new ideas – relating to the duty of rescue, safe havens, autonomy in exile, and post-conflict incubation – with a chapter for each of them beginning with moral values. There, and throughout the book, we eschew moral grandstanding: we do not preach the moral standards of sainthood. Far from it: we set out the minimal moral norms that are necessary for a refugee response that meets a few basic requirements. A disastrous consequence of the crisis is that the refugee issue has got tangled up with the amorphous and divisive topics of globalization and migration. Part of our purpose is to restore refuge to its proper place as a well-defined task that is well within our capacities to undertake, and that an overwhelming majority of mankind can agree upon.

Dag Hammarskjöld once said of the United Nations, it 'was not created to take mankind to heaven, but to save humanity from hell'. We have an analogously modest ambition. The saintly can go beyond what we propose, and we will cheer them along; but our book is for people who privately might recognize that their moral standards are typical rather than exceptional.

Just as we eschew moral grandstanding, so we eschew dreams of global government. The world is as it is: a menagerie of states with different interests and different capacities. They find cooperative action difficult. We try, within the constraints of being thinkers rather than doers, to suggest how such world might go about meeting the needs of refuge. It does not require grand new structures, just that enough politicians focus on it for a while. In Part III we rerun the history of the crisis and show how the approach we suggest would have made a difference. While that is water under the bridge, there is a lot of the future left.

PART I: WHY IS THERE A CRISIS?

I

Global Disorder

Global refugee numbers are at their highest since the early 1990s:[1] 21.3 million people. As if this were not bad enough, the typical focus on refugees leads to a radical underestimation of the disruption to people's lives caused by violent disorder. To be classified as a refugee you have to cross an international border. Many people fleeing violence are in no position to do that. The pertinent underlying phenomenon is displacement, not refuge. Measured by the number of people who have been displaced from their homes by violence, the total is far higher: 65.3 million. This is the highest figure ever recorded. It is even the highest proportion of the world's population ever recorded: one person in every 113.[2] Global modernity has not only produced technological miracles like the iPhone, and more than 1,800 billionaires; it has broken all records for the human tragedies that constitute displacement. How can this be?

In the past seventy years the world has experienced the most extraordinary period of sustained economic growth in history. This has transformed living standards. People not only have higher incomes, but have much better health, and are much better educated and informed. That this unprecedented spread of prosperity has coincided with a massive increase in the numbers seeking refuge is even more extraordinary. It demands explanation.

It is tempting to relate the record number of displaced with the record number of billionaires. But facile explanations about the rich getting richer while the poor have got poorer will not do. Most people today, not just the billionaires, are much better off than our forebears alive in 1945. Furthermore, in terms of global divergence, the bad decades were those early in the period when around a score of rich countries left everyone else behind. By the 1980s there was a grim cliff between a rich world and a poor world with little in between. Since the 1990s, global inequality has been falling rapidly as most other countries have started to catch up. The most spectacular cases have been China and India, home to a third of mankind. But this trend is widespread; once impoverished and conflict-devastated societies like Vietnam, Rwanda and Colombia are now peaceful and have achieved rapidly rising living standards. Most countries are now somewhere in the middle. So, global economic developments look to be unpromising as an explanation for the upsurge in displacement. What else might it be?

WHAT DRIVES DISPLACEMENT AND REFUGE?

People seeking refuge are not fleeing poverty, *they are fleeing danger*. The flight for refuge happens when a society ceases to provide security for its people. For one reason or another, it falls into violent disorder. During the decade 1935–45 Europe fell into such disorder. The rise of fascism made Germany dangerous for Jews, and triggered a civil war in Spain. An analogous ideology in Japan supported an invasion of China. Each of these events created huge civilian dislocations. Then the Second World War ravaged entire regions. But the dangers that have produced the current vast refugee problem have had very different origins.

This, indeed, is the first big awkward fact about mass violence: many different circumstances can bring it about. Violent societies are analogous to Tolstoy's unhappy families: they each become violent in their own way.[3] They are best defined by what they are not: safe for ordinary people.

No society is completely safe. In the USA black men face a heightened risk of being shot by the police; in Saudi Arabia adulterous women are at risk of being stoned; in Russia it would be unwise to denounce President Putin. Each of these is reprehensible, and a worthy focus of concern. In some cases, when individual risk is severe and targeted, people may need to seek asylum. But, for the most part, this is not what is driving the flight to refuge – it is vital to distinguish mass violence from such manifestations of individual insecurity. Mass violence is rare; insecurities are pervasive. A failure to delineate mass violence properly would drive us to seek 'solutions' in the construction of some imagined idyllic society: idealized versions of Sweden or Montana according to taste. The desperation that leads people to abandon their homes to seek refuge is too serious a phenomenon for such romanticism. So our focus is on the circumstances in which a society collapses into mass violence; not those in which awful things happen to some people.

Even with this tourniquet around the problem, mass violence has numerous causes.

The traditional source of violence is inter-state conflict. The violence that dislocated civilian life in China in the 1930s, Russia in the 1940s, and Korea in the 1950s happened because of invasions from hostile neighbours. Hence, one condition for security is that a country be sufficiently strong militarily to protect itself from invasion by foreign enemies. Many countries may not even have such enemies.

If mass violence is not brought from abroad, it must originate at home. Such disorder is unusual and only comes about if two very different sources of internal security both fail at the same time.

The most attractive source of internal security is legitimacy. Most states, whether democratic or not, have sufficient legitimacy in the eyes of their citizens for people to be willing to comply with the rules. Those states whose legitimacy is accepted by a large majority of citizens need far fewer resources in order to enforce their rules. Britain can get by with a small and unarmed police force; North Korea needs the capacity for state violence against individual citizens to be so substantial as to be a constant reminder.

Yet, despite lacking legitimacy, North Korea has not collapsed into mass violence. Kim III maintains order in the same way as Kim II and Kim I: by brute repression. Brute repression threatens mass violence against citizens: were there to be an uprising, people would probably be slaughtered in their thousands, but the threat is *latent*. It is so awful, and so credible, that it does not need to be used.

Evidently, what matters for domestic security is the extent of state legitimacy relative to the capacity of the state for coercive force. All states need *some* coercive force because no government, however inclusive and responsive, wins universal acceptance. All societies include recalcitrant oddballs who regard their grievances as licence for violence. On conventional criteria, Sweden in the 1980s is about as close as any state has ever come to Earthly perfection. But this did not prevent its Prime Minister, Olof Palme, from being shot dead in the street. Both legitimacy and coercive force reduce the risk of collapse into mass violence, and so there is a trade-off. A state can maintain the security of its citizens with very little coercive force if it has high legitimacy, or with very little legitimacy if it has sufficient coercive force.

In delineating the conditions for security we have also delineated its antithesis: fragility. A fragile state is a poor country marked by weak state capacity and legitimacy. There is a striking correlation between levels of fragility and levels of displacement. Fragile states are those that have no defence against mass violence. They are not invariably beset by mass violence: but each is a house of cards.

Fragility is the single most salient cause of displacement around the world today. Even factors that may become increasingly common drivers of flight like climate change and natural disasters are only likely to cause mass cross-border movements if they affect fragile states. When Hurricane Katrina struck New Orleans it did not require people to leave the United States. In contrast, when the earthquake struck Haiti many people fled to the neighbouring Dominican Republic because they could not find a domestic remedy or resolution to their situation.

Our opening question, however, was not 'which states are fragile?' but 'why has mass violence increased?' In effect, why might exposure to fragility have increased despite the wide diffusion of global economic growth?

WHY HAS FRAGILITY INCREASED?

The reasons for fragility are complex. We will not find a single big cause, which if only it was fixed would reverse the upsurge. Even Bush and Blair will not serve, other than as being responsible for those refugees from Iraq. President Obama and virtually all other leaders agree that Afghanistan was a 'war of necessity', and by the time of the Arab Spring both Bush and Blair were out of office. We need to look beyond pantomime villains. Fragility has increased because of a combination of several major global changes: we suggest five of them. In each case, their effects on fragility have been incidental to their rationale. An implication is that there are no easy fixes. Humpty cannot be restored to his seat on the wall.

MAD no more

Paradoxically, one factor might have been the end of the Cold War between the Warsaw Pact and NATO. The Cold War was defined by fear of 'mutual assured destruction' (MAD) from nuclear weapons, something that people who have grown up after 1991 find it hard to appreciate. Both sides recruited allies, so a conflict almost anywhere might draw in the superpowers and escalate, as had happened at the onset of the First World War. This made even conflicts in out-of-the-way places potentially so dangerous that they were discouraged. Broadly, each superpower was allowed to keep its client regimes in power. Low-level proxy wars took place across client countries, but governments across Africa, Latin America, and South-East Asia maintained relatively strong state capacity as the US and the Soviet Union poured in money and weapons. With the end of the Cold War there was no longer an overarching need to do so: the lid was taken off. From Sierra Leone to Somalia to Bosnia, reduced state capacity contributed to mass violence.[4]

Quite possibly this mattered in Syria, which had long been a client state of Russia. During the Cold War it would most likely have been understood by Washington and its allies that significant regime change in Syria would be resisted militarily by Russia and so was too dangerous to encourage. But by 2011 such behaviour seemed long past. When the Arab Spring first spread to Syria, the American Ambassador did not feel inhibited in addressing a protest with expressions of support. Nor was the rejection of the notion of a Russian sphere of influence confined to the Middle East. The European Union embarked upon encouraging Ukraine to take the first steps towards membership. In each case this led to two distinct phases of mass violence. In the first phase, there was violent internal resistance: in Syria the regime used violence against the protesters, while in Ukraine a violent insurgent group emerged in the eastern provinces opposed to the protest-generated new government in the west. In the second phase, Russia intervened militarily: in Syria with its air force, and in Ukraine with disguised ground troops.

The democratic peace?

A second paradoxical factor might have been the spread of democracy following the fall of the USSR. In Western societies democracy, understood as elections matched by checks and balances on the use of power, has long been accepted as conferring legitimacy, and, with the West triumphant, it was somewhat glibly assumed that this was a global truth. Democratic accountability of governments to their citizens would eliminate the grievances that were the cause of internal violence against the state.

Following the fall of the Soviet Union, democracy appeared to spread rapidly around the world. But what actually spread around the world was the practice of holding an election. Elections are events that can be held in virtually any circumstances. In contrast, the checks and balances on the use of elected power which are an integral part of the long-established democracies are not events but processes, and they take time and continuous struggle to establish. Currently, many societies have a lopsided democracy in which checks on power are too weak to prevent majorities from abusing minorities. In around a third of elections the checks on power are too weak to prevent voting malpractices that can enable minorities to abuse majorities.[5] Further, in some societies there is too little sense of shared identity to give life to the notion of the common good: 'we' means 'our group' not 'our nation'. Power, whether won through violence or an election, is used for the same end: redistribution to 'us' from 'them'. In none of the above circumstances will an election turn power into legitimate authority, and so the costs of enforcing compliance with the state will not fall.

However, while the rapid spread of lopsided democracy did not turn out to be the holy oil that anointed governments with legitimacy, it did reduce the coercive power of the state. For literally thousands of years autocrats have understood the most effective forms of coercion. One tried-and-tested rule is to act pre-emptively. It is too risky to wait until your opponents have acted: they might succeed. Act on suspicion, albeit this requires punishing the innocent along with the guilty. A second rule, also tried and tested, is to use violence not as a last resort but routinely: it is an effective reminder of the dangers of non-compliance. Even modest adherence to democracy precludes these methods.

Bringing these two effects together, the rapid spread of democracy after 1991 probably left many societies more susceptible to mass violence. Even after a government had won an election, many people who felt alienated continued to regard state power as illegitimate, while the state was less able to restrain such opposition from becoming violent.

The best-known demonstration of the failure of elections to produce a government seen as legitimate by its citizens is Iraq. Iraq has had more elections than we can readily recall, but by 2011 they had yielded a sectarian government of the Shia under the Prime Minister, Nouri al-Maliki. He attempted, with diminishing success, to coerce an alienated Sunni minority. By 2011 democratic Iraq was fragile in the extreme.

But the most dramatic example of the inability of an election to achieve acceptance of government was Libya. Having liberated themselves from the brutal and grotesquely self-serving regime of Colonel Gaddafi, Libyans elected a government-of-reason. But instead of the country developing, it rapidly descended into rival violent factions. The state completely collapsed, with wide-ranging repercussions that we will encounter in the next chapter.

Yes we can!

A third factor leading to increased fragility is technological. Changes in technology have long been a standard explanation for international warfare: at times technology favours defenders – think of castles – and at times it favours attackers – think of tanks. One explanation for the First World War is that the technology of the time favoured attackers and so during July 1914 there was a self-fulfilling rush into military escalation. There are equivalent technological shifts between state coercion and insurrection. Tear gas and phone tapping have long enhanced coercion, but, starting around 2005, the explosive global spread of mobile phones and social media radically enhanced many forms of social protest, from rallies to insurrection. The first political manifestation of the new power of social networks was the victory in 2008 of the outsider Barak Obama in the primary contest against Hillary Clinton: social media, exemplified by 'Yes, we can!', defeated a conventional political campaign. But where the power of social media mattered most was in confronting state violence.

Protest does not depend exclusively, or even primarily, upon the extent of grievance. It depends upon the likely consequences of participation. The consequences if you are taking part in a public demonstration against a coercive state are straightforward. If few other people take part, the likelihood of being caught and punished is very high, whereas if a million others come into the square the forces of coercion will be so outnumbered that the risk of punishment is very low. The consequences for the regime are similarly dependent upon numbers. If the protest is small the regime will brush it off, or even double-down, whereas if it is massive there is a good chance that it will be toppled. The payoffs to participation are therefore highly sensitive to the expected participation of others.

The advent of the mobile phone and social media, adopted predominantly by the urban young, suddenly transformed the payoff to protest. Around the Middle East, grievances against the authoritarian regimes that were serving narrow interests were longstanding: the situation in 2011 was similar to that in 2001 or indeed to 1991, or even 1981. But whereas taking part in a protest at any of the earlier dates would have been quixotic, by 2011 to millions it became 'Yes, we can too!' Nor was this a uniquely Arab phenomenon: three years later the same thing happened in Ukraine.

However, its international spread first became an Arab phenomenon because the transmission of behaviour from one country to another through social media depends on the extent to which different national networks overlap. Evidently, urban youth in Tunisia,

Libya, Egypt, and Syria were linked by language, culture, and spatial proximity as well as by political context.

The resource booms

A further likely factor in the rise in fragility is the period of continuous increase in the price of natural resources – known as the 'super-cycle' – in the decade up to 2013. For countries that were resource exporters this raised national income but had other effects that were not so benign.

In a brilliant new study, the economist Nicolas Berman and his colleagues have geo-referenced all the mineral resources extracted in Africa, and linked them geographically to all the outbreaks of organized violence on the continent.[6] Although the link has been studied by many scholars for over a decade, this study has finally produced incontrovertible evidence that resource extraction increases the risk of violent conflict, and also gone a long way to understanding why it does so. While the study is only of Africa, there is no reason to think that its results are not more general. It finds that the surge in prices during the super-cycle increased the incidence of organized violence. It did so primarily by enabling rebel groups to tap into mines as sources of finance, which they then used to buy armaments. Such an effect clearly became important in Syria, since ISIS managed to gain military control over the Syrian oilfields and used the revenues from oil to escalate the violence.

High resource prices also have political effects. The governments of resource-dependent countries are more likely to be autocratic. Even when a resource-exporting country holds an election, new research finds that an increase in the price of the natural resource makes it less likely that the election will be free and fair.[7] The largest current displacement problem in Africa, in South Sudan, is inextricably linked to oil. The conflict is essentially a conflict over the control of oil wells. And it has not just been oil; mineral extraction – from diamonds to coltan – has shaped two decades of mass violence and fragility in the Democratic Republic of Congo.

High resource prices, and associated new discoveries, may also have psychological effects. Citizens may become dissatisfied because their expectations rise by more than what the government manages to deliver.[8] That the uprisings of the Arab Spring occurred around the peak of the global oil price may be more than coincidence.

Islamic extremism

Over a long period, a supremacist Islamic ideology had been promoted internationally by Saudi Arabia. This had initially been encouraged by the USA as a means of stimulating an insurgency against the Soviet occupation of Afghanistan: thus were born the Taliban. In societies in which the state was well equipped to keep large-scale organized violence at bay, the supremacist ideology manifested itself as terrorism; for example, in Bangladesh. But societies in which the government had less military capacity became exposed to the far more serious threat of mass violence.

The Sahel, the geographical area of transition south of the Sahara and the poorest region on the planet, is divided into countries whose tiny economies can barely support a viable state. As the new ideology took root in the region, societies became yet more fragile. The situation was exacerbated by the fall of Gaddafi's regime in Libya. In his death-throes Gaddafi had recruited mercenaries from the Sahel. His recruits had little interest in risking their necks for such a ridiculous cause, but as he fell they took the opportunity to loot his armoury. Oil wealth and paranoia had made Gaddafi a soft touch for any international arms salesman without scruple, and so he had amassed a spectacular trove of modern weaponry. Compared to the toy armies of the Sahelian governments, Gaddafi had been Goliath. The mercenaries had their own agenda: grievances against their governments. As they demolished the Malian army, Islamic supremacists recognized an opportunity and exploited it. Posing as allies of the ragbag mercenary forces, they marginalized them and usurped power. As the Malian state crumbled many thousands of civilians were displaced. Two years later, a similar process happened in the Central African Republic, producing a much larger displacement. Somewhat similar processes happened with the rise of Al-Shabaab in Somalia and Boko Haram in Nigeria.

But such opportunistic exploitation of a fragile situation by Islamic supremacists found its apotheosis in Iraq. The large, disaffected

Sunni minority produced by lopsided democracy, repressed by a state characterized by venal incompetence, was ready prey for ISIS. As ISIS built a brutal mini-state in northern Iraq, it set its sights upon an invasion of Syria.

CRYSTALLIZING MASS VIOLENCE

Many societies are fragile, but only in some of them do the risks crystallize into the mass violence that gives rise to displacement. As with other forms of organized violence, what drives the numbers are the tail risks: the outliers. This can make it misleading to talk about 'trends'. Totals are dominated by a few low-probability events that nevertheless happened. It is tempting to discern the unavoidable march of history in such numbers, but the world is not like that.[9] Refuge is what statisticians call a 'fat tails' phenomenon: a very low likelihood event but with catastrophic consequences that create a thick tail to a distribution curve.[10]

The lists of fragile states typically include between forty and sixty countries around the world but only three of them account for half of all the world's current displacement. Even within those three, one is dominant: the conflict in Syria alone has generated over 11 million displaced people. The accounts of the violence in Syria typically read as though it were inevitable, but it could not reasonably have been predicted. Syria was a repressive autocracy initially destabilized by the Arab Spring: a phenomenon that was not widely foreseen. The flight to refuge was subsequently exacerbated by the external intervention of ISIS: the horror of ISIS took the international community by surprise. It was then greatly amplified by Russian bombing: an intervention that caused international astonishment. Syria has evidently been a 'fat tails' event.

The other two conflicts that with Syria account for half of all displacement are Afghanistan and Somalia. The origins of their fragility were very different from Syria's. The surge in Afghani refugees resulted from the American invasion and continuing warfare with the Taliban. But Afghanistan was already a failed state: the insurgent Taliban had recently gained control of most of the country, but were recognized as a government only by Saudi Arabia, Pakistan, and the United Arab Emirates. Violent internal disorder had long been endemic. Somalia has also been a failed state for a generation, prone to organized violence, but with only limited and sporadic international intervention from its neighbours, Ethiopia and Kenya.

But while the grand total is dominated by these tail events, with 40–60 societies that are fragile, some risks will always be crystallizing. The other half of the world's total displacement comes from this steady drizzle of mass violence, not sufficiently dramatic to dominate the daily news, but still the stuff of tragedy. The recent such collapses into mass violence and flight are South Sudan, Sudan, Yemen, Burundi, Ukraine, the Central African Republic, Myanmar, and Eritrea. As with the population of fragile states from which they are drawn, this is a very disparate collection united by little beyond violence. The Tolstoy analogy is inescapable; at best we can cluster them.

Three situations are predominantly attributable to the tensions generated by lopsided democracy. In South Sudan the national government has failed to create sufficient sense of shared identity between the two major ethnic groups, the Dinka and the Nuer. As was explained to one of us in a meeting with a presidential adviser, before the latest conflict began, the problem as perceived by the Dinka-dominated government was that the Nuer did not recognize the authority of the government despite its being duly elected. The Nuer had indeed created their own substantial armed group. The solution determined by the government was to purchase arms. In Burundi, despite initially being democratically elected, the president never accepted a national mission, as opposed to governing on behalf of his own group. But the trigger for the refugee crisis was his insistence on a third term, won through an election that was not recognized as free and fair. The resulting mass protests were met with state mass violence, which in turn led to displacement. While lopsided democracy could not deliver legitimacy, the tiny economies of these two small and impoverished societies could not support the apparatus of repression that would have been needed to keep insurrection at bay through intimidation. The fragility of South Sudan was further compounded by an oil cycle of boom and bust.

Much as this will arouse indignation, Ukraine is also a case of lopsided democracy. As in some other recent countries, it is existentially divided. Elections reveal a split between a West-admiring western part and a

Russia-admiring eastern part. Under a Russia-admiring government, duly elected but unencumbered by checks and balances, the President became a world-class looter. An Arab Spring-style mass youth uprising in the capital toppled him, replacing him with a similarly unencumbered West-admiring government. Thereupon an insurgency began in the eastern provinces. With Russian support for the insurgency the violence escalated, with the West-admiring government resorting to bombing the civilian supporters of the insurgency.

A different cluster of countries is predominantly characterized by an inherently weak state such as typifies the impoverished small countries of the Sahel. Misgoverned for decades, the Central African Republic has been continuously fragile, but the same conjunction of supremacist Islam and spill-over from the fall of the Gaddafi regime that produced mayhem in Mali pushed the society over the edge. Military intervention by France prevented a prospective meltdown into genocide.

Yemen was the worst global displacement disaster of 2015 in terms of the numbers displaced that year; so understanding it matters. Around 2.5 million people became displaced, 9 per cent of its entire population. Like the Central African Republic, it is analogous to a Sahelian country. It has never managed to function as a state for more than a few years at a time and is riven by rivalries between clans. Also like the Sahelian countries it has been ready prey for supremacist Islam. The polity was further stressed by an oil boom–bust cycle. In a final twist of the knife, Saudi Arabia intervened to support the government, undertaking a bombing campaign against the civilian population of the insurgent side closely analogous to the intervention of Russia in Syria.

Sudan, though much larger than the other Sahelian countries, shares their essential features: the capacity of the state is too weak for it to be other than fragile. Its fragility certainly cannot be attributed to lopsided democracy: there has been nothing remotely democratic about the Sudanese regime. Lacking even a semblance of legitimacy, the state is entirely reliant upon coercion. It would need a North Korean scale of violent menace to cow its population into continuous acquiescence in state power. Like Yemen, tensions were compounded by an oil boom–bust cycle.

For decades Myanmar was a weak state over-reliant upon repression that periodically resorted to mass violence against its own citizens. But the latest upsurge in refugees was more attributable to inter-ethnic tensions than to state repression. The Rohingya, a Muslim minority in a Buddhist-majority society, became the victim of majority violence from which the state was unwilling, and possibly unable, to protect them. Wanting to win an election with the votes of the majority community, even the longstanding civil-rights campaigner Aung San Suu Kyi did little to reduce tensions.

Finally, Eritrea belongs in its own unique category. A repressive state, with considerable capacity for mass violence, it had relied upon the technique of incarcerating its potentially disaffected youth in the army to serve long terms as conscripts. For around a decade this worked: the rhetoric of unity in the face of the powerful neighbouring enemy, Ethiopia, lent a degree of legitimacy. Gradually, this narrative has lost its power to ensnare. While Eritrea's economy has stagnated, despite its excellent coastal location, the economy of landlocked Ethiopia has been well run for ordinary people and delivered rapidly rising living standards. It has also become home to thousands of Eritreans. To the bottomless dismay of the heroic people who fought for the secession from Ethiopia, their struggle succeeded only to be revealed as pointless. With the demise of the rationale for a society kept permanently on a war-footing, the ordinary people who worked as the jailers of the nation's youth lost their dedication. Junior officers and border guards began to accept bribes from reluctant conscripts keen to escape. What began as a trickle has gradually further eroded norms of obedience to power and has become a flood. There is no mass violence within Eritrea. The people who are fleeing the country are not families whose homes have become unsafe. There is no breakdown of order. Faced with a choice between the quasi-prison conditions of conscription, and the actual prison conditions that would result from non-compliance, young people have used their ingenuity. What we are witnessing is a mass breakout from a nation that has become a jail.

THE OPTIONS FOR FLIGHT

Where fragility crystallizes into mass violence, civilian populations need to flee their homes. The focus of international refugee law remains the antiquated notion of 'persecution' but the practical reality is that fragility ultimately underlies most of today's refugee movements. When we turn to the ethics of international response, in Chapter 4, we will argue that the defining feature of need is this flight from violence. The targets of that violence may be an identifiable group of people, as with Germany's Jews, or a particular location, as with the bombing of Aleppo. In either case, people must flee to safety.

The people displaced from their homes may be able to find sanctuary elsewhere in the country, or they may need to leave it. The concept of an 'internally displaced person' (IDP) describes somebody who is displaced in his or her own country. Often, a displacement leads to some people opting to move within the country as IDPs, and others opting to leave it as refugees. Sometimes people do not have an option. German Jews were at one extreme: terrorized by the fascist government, they were at risk everywhere in Germany, and so flight abroad was the only safe resort. In contrast, the people terrorized by Boko Haram, a supremacist Islamic insurgency operating in northeast Nigeria, may have the option of moving elsewhere within Nigeria. Boko Haram is confined to a small and relatively lightly populated portion of the country, though since that area is a border region, for some crossing the border will be the safest option.

In Syria most of the 11 million displaced have remained in the country. This was probably inherent to the nature of the violence, which has been predominantly territorial. Although it began as a regime witch-hunt against protesters, the conflict rapidly escalated into a conventional struggle to control territory. Consequently, many people whose homes were in dangerous areas have sought sanctuary in the safe ones. Perhaps they are able to live with relatives, making their relocation less disruptive than fleeing abroad. For others, relocating within Syria may have been the only option because periodically the borders have been closed.

Only those who cross the border qualify for the legal designation of 'refugee'. International agencies and the international media tend to focus mainly on those who cross borders. But those people displaced from their homes who seek sanctuary elsewhere in their country should not drop off the international agenda, and their practical needs of sanctuary often go unmet. Since mass violence occurs in states that are fragile, even though much of a country may remain safe the state is unlikely to have the capacity to cope. Although the international community has developed guidelines on how states should respond to internally displaced people, institutional responses remain weak and uneven.

That same distinction as to whether a border is crossed delineates internal and international migration. In poor countries most migrants move from rural areas to towns and cities within the country, but some cross a border. Those that become international migrants share the same directly observable phenomenon that determines whether someone fleeing for safety is classified as an IDP or a 'refugee'. But refugees are not migrants. Although the difference cannot be discerned from the physical act of crossing a border, it is no less real. At its core is the psychological impetus for the decision. Migrants are lured by hope; refugees are fleeing fear. Migrants hope for honeypots; refugees need havens.

Among the global population of 7 billion, only one person in seven lives in a honeypot country.[11] Many of the other 6 billion would like to move to one of them. In contrast, less than 1 per cent of the world's population are displaced, and less than half of them are refugees. Were the international community to be too intellectually lazy to distinguish the quest for refuge from the desire to migrate, a vital need which it is manageable to meet would get drowned in a tidal wave of would-be migrants.

Refugees need havens: where do they find them?

HAVENS OF REFUGE

If you think that the distinction between havens and honeypots is contrived, you are about to confront your prejudices. We suggest that you jot down a list of the most desirable countries in which international migrants might dream of living: the top ten honeypots. It is not difficult: most of us dream such dreams, and migrants take the next step and enact them. Now try to jot down a list of the top ten havens: the countries to which refugees flee. How similar are your lists?

The top haven country for the past four decades has been Pakistan.

Did you get it right? Indeed, did Pakistan even feature on your list of the top ten honeypots? Probably not. We will work a little down the list, turning to the runner-up haven country, which was indeed a very close second. It is Iran. Some people find modern Iran alluring, but it scarcely fits the Western image of a desirable country to relocate to. The next four are all African: Ethiopia, Kenya, Uganda, and Tanzania.[12]

One strikingly counter-intuitive feature that these six countries have in common is that while they are the top-ranked countries for the inflow of refugees, they are all countries of emigration. Far from being honeypots, the more affluent members of their societies tend to seek honeypots elsewhere. One was, of course, the father of President Obama. Vying for the remaining places in the top ten havens, depending on the year of measurement, are Thailand, Turkey, Jordan, Lebanon, the Democratic Republic of Congo, and Chad.

To return to our opening point: the concept of a haven is utterly different from that of a honeypot. Honeypots are economically much alike: they are rich. So what, if anything, do havens have in common?

If you are trying to find similarities in government humanitarian policies, or in the generosity of local peoples, you are looking in the wrong place. Neither the governments nor the peoples of Thailand, Jordan, and Kenya have more in common than they would with any other randomly drawn grouping. What haven countries have in common is their locations. They are not close to each other, but they are all close to fragile states, and often to clusters of such states. Driven out by fear, rather than lured on by hope, refugees overwhelmingly head for havens that are proximate.

Countries such as Pakistan and the Democratic Republic of Congo did not become haven countries because they put up 'welcome' signs at railway stations. They became haven countries by default: refugees flocked to them because they were close by. Their states would have had to organize their capacities for coercion to the limit, and indeed most likely beyond the limit, to avoid becoming havens. Whether or not they are well equipped to cope with a massive influx of refugees, and most of them are not particularly able to do so, that is what they have got. Indeed, some of them are among the poorest countries in the world. A few of them are themselves high on the list of fragile states.

We began this chapter with an astonishing fact. Our new century, which will deliver wonders like unprecedented longevity, leisure, prosperity, and connectivity, is also delivering record levels of displacement. Sixty-five million people have fled from their homes in fear of violence. What, if anything, can the rest of us do to remedy this situation?

Tony Blair sprang to political prominence with a compelling phrase: he would be 'tough on crime, and tough on the causes of crime'. The twin approach, not just reaction but *prevention*, sounded smart. It is similarly appealing to start from the notion that the best policy towards displacement is to prevent it from happening.

We have seen that displacement arises from fragility: so could states be made much less fragile by international assistance? This is indeed now the priority for much international public policy. Aid agencies are focusing their resources more heavily on fragile states: for example, Britain's Department for International Development, widely regarded as currently the most sophisticated of the development agencies, has increased the share of its budget ring-fenced for fragile states, first to 30 per cent, and in 2015 to 50 per cent. The security services are also focusing more heavily on such states: intelligence services are working with their governments to counter supremacist Islam, and the armed forces are training their armies. But there are limits to what is possible. Recall that the big numbers are generated by 'fat tail' events that are not readily predictable.

Beyond that, helping countries to become resilient is not easy. States need to enhance their legitimacy in the eyes of their citizens, and also enhance their capacity to maintain security. International actions may be able to assist these processes, but each is primarily a domestic struggle. Since each fragile state is distinctive – an 'unhappy family' with its own peculiarities – cookie-cutter interventions are liable to do harm in some contexts. But even if it is generally accepted that each situation needs its own context-specific international support, this risks giving each of the many international agencies a licence to invent its own approach. So we should not expect too much of international risk prevention. The causes of earthquakes are far less complicated than those of mass violence, but despite enormous research effort we still cannot usually predict them even by a few hours. Instead, the best policy for earthquake-prone areas is to construct for resilience.

So probably the international community's main responses to the risks of mass violence are going to be reactive. The key message to take from this chapter is that effective international reaction to displacement and refuge is going to be needed for decades to come. This does not depend upon some precarious projection of likely refugee numbers: the grand totals are likely to go up and down unpredictably. But the underlying process of refugee generation is clear enough: a large group of fragile states is each exposed to a small but significant risk that it will implode into the mass violence against civilians that generates displacement. Many of those displaced will probably remain in their own countries, but many others will seek havens beyond the border. For the next few decades the international community will need to react to the needs of the internally displaced and the refugees. The essential question that we now address is whether the capacity for effective reaction is already in place or will need to be built.

2

The Time-Warp

Seventy years ago, the international community faced the largest displacement crisis in its history. Millions of people found themselves uprooted in the aftermath of the Second World War, with borders being redrawn across Europe. Solutions were urgently needed both for the people displaced and for governments seeking to restore stability. A United Nations refugee regime was hastily created, reflecting the onset of the Cold War in the late 1940s. It comprised two core elements: an international treaty offering a definition of a 'refugee' and the rights to which such people should be entitled, and the creation of a UN specialized agency with a mandate to protect and find solutions for these refugees.

The deal reached reflected the politics of the time. Even though the initial impetus for the regime stemmed from the aftermath of the Holocaust and the collective failure to provide protection to fleeing Jews during the 1930s, the architecture of the regime was profoundly shaped by the early-Cold War context in which it was created. It was generated because the norms of revulsion at the Holocaust happened to align with the strategic interests of the US in the containment of Communism. Key decisions like how even to define a 'refugee' were shaped by the concerns of the US and its Western allies to avoid the return of displaced people to Communist Soviet bloc countries. The outcome was in many ways a pragmatic compromise designed as a temporary stop-gap solution for a particular historical juncture.

And yet, in a classic instance of Eurocentric policy formation, that European regime was subsequently extended, without significant adjustment, to the rest of the world. Over time, it became the global refugee regime, shaping the response to refugees in Africa, the Middle East, Latin America, and Europe decades later. Although there has been incremental change, this has generally been piecemeal, relying mainly upon court decisions to reinterpret refugee law or episodic shifts in organizational mandates to address particular displacement challenges. At no point has there been a major reform process to consider the ongoing relevance of the post-war framework in a radically different world. The trajectory has been highly path-dependent: decisions in the present have been limited by the decisions made in the past, even though past circumstances may no longer be relevant.

Subsequent change has been slow and haphazard. Legal adaptation has come from layers of reinterpretation of the language of a convention created for a bygone era. Courts have contrived to fit a host of circumstances into the arcane notion of 'persecution' but in ways that have been varied and inconsistent, and that have left omissions. Organizational adaptation has come from responses to new emergencies often being ossified as permanent policy. These incremental shifts have, over the intervening seven decades, created a growing gap between institutions and needs.

The result is a regime that is no longer fit for purpose. It fails to engage adequately with contemporary challenges. Even though factors such as climate change and state fragility will drive future displacement, they are sidelined by the existing regime. Even though most refugees are now in urban areas, it provides a model premised mainly on assistance in camps. Even though refuge is inherently political, the main UN refugee agency has been prescribed a 'non-political' character in its founding statute. A clause intended to ensure the organization did not take sides in the Cold War too often now prevents it from proactively engaging with the political barriers to refugee protection. Furthermore, it also struggles to adequately utilize new opportunities that have opened up as the world has progressed, including leveraging globalization, technology, the role of business, and the capacities of refugees themselves.

Existing institutions are premised upon a simple and valuable idea: that people have a right to flee serious harm, and receiving countries have a corresponding obligation to admit them. But there are also elements of the regime that are incontrovertibly dysfunctional. The European migrant crisis triggered in April 2015 has lifted refugees to the top of the political agenda for virtually the first time since the end of the Cold War. With the global spotlight on the regime, and a widespread sense of crisis, there is a moment of opportunity for change. This chapter therefore aims to make sense of the institutional trajectory of the refugee regime, and explore which elements have endured because they have value and which have lasted simply because of inertia or lack of imagination.

A REFUGEE REGIME FOR COLD WAR EUROPE

For as long as there have been political communities, there have been persecuted groups forced to flee in search of rights. Since the establishment of nation-states in Europe following the Peace of Westphalia in 1648, governments have sought ways to govern refugee movements. The Huguenots, for example, as Protestants expelled from France following the revocation of the Edict of Nantes in 1685, were accepted as refugees in Britain. Throughout the revolutions of the eighteenth and nineteenth centuries, European states worked bilaterally to ensure safe passage and population exchange for the victims of state formation and dissolution who better fitted the ethnic or religious criteria of newly emerging states.

It was not until the twentieth century that states recognized the reciprocal sharing of responsibility for refugees as a humanitarian obligation. During the inter-war years, with the collapse of the Ottoman Empire, in 1921 the newly launched League of Nations created the position of High Commissioner for Refugees (LNHCR). The organization the Commissioner headed was modest but effective in form, simply providing travel documents (known as 'Nansen passports') to designated groups of stateless and displaced people: Russians, Greeks, Turks, Bulgarians, and Armenians.[1]

The first large-scale multilateral attempt to manage refugees only emerged in the aftermath of the Second World War, with tens of millions displaced across Europe. It was at this moment that the modern refugee regime, the bulk of which remains intact today, was born. Like much of the post-war architecture of multilateral order, it comprises two main elements: a treaty and an international organization.

The 1951 Convention is a simple document. It provides a definition of a refugee and outlines the rights to which such people are entitled. It defines a refugee as someone outside his or her country of origin because of a 'well-founded fear of persecution' because of race, religion, nationality, membership of a social group, or political opinion. It then sets out a series of claims refugees can make against states: principally, the right not to be forcibly returned to a country in which there is a risk of serious harm (*non-refoulement*), as well as key civil and political, and economic and social, rights.

UNHCR's founding statute, adopted by the UN General Assembly on 14 December 1950, created an organization with a mandate of 'providing international protection' to refugees and 'seeking permanent solutions' to their plight by assisting governments and private organizations to facilitate voluntary repatriation or assimilation within new national communities. The only other element of note in the statute is the designation of the organization as having a 'non-political character'.

This refugee regime was certainly not intended by the negotiating states to endure, let alone to be disseminated around the world. Participants recognized that they were reacting to a unique situation that required a highly specific solution. To make this clear, states imposed a series of limitations. UNHCR's work was temporally limited: it was set to expire at the end of 1953. Moreover, both UNHCR and the Convention were temporally restricted to what had already happened: they were to apply only to people who were refugees 'as a result of events occurring before 1 January 1951'. To make its limitations crystal clear it is also spatially bounded: the 1951 Convention was created with a geographical limitation, allowing its signatories the option to apply it to people displaced 'owing to events in Europe'.

Furthermore, the *travaux préparatoires* – the published records of the negotiations – reveal that even the relatively limited choices of the day were the outcome of awkward political compromise among the twenty-six negotiating governments. The United States was the most keen to impose tight restrictions on the regime. Eleanor Roosevelt and the State Department delegation had argued that the regime should be temporary and not apply to other, emerging refugee crises of the late 1940s and early 1950s in India, Korea, and Palestine. They also insisted – against the requests of India, Pakistan, and many directly affected Western European countries like France and Belgium – that UNHCR should have no role in the direct provision of material assistance but should simply provide legal guidance and expertise to governments.[2]

The negotiating positions of key governments were interest-based and not the result of lofty humanitarian principles. The US was primarily motivated by a desire to control and discredit Communism. The adoption of a definition of refugees based on individualized 'fear of persecution' emerged because of the US's vehement rejection of repatriation to Communist countries being a viable solution for those who had been displaced from Eastern Europe. This was a reaction to the immediate antecedent to UNHCR – the UN relief and rehabilitation agency, operational between 1943 and 1946. That agency had indeed sought to facilitate repatriation. But in 1947 the US terminated the agency and briefly created its own International Relief Organization (IRO) with a focus on resettling those who risked return to the East. Its condition for backing the embryonic UNHCR regime was that it too held this focus on non-return to persecution.[3]

Other governments had different goals that were also the result of their particular interests, but these were largely thwarted. Against the US position, the refugee-hosting countries of Western Europe wanted UNHCR to operationally provide material assistance to populations on their territories. But in the context of already receiving huge assistance through the US-led Marshall Plan of 1948, they were forced to defer to the US's wishes. The UK was alone among Western states in pushing for UNHCR and the Convention to have immediate global scope, mainly because of its concerns with managing its empire and the immediate legacy of post-colonial displacement on the Indian subcontinent.

Yet, despite US dominance, Western European governments did manage to sow the seeds for the possible survival of the regime. Unlike the 1951 Convention, UNHCR itself had no geographical limitation, discretion was given to governments to apply the 1951 Convention to 'events in Europe *and elsewhere*' if they so wished, and it was understood that UNHCR's mandate might well be renewed. The drafters envisaged that it might endure and adapt, recognizing that its definition of a refugee would not cover all situations but might evolve dynamically through at least two routes: the interpretation of national courts and supplementary international agreements.

Over the next several decades, this hastily negotiated and ostensibly temporary regime survived largely intact, adapting incrementally – through opportunistic and occasionally pathological means.[4] A regime initially not intended to last a decade would become the basis of global refugee governance.

Central to its survival was the opportunity afforded by the Cold War. Initially viewed as temporary by the US and functioning on the basis of private foundation grants, UNHCR was able to demonstrate its strategic value to the US through its response to two events. In 1953 it tackled the West Berlin crisis. Faced with a strike in East Berlin and exodus to the West, UNHCR conceived a plan of action to support international and German voluntary agencies to meet the present emergency caused by the influx of refugees through Berlin, supporting emigration, immediate relief in Berlin, and integration of refugees in Western Germany. The second event was in 1956, when the invasion of Hungary by the Soviet Army led to the mass exodus of nearly 200,000 refugees to neighbouring Austria and Yugoslavia. Overwhelmed by the influx of refugees, Austria formally requested UNHCR to appeal to governments on its behalf for assistance in responding to the emergency, providing the organization with the chance to prove to the US that it could play a key strategic role in helping those fleeing Communism.

EUROCENTRISM GOES GLOBAL

The big turning point was geographical expansion. The 1967 Protocol Relating to the Status of Refugees expanded the scope of a regime originally designed for Europe to the rest of the world. Against the backdrop of anti-colonial struggles, decolonization, and emerging Cold War proxy conflicts, the West was concerned to manage the potentially destabilizing consequences of refugee movements in the Third World. UNHCR had already been called upon on an ad hoc basis to respond to the crises for Chinese refugees in Hong Kong and Algerian refugees in Tunisia in 1957, for example, and the Protocol brought the 1951 Convention into line with the universal scope of UNHCR's statute.

The decision to apply Europe's refugee regime unaltered to the Third World was pragmatic, hasty, and again largely dictated by Cold War strategic interests. By the mid-1960s, and with the advent of the Vietnam War, the Third World had come to be seen as a volatile source of instability for the West. From South-East Asia to Southern and Eastern

Africa, newly independent states were perceived as potential targets for Soviet alignment and unprotected refugees as a potential vector for cross-border insurgency. It was concern with 'refugee warriors' rather than a benevolent desire to protect the vulnerable that lay behind the globalization of Europe's regime.

The mismatch was immediately obvious. Refugees fleeing liberation wars or post-colonial violence in situations like Rwanda's 1959 revolution, Angola's post-1961 civil war, or the emergence of violence in Sudan from the late 1960s were in a very different situation compared to those dispersed across Europe after the Second World War. The same applied to those fleeing proxy violence, military coups, and juntas in Latin American countries like Guatemala, El Salvador, and Nicaragua. The European regime's focus on individualized 'persecution' simply did not fit the circumstances of war refugees in other parts of the world.

Despite the obviously poor fit, adjustments to the post-war European framework were piecemeal and on a region-by-region basis. In 1969 African governments agreed the Organization of African Unity (OAU) Convention Relating to the Status of Refugees, applying the 1951 Convention to the African context but with some significant changes. It expanded the definition of a refugee to include 'persons fleeing events seriously disturbing public order in either part or the whole of his country of origin'. Later, in 1984, Latin America followed suit when the Organization of American States (OAS) agreed the Cartagena Declaration on Refugees, expanding its regional definition to include people threatened by 'generalized violence, foreign aggression, internal conflicts, massive violation of human rights or other circumstances which have seriously disturbed public order'.

Tweaks aside, the core practices of the global refugee regime have emanated from its post-war European origins.[5] The biggest change within the refugee regime has arguably been the most detrimental to it: the move towards a 'care and maintenance' model. The 1950 decision that UNHCR should not engage in the direct provision of material assistance began to change from the 1980s. Until that point, the regime's primary role had been to offer legal and operational guidance to states relating to the provision of protection and solutions. During the 1960s and 1970s, in most of the developing world, refugees were mainly self-settled in rural areas and de facto integrated among local host populations. But from the 1980s the refugee camp – long used by some governments – became the default instrument of formal refugee assistance in the developing world. Vast areas in often remote, arid, and dangerous border locations were annexed as spaces for emergency protection that became enduring residences for the long-term displaced.

Dehumanizing camps became the default response for a combination of reasons. First, with democratization, debt crises, and the 'Structural Adjustment' programmes of the 1980s and 1990s through which the International Monetary Fund and the World Bank imposed economic liberalization and cuts in government spending across much of the developing world, host governments became increasingly constrained in their ability to allocate scare resources to non-citizens.[6] Camps offered a means to place refugees 'out of sight and out of mind' while abdicating financial responsibility to the international community. Second, with the end of the Cold War, UNHCR needed to remain relevant to its core donors. Without a role to play in meeting the US's Cold War strategic interests, it sought to reinvent itself as a humanitarian organization. The camp made this possible, allowing the organization to dramatically expand its staff numbers and budget through its growing and visible role in both emergency assistance and long-term camp management. UNHCR staff numbers grew from 500 to over 9,000 between 1950 and 2016. Camps provided jobs: just not for refugees.

While the refugee regime has not been entirely static over the last several decades, it has certainly been path-dependent, and today's system still resembles that created for the particular circumstances of post-war Europe, albeit in a radically different world.

THE SILENCES OF THE 1951 CONVENTION

The 1951 Convention sets out the morally incontrovertible idea that people who face serious harm in their country of origin should not be forced to go back until it is safe to do so. It identifies that such people should be able to access basic rights and freedoms while in exile and ultimately be able to either go home or be integrated in another society. In that sense, its central idea is that when people's own countries are unable or unwilling to ensure their most fundamental rights they should be allowed to cross an international border in search of a safe haven.

However, its limitations have become increasingly more obvious over time. Generally, the value of international legal norms resides in their ability to build a shared set of expectations about appropriate state behaviour over time. But the problem today is that the 1951 Convention no longer generates a shared commitment and nor does it adequately prescribe behaviours that fit today's displacement challenges. Never truly global, it is more adrift than ever from current needs.

Today, most countries fail to comply with the 1951 Convention. Signatory states in the developed world find ever more elaborate ways to disregard or bypass the principle of *non-refoulement*, adopting a suite of deterrence or *non-entrée* policies that make it difficult and dangerous for refugees to access their territory: carrier sanctions, razor wire fences, interception en route. Signatory states in the developing world do tend to admit refugees more because of geographical necessity and international pressure than law, and when they do, they still almost universally fail to implement the socio-economic rights in the Convention. And, yet, paradoxically, many of the most generous host countries in the world are not even full signatories: Jordan, Lebanon, Thailand, Nepal, and Turkey, for instance. Countries in the Middle East and Asia have argued that the Convention does not meet the realities of displacement in their regions, and that their own cultural and legal practices in any case provide sources of sanctuary. Meanwhile, Turkey has signed the 1951 Convention but not its 1967 Protocol, meaning that it has no international legal commitment to recognize refugees who come from outside geographical Europe.

The way that different states interpret key ideas in the Convention has changed gradually over time through the mechanisms envisaged by its drafters: court jurisprudence and supplementary international agreements. For example, in some jurisdictions, the interpretation of a well-founded fear of persecution has broadened to include war refugees, people fleeing persecution by non-state armed actors, or certain extreme forms of socio-economic rights deprivation. Meanwhile, the so-called nexus-grounds such as 'membership of a social group' have expanded to include additional groups: for example, those fleeing persecution based on sexual orientation.

On the other hand, however, these updates have been slow, patchy, and inconsistent. They have depended almost entirely on decisions in particular regions or by individual countries to stretch the scope and interpretation of key parts of the 1951 Convention. This has had a number of consequences. It has meant that the definition of a 'refugee' can mean something quite different from one country to another. More fundamentally, the slow pace of adaptation, mainly through courts, has left the dominant interpretations of the 1951 Convention poorly adapted to meet the displacement challenges of the contemporary world.

It's not that the 1951 Convention need necessarily be abandoned. It may well play a useful residual role insofar as it still encourages commitment and compliance. The problem is when an overriding obsession with it risks expending finite political capital on a digression. In particular, there are three broad areas in which there is a gap between what the current refugee regime offers and practical needs in the contemporary world.

MISSING PEOPLE: WHO NEEDS TO BE A REFUGEE?

Although the drafters of the 1951 Convention recognized that the definition of a 'refugee' would need to adapt over time, it has become increasingly out of touch with the realities of displacement in the twenty-first century. Like most legal regimes, the refugee regime identifies a category of people (refugees) and a set of rights to which such people are entitled. The 1951 Convention sets the threshold for being part of the category of people entitled to a privileged immigration status as 'persecution'. It establishes that such people not only have a right to *non-refoulement*, but rights in exile and, where needed, a pathway to citizenship. Yet 'persecution' no longer seems the right threshold for a privileged immigration status and the rights associated with it.

The original reason for privileging persecution is historical: not returning people to Communism was the primary concern of the emerging global superpower at the time the Convention was drafted. Today, though, there are a range of reasons why extremely vulnerable people cross international borders that fall outside the traditional understanding of persecution. Environmental disturbance, including that due to climate change; generalized violence, whether because of war or drug- and gang-related violence; and food and water insecurity – these have all have been identified among the 'new drivers' of displacement. For many people affected by these challenges, there will be opportunities to relocate domestically; for others there may not be.

Connecting many of these drivers of displacement is a central underlying trend: a growth in the number of fragile states, for the reasons we saw in the previous chapter. In these states people generally face chronically poor living standards. With increased global opportunities for mobility, many choose to move. This dual trend of increased fragility and growing mobility has created an emerging phenomenon that might be described as 'survival migration' – people who leave their countries because they simply cannot secure the minimum conditions of human dignity in their country of origin.[7] Many find themselves in a neither/nor situation – neither are they generally recognized as refugees, nor are they simply voluntary economic migrants.

For some scholars, like Matthew Price, the answer would be that asylum should prioritize the persecuted over and above the broader category of people fleeing fragile states. His claim is that when a tyrannical government is deliberately 'out to get you', this leads to a severance in the basic social contract between state and citizen. This severance makes effective redress within that person's own state extremely unlikely, requiring territorial asylum and, in all likelihood, a pathway to alternative citizenship. On that basis, it has been argued that those fleeing persecution are the most deserving of the deserving.[8] But this argument no longer stands up to scrutiny.

It is not clear that those fleeing this narrow understanding of persecution are necessarily more deserving than other displaced populations. From an ethical perspective what should matter is not the particular cause of movement but the threshold of harm that, when not addressed in the homeland country, necessitates border crossing as a last resort.

One way of grounding how we should identify refugees in a changing world is through the concept of *force majeure* – the absence of a reasonable choice but to leave.[9] More specifically, the threshold for refuge would be fear of serious physical harm.[10] And the test would be: when would a reasonable person not see her- or himself as having a choice but to flee? In other words, if you were in the same situation, what would you do?[11]

The value of 'fear of serious physical harm' is that it is a universal concept. While 'persecution' is a historically and culturally contingent idea, 'fear from physical harm' is a universal common denominator. Why would someone not see her- or himself as having a choice but to flee? Because she or he is afraid, as you would be. Fear is not country-specific. Unlike migration, which is usually about an upside, refuge is needed when horrible things have happened to you and your family: members of your family have been attacked by militias, your daughters have been raped, or your village has been destroyed by serious flooding and there is nowhere else to go.

The standard should be intuitive and universal, rather than relying upon the shoehorning of circumstances into an arcane and regionally specific language of the past. An additional advantage of the *force majeure* standard is that it reflects the direction of travel that the refugee regime has gone in wherever developing countries have adapted the European norms of the late 1940s to meet their own regional circumstances. The regional refugee regimes for Africa and Latin America include a greater emphasis on ideas like 'generalized violence' and 'serious disturbances to public order', for instance. If we had a more universally applicable standard, perhaps even current non-signatory regions like the Middle East, South Asia, and South East-Asia might have greater reason to commit to regional or even international standards for refuge.

Take the example of Zimbabwe. Between 2003 and 2009, up to 2 million Zimbabweans fled to neighbouring South Africa to escape Robert Mugabe's regime and a serious set of socio-economic rights deprivations, resulting from hyperinflation, famine, drought, and the collapse of the national economy. Many fleeing were in an almost identical position to refugees in having to leave the country simply in order to survive. However, the legal problem was that most were not fleeing the political situation so much as the economic consequences of the underlying political situation. As a result, when in South Africa, most were not recognized as refugees. At the peak of the crisis, South Africa recognized fewer than 10 per cent as refugees and was deporting around 300,000 Zimbabweans a year back to the country. The outcome was clearly unjust but it reflected South Africa's use of the 'persecution' standard of the 1951 Convention's definition of a refugee, which excluded most Zimbabweans.[12]

Further, Price's argument assumes the existence of a functioning state, and a 'social contract' between the citizen and the state which it has breached through persecution. But in many fragile societies the 'state' as such is a shadow. Somali refugees are not fleeing persecution by the state, but the consequences of a society without a state. The resulting disorder and violence are no less *force majeure*; nor is the need for post-flight support less urgent. In such cases, the original anti-Communist emphasis upon resettlement away from the persecuting state has also lost much of its pertinence. In contrast to expectations during the Cold War, political transitions and opportunities for repatriation take place in both Price's archetypal authoritarian regimes and many fragile states.

Contrary to many international public policy assumptions, there are practically no weak states that should be permanently written off. In the twenty-first century it is feasible for all societies to become reasonably viable. The global tragedy of the 1980s was Ethiopia; that of the 1990s was Rwanda: both are now thriving. Many societies will remain fragile for many years, and so long-term provision must be made for those who flee the fallout from anarchy. Sometimes this will persist for so long as to make assimilation into other societies the best option, but, as we discuss in Chapter 7, a refugee strategy that incubates the restoration of a functioning state has an important role. Whether people have been persecuted by a state is essentially immaterial to which of these options is appropriate.

A final weakness with the emphasis upon 'persecution' is that in practice its meaning has been stretched far beyond the logically minimalist way in which it is described by Price. Some states have restrictive interpretations; in others it is more commonly understood as a threshold of 'serious harm' rather than the original idea of a state being 'out to get' its own citizens. But the fact that this expansion has emerged through the often conservative and inconsistent pathway of the jurisprudence of national and regional courts has led to huge variation, in ways that frequently appear ethically arbitrary. In some states, war refugees are recognized; in others they are not. In some states, those fleeing attacks by non-state-armed actors are recognized; in others they are not. In some states, those fleeing conscription are recognized, in others they are not. Even across Europe, where there are supposedly harmonized asylum standards, there is huge variation in practices: for example, in 2014 the recognition rate for Iraqis was 14 per cent in

Greece and 94 per cent in France; for Eritreans it was 26 per cent in France and 100 per cent in Sweden.[13] When persecution has no coherent or consistent meaning, how can it be a credible threshold for determining who gets to cross a border in search of rights?

A key question faced by the international community therefore remains, 'Who is a refugee?' Among the millions of people crossing international borders in search of refuge, who should be prioritized and on what basis? What should be the threshold for access to a safe haven? In a changing world, the old answers provided by 'persecution', and the conservative and inconsistent role of courts in incrementally reinterpreting it over time, seem inadequate to respond clearly and decisively to these questions.

Where and how to determine the threshold are decisions that should be in the hands of policy-makers rather than just the courts. While lawyers take such decisions based on individual rights, policy-makers must consider the implications for entire societies. As we show in Part II, unless policy is properly thought through, the 'rights' exercised by the few can have adverse repercussions for the many. For example, wherever the threshold is placed, policy-makers will need to openly confront the challenge of how to reconcile the quantity and quality of protection. On the one hand, in a world of survival migration, the scope of protected categories will inevitably need to broaden. Governments will simply have to collectively find ways to protect those fleeing new forms of fragility. On the other hand, in order to increase the numbers and categories of protected people, new ways will have to be found to offer protection more sustainably and at scale.

MISSING PROVIDERS: WHO SHOULD BEAR THE BURDEN?

So who should provide havens? The 1951 Convention is silent on both where and with what resources refuge should be provided. The question of which state has primary responsibility for providing refuge is simply not answered explicitly by the existing regime. Consequently, it is politics – and more specifically power – rather than law or principle that primarily determines who takes responsibility for refugees and on what basis.

In principle the regime recognizes that refugees should be a shared global responsibility. The Preamble to the 1951 Convention explicitly recognizes that international cooperation is a necessary condition for the achievement of protection, assistance, and solutions, stating that 'the grant of asylum may place unduly heavy burdens on certain countries', and that 'a satisfactory solution of a problem of which the United Nations has recognized the international scope and nature cannot therefore be achieved without international co-operation'. In practice, though, there are no clearly specified principles or operational mechanisms for what has been called burden- or responsibility-sharing.

On the one hand, the refugee regime offers relatively clear norms relating to 'asylum' – the obligation to admit refugees onto the territory of a state. On the other hand, it has relatively weak norms relating to 'responsibility-sharing' – the obligation to contribute to supporting refugees who initially arrive on the territory of another state. Despite repeated attempts by the international community to negotiate supplementary agreements on responsibility-sharing, clear and authoritative principles and mechanisms have proved elusive. In the absence of a clear allocation mechanism for spreading responsibility, proximity has de facto shaped its distribution, which is why, as we have seen, states that neighbour conflict and crisis take in the majority, and those that have the luxury of hiding behind territory and water have historically been able to shirk responsibility.

While proximate countries are left with a legal obligation to admit refugees, more distant countries have had almost total discretion in determining whether, and to what extent, they are prepared to contribute, whether by offering resettlement places or financial support. This leads to the inequitable outcome that a relatively small number of some of the poorest countries in the world take on the greatest responsibility.

These geographical dynamics, reinforced by the existing institutional architecture, create perverse incentives. Southern host states face legal obligations and significant international pressure to open their borders and provide refugees with access to their territories. But they also face strong domestic incentives to offer only the most minimal forms of protection and material assistance. Northern donor states have strong incentives to shirk responsibility and to free-ride on the contributions of more proximate states.

The result is a regime that is perennially characterized by collective action failure. Refugee protection is a global public good: all countries benefit to some degree from the human rights and security outcomes it yields, irrespective of whether they contribute. As with all public goods – like street lighting at the domestic level – free-riding and under-provision are inevitable unless some kind of centralized institution creates rules for effective cooperation. Yet existing institutions offer insufficient mechanisms to ensure adequate overall provision. The cooperation problem in the refugee regime can be thought of as what game theorists would describe as a 'suasion game': one in which weaker players are left with little choice but to cooperate and stronger players are left with little incentive to cooperate.[14]

This explains in part why fewer than 1 per cent of the world's refugees get access to resettlement in third countries beyond their region of origin. It explains why UNHCR's assistance programmes around the world are chronically under-funded. It explains why distant countries in the global North, who take a relatively tiny proportion of the world's refugees, constantly compete with one another in a 'race to the bottom' in terms of asylum standards in order to encourage refugees to choose another country's territory rather than their own.

In the absence of clear rules, attempts by UNHCR to overcome this collective action failure have had to be ad hoc and episodic. The organization relies upon annual voluntary contributions for almost all of its budget, rather than having access to assessed, multi-year funding contributions. This makes it easy for governments to change their priorities but difficult for UNHCR to plan. Meanwhile, in order to address long-standing or large-scale refugee crises, it has relied upon the UN Secretary-General convening international conferences such as the International Conferences on Assistance to Refugees in Africa (ICARA I and II) of 1981 and 1984, the International Conferences on Indochinese Refugees of 1979 and 1989, and the International Conference on Central American Refugees (CIREFCA) of 1989, intended to generate reciprocal governmental commitments for a particular crisis.[15]

To take an example, after the end of the Vietnam War in 1975, hundreds of thousands of Indochinese 'boat people' crossed territorial waters from Vietnam, Laos, and Cambodia towards South-East Asian host states such as Malaysia, Singapore, Thailand, the Philippines, and Hong Kong. Throughout the 1970s and 1980s, the host states, facing an influx, pushed many of the boats back into the water and people drowned. Like today, there was a public response to images of people drowning on television and in newspapers, but addressing the issue took political leadership and large-scale international cooperation. In 1989, under UNHCR leadership, a Comprehensive Plan of Action (CPA) was agreed for Indochinese refugees. It was based on an international agreement for sharing responsibility. The receiving countries in South-East Asia agreed to keep their borders open, engage in search-and-rescue operations, and provide reception to the boat people.

However, they did so based on two sets of commitments from other states. First, a coalition of governments – the US, Canada, Australia, New Zealand, and the European states – committed to resettle all those who were judged to be refugees. Second, alternative and humane solutions, including return and alternative, legal, immigration channels were found for those who were not refugees in need of international protection. The plan led to over 2 million people being resettled and the most immediate humanitarian challenge was addressed, partly because of the political will generated at the end of the Cold War and partly because of exceptional leadership by UNHCR.[16]

As the Indochinese example highlights, these ad hoc initiatives have sometimes succeeded when they have been accompanied by decisive leadership and a clear framework for collective action, and have met the interests of states. But such initiatives have been rare and their very existence is indicative of a broader structural weakness in the refugee regime: the absence of norms for responsibility-sharing.

In the twenty-first century, increasing opportunities for mobility and migration have further complicated the question of 'Where to protect?' Rather than waiting passively for governments to decide where protection should be provided, more and more refugees have been making this decision for themselves. 'Spontaneous arrival asylum' – including moving directly onwards to more distant countries in the North by using the service of human smugglers – has become the primary means by which refugees are redistributed beyond their 'regions of origin'.

*

In response, those receiving countries in the developed world have created a range of new practices relating to where refugees should receive protection. Most of these have had in common the aim of reasserting, by fiat or coercion, the idea that refugees should have received protection nearer to home rather than embarking on independent journeys. One such example is the advent of the 'safe third country' concept – the idea that refugees should seek asylum and remain in the first safe country they reach and if they have passed through such a country they can be subject to removal. Another example is the idea of 'outsourcing', with countries seeking bilateral agreements in which they pay another country to admit spontaneous-arrival asylum-seekers and process their claims. Australia's bilateral agreement with Nauru is perhaps the most infamous example. These techniques may well offer a convenient means to contain refugee populations but they are neither supportive of refugee protection nor sustainable.

Australia's approach to the extra-territorial processing of asylum-seekers illustrates the worst of all policy outcomes when a government unilaterally attempts to reconfigure the political geography of asylum. Its so-called Pacific Solution, run between 2001 and 2007, turned away all spontaneously arriving asylum-seekers arriving by boat and sent them to detention centres on Pacific island states – notably Nauru and Papua New Guinea. Amid catastrophic human rights consequences, including prolonged child detention and high suicide rates, the scheme was abandoned, only to be reintroduced in 2012. Australia has also tried to develop similar bilateral agreements with states like Malaysia and Cambodia to receive and process Australia-bound asylum-seekers. Crucially, the 1951 Convention itself does nothing to prohibit the transfer of responsibility for refugees and asylum-seekers – although it has generally been interpreted to place absolute responsibility on the transferring state to ensure those moved receive full access to their rights, not only under refugee law but also under international human rights law.

Such emerging trends put forward increasingly unilateral answers to one of the key areas in which the 1951 Convention is largely silent, 'Who should bear the burden?' Yet it is crucial that if refugee protection is to be sustainable, better answers be found, premised upon collective rather than unilateral action and reinforcing rather than undermining the quantity and quality of protection available to refugees. It is in the historical absence of a clear set of principles and mechanisms for responsibility-sharing that, gradually, almost all states have found themselves in a race to the bottom in term of standards of protection.

MISSING MODELS: WHY CAMPS ARE NOT ENOUGH

The principal way in which the refugee regime provides protection is ineffective and outdated. Since the 1980s the dominant model has been the long-term provision of assistance in refugee camps and closed settlements. A model designed to provide immediate access to food, clothing, and shelter during humanitarian emergencies has become the way in which the international community provides refugees with long-term support. Frequently located in remote and insecure border areas, the 'camp' has become the primary means of protection for refugees around the world.

Until the 1980s, the main way of protecting people was a reflection of the Convention's aspiration to support autonomy. In the North, resettlement was accepted as the dominant durable solution for refugees. Most refugees were moving East–West, fleeing Communism, rather than coming from the South. Repatriation was therefore seen as impossible and immediate, long-term integration as the most politically desirable option. In the South, refugees were generally allowed to spontaneously settle in rural areas. From Julius Nyerere's Tanzania to Kenneth Kaunda's Zambia, Africa's benevolent authoritarian rulers saw it as a pan-African duty to openly provide access to their territories. But this was also the case in other parts of the world – for Afghans in Iran and Guatemalans in Mexico, for instance.

Since the 1980s, though, a very different model has emerged with the advent of a global humanitarian industry intent on distributing food, tents, and blankets. Gradually, UNHCR was asked by governments to provide organized assistance and all too willingly obliged, especially once it found itself without purpose and without money at the end of the Cold War. Host governments in the South, challenged by democratization and structural adjustment, found a means to avert public concern about pressure on resources by abdicating responsibility to internationally managed enclaves in peripheral areas of their countries. Moreover, as new opportunities emerged for 'jet age' asylum-seekers to move from South to North, Northern donor states began to view refugee camps as a means to contain refugee populations who otherwise might try to turn up at their borders.

To take an example, following independence from British rule Tanzania had, under the one-party state rule of Nyerere, opened its borders to allow refugees from across the continent – notably Burundians, Rwandans, and those fleeing liberation wars across Southern Africa – to self-settle in rural areas. It afforded them access to the same agricultural, educational, and health opportunities as those available to host nationals under the country's socialist *Ujamaa* model. International development actors – and not humanitarian actors – provided integrated development support that simultaneously benefited citizens and refugees alike. The example has been widely cited as illustrative of a 'golden age' in African refugee policy. It was only with the introduction of competitive elections and the move towards privatization and retrenchment of public services that Tanzanian governments began to shift towards encampment policies, calling upon the international community to take on a 'care and maintenance' role, and that refugee camps began to emerge across the country.[17]

In Kenya, for instance, the Dadaab refugee camps were created in 1993 to host the mass influx of Somali refugees who arrived following the outbreak of the country's civil war in 1991. The cluster of three camps were designed with a maximum capacity of 120,000 people, but in 2011 the combined populations swelled to host over 500,000 Somali refugees and today it hosts over 300,000 in dire conditions, after some went home or moved onwards. The camps are located in the remote border region of the North Eastern Province, and are the subject of violent cross-border incursions from warring factions and terrorist groups operating in Somalia. Concerned with security and competition for resources, the government has adopted a strict encampment policy, generally requiring Somalis to remain in the camps and denying them access to the formal economy. The international community provided seemingly indefinite humanitarian assistance, which was inevitably inadequate. A funding model based on a short-term emergency response is being used to pay for permanent needs.

Dadaab is illustrative of so-called protracted refugee situations, in which refugees have been in exile for at least five years, and are often denied access to the right to work or to freedom of movement. Today, 54 per cent of the world's 21.3 million refugees are in such situations. UNHCR is responsible for refugees in thirty-two separate protracted refugee situations around the world, with an average length of exile of twenty-six years. Twenty-three of these have lasted more than two decades. In principle, refugees should have timely access to 'durable solutions': a pathway towards permanent reintegration into the state system. But in practice they are getting trapped in indefinite limbo without even the most basic sources of autonomy and opportunity. In 2015, for instance, fewer than 300,000 of the world's refugees received access to either resettlement, repatriation, or local integration. The rest were forced to remain in limbo for another year; the majority without even the right to work. They risk becoming perpetual refugees.

From a refugee's perspective, long-term encampment has been described as a 'denial of rights and a waste of humanity'.[18] Wuli, for example, is a refugee from Somaliland. He has lived in the Ali-Addeh refugee camp in Djibouti since fleeing his own country at the age of eighteen in 1988. Nearly three decades later, he still lives in the same inhospitable camp, in an arid and remote area where temperatures regularly exceed 40°C. Ali-Addeh, home to around 12,000 refugees, has no markets nearby and refugees are not allowed to work. Post-primary educational opportunities are limited, so Wuli provides informal education to young refugees, many born in the camp, in his own tent. He explained: 'Man does not live on food and water alone but on hope. My hope is gone but I pass it on to the next generation.' His situation is typical of so much wasted talent across the world's refugee camps.

These protracted circumstances are bad not only for refugees, but also for host states and the rest of the world. They represent not only a human rights issue but also a security challenge. Without opportunity, they risk creating a lost generation – with people sometimes being born in, growing up in, and becoming adults in camps. They provide ideal nurturing grounds for recruitment and radicalization by rebel groups, militias, and terrorist organizations, who can exploit the presence of an alienated, unemployed, and bored youth population. A range of studies have shown how protracted refugee camps in border locations may serve as vectors for the spread of conflict and violence. We heard stories in the Za'atari refugee camp of parents explaining how their grown-up children had chosen to return to fight in Syria rather than wait passively in the camp.

There are very few viable alternatives to the dominant camp-based 'care and maintenance' model. But the model is so inadequate that refugees are moving onwards of their own accord. To take the example of Syrian refugees, just 9 per cent actually live in camps, because they offer such limited prospects. Only around 10 million of the world's refugees now live in camps.

Cities like Beirut and Amman have become the most common alternative to camp life. Reflecting a wider trend, urbanization is shaping the lived reality of refugees – and large numbers live in global metropolises like Nairobi, Johannesburg, Bangkok, São Paulo, Istanbul, and Cairo. Over half the world's refugees, including 75 per cent of Syrians, live in urban areas in neighbouring countries. But, in cities, assistance is limited and the formal right to work is usually restricted. Although UNHCR has an Urban Refugee Policy, it offers very little assistance in practice, with most urban refugees receiving no tangible help. By moving to cities, most refugees relinquish all formal support but also end up locked out of the formal economy. The world simply has not created a refugee assistance model compatible with a world of global cities. The actors who really matter for urban life – municipal authorities, employers, refugee-led community organizations – are too often excluded from such models. The result is that too many refugees in cities find themselves without aid and facing destitution.

There is another option, which increasing numbers of Syrians and others around the world are taking: risking death to travel onwards to another country. And that's what we're seeing in Europe now: the growth in secondary movements impelled by the inadequacies of the global protection system. Around the world, refugees are effectively offered a false choice between three dismal options: encampment, urban destitution, or perilous journeys. For refugees, these inadequate options – camps, urban destitution, and boats – *are* the modern global refugee regime.

UNHCR AND THE TWENTY-FIRST CENTURY

International regimes are about organizations as well as just norms. UNHCR has not been static since its creation in 1950. Its entire history has been one of adaptation and change. For example, at its creation, it was a temporary organization with no funding and a staff of just a few hundred. Sixty-five years later it has offices in almost every country and an annual budget in excess of $5bn. The scope of its work has expanded dramatically from its being a mainly legal organization focused just on the protection of refugees to becoming an operational one engaged in the protection of refugees, stateless persons, internally displaced persons, and victims of natural disaster.

The pre-eminent historian of the organization, Gil Loescher, shows how successive UN High Commissioners for Refugees have confronted a common challenge: how to walk the 'perilous path' between being beholden to major donor states simply to sustain operations and yet needing to carve out sufficient autonomy to persuade states to contribute to protection and solutions for refugees, occasionally against their own self-interest. Faced with competing obligations towards donor states, host states, and refugees, and the need to ensure the organization's own corporate survival, the most successful High Commissioners have had the strategic awareness to translate the prevailing politics of the day into commitments to refugees.[19]

However, the metric by which any international organization should be assessed is its ability to facilitate collective action within its given policy field. In UNHCR's case this relates to its ability to facilitate collective action to ensure refugees have access to protection and solutions. This involves ensuring governmental commitment and compliance to the core norms of the regime: *non-refoulement* and refugees' access to rights. It also involves supporting international cooperation to ensure there is adequate funding to supply refugees' basic material needs, as well as their timely access to durable solutions like resettlement, local integration, and repatriation.

Of course, one of the challenges is that not all of these outcomes are uniquely within the control of UNHCR and so passing judgement on organizational performance must allow for this limitation. Neverthe-less, it has at its disposal a range of tools to influence state behaviour and guide these types of outcomes. It has the moral authority that comes from having supervisory responsibility for the 1951 Conven-tion, the expert authority that comes from over six decades of working in this area, a virtual monopoly on the refugee mandate across the UN system, convening power and the ability to create special initia-tives, the authority to raise funding directly, and a presence in virtually every country in the world.

UNHCR's capacity to facilitate collective action has depended in part upon the wider context of global order and the distribution of power in the international system. During the Cold War, it was far more viable for UNHCR to have an explicitly 'non-political' mandate. It had the backing of and, to a large extent, worked on behalf of the United States government and its Western allies. Facili-tating resettlement from East to West and supporting frequently authoritarian – but often aligned – satellite countries around the world in creating stable hosting conditions for refugees posed rela-tively uncomplicated political challenges for UNHCR.

In the immediate post-Cold War era, the world changed significantly but UNHCR was at least able to reinvent itself in a context in which the United States, as its main backer, was the pre-eminent superpower, and the appetite for multilateralism was widespread. There was a sig-nificant demand from governments for UNHCR to facilitate durable solutions for populations who were displaced in regions that had pre-viously been afflicted by Cold War proxy violence – South-East Asia, Central America, and Southern Africa, for example. From Cambodia to Mozambique, UNHCR helped people to go home and it scarcely needed to lift a finger to get donors to pay for it. Meanwhile, with the advent of so-called 'new wars' from the Balkans to sub-Saharan Africa, donor states looked to humanitarianism as a new feature of their foreign policy toolbox, a fig leaf for the unwillingness to engage in more direct military intervention.

It is in the twenty-first century that the global order has gradually become a far less auspicious environment for UNHCR to be an effective facilitator of collective action. On the one hand, the terrorist attacks of 11 September 2001 contributed to a new demand for

UNHCR's humanitarian engagement following military intervention and failed state-building in Afghanistan and Iraq. On the other,
it contributed to a growing fear of Islam across the developed world.
Whereas previously Europe had been relaxed about allowing entry to
Muslims fleeing Bosnia and Kosovo during the 1990s, 9/11 unleashed
a political toxicity around the admission of Muslim refugees.

In the global North, UNHCR has faced a fundamental and growing
challenge to the core tenets of the refugee regime. Fear of immigration,
the structural collapse of manufacturing jobs, and post-2008 auster-
ity measures have contributed to a resurgence of popular nationalism
in the liberal democratic world, with significant implications for refugees. In the South – from Kenya to Thailand – UNHCR has similarly
started to encounter states prepared to engage in copycat defiance of
refugee law, increasingly threatening to close their borders or expel
refugee populations.

In a multipolar world of populist nationalism, UNHCR is struggling to reinvent itself. Throughout the post-2015 European refugee
crisis, it has lacked visible influence at a political level, being reactive
to major changes in Europe and elsewhere rather than proactively
driving the agenda. There can be no doubt that many of the organization's staff do extraordinary work, saving lives every day. But to
continue to be relevant in a changing world, UNHCR will need to
fundamentally update its business model. The organization excels in
the areas on which it focuses – providing humanitarian aid in camps
and legal advice to governments – but these are no longer the primary
skills needed to ensure refugee protection in the twenty-first century.

The problem is in part that UNHCR has not had the opportunity
for systematic reform. Its primary mechanism of historical adaptation
has been what might be called panic legacies. It has adopted emergency
responses to address particular crises, and these have often then
become ossified as permanent responses. Over time, these legacies of
ad hoc response have deepened like coastal shelf. And yet despite this
layering, core elements of the organization's role and mandate have
never been subjected to serious reflection by member states. Examples
of these legacies can be found in UNHCR's own relationship to each
of the three broad types of gaps we discussed above.

In terms of models, the most obvious example of an ad hoc response that has become entrenched is camps. As we have explained, camps were not a significant part of the UNHCR toolkit for the first three decades of its existence. UNHCR gradually started to use them in South-East Asia in the early 1980s because it needed to temporarily house people leaving Vietnam and Cambodia in host countries that were not signatories of the 1951 Convention and from which rapid resettlement to the West was anticipated. But with UNHCR facing a near crisis of funding and relevance by the late 1980s, an initially exceptional approach was rolled out as UNHCR expanded its 'care and maintenance' role. By the early 1990s, this was the dominant policy response to mass influx: from the movement of Iraqis into Turkey in 1991, to Somalis entering Kenya after 1991, to Rwandans entering Tanzania in 1994. Camps quickly overshadowed prior settlement options.

The organization does now have a Policy on Alternatives to Camps but there remains a significant gap between policy and practice.[20]

In terms of people, a similar story can be told of how UNHCR's 'population of concern' has evolved. Take for example victims of natural disaster. In the aftermath of the Asian tsunami of 2004, the UN Secretary-General asked UNHCR to stand in and provide assistance in Sri Lanka and Indonesia. UNHCR made clear that this was an 'unprecedented' and exceptional move, stating that what it was doing was outside its mandate. And yet the exception soon became the rule. Over the next six years it took on a further six similar roles in Pakistan, Myanmar, the Philippines, Pakistan again, Sri Lanka, and Haiti.[21] By 2010, the High Commissioner at the time was regarding the practice as policy, and UNHCR was effectively the lead agency for protecting people displaced by natural disasters. But this left UNHCR with a responsibility that it has been poorly resourced to meet. It donors and staff have subsequently wondered if this was a rational move for an organization struggling to meet the needs of its primary constituency.

In terms of providers, UNHCR's current funding model is also a panic legacy that has become dysfunctional. Its single-year government-driven funding model is the product of historical contingency. In a world in which predictable, multi-year funding is needed, the primary source of refugee funding remains the 'annual voluntary contribution'. UNHCR writes an annual appeal outlining its budget. After much bilateral discussion, governments commit to fund part of the budget – usually just for one year – whether on an earmarked or an unearmarked basis. Each year the cycle repeats. The approach leads to huge unpredictability and wasted resources. Unsurprisingly, it too is an anachronistic legacy of the past, and initially began because the UNHCR of the 1950s was created with only a temporary mandate and with extremely limited government support. This is a tragedy when other, more predictable financing models are now so widely used in other sectors. Such mechanisms include catastrophic risk financing through government-backed catastrophe bonds, public–private partnerships based on a user-fee model or guaranteed annual subsidy, and political-risk insurance – all of which are used elsewhere to encourage business investment in contexts of uncertainty.[22]

CRISIS AND THE OPPORTUNITY FOR REFORM

So although the global refugee regime has historically adapted, it has done so incrementally and conservatively, following a broadly path-dependent trajectory. The core elements conceived after the Second World War – the 1951 Convention and UNHCR – remain significantly unaltered since their creation. At no point has there been a systematic or fundamental reflection on whether these institutions need to be reformed or updated, and if so how far.

We are not suggesting that either the 1951 Convention or UNHCR should be abolished. Nevertheless, the 1951 Convention fails to adequately answer the most basic contemporary questions on 'who to protect', 'how to protect', and 'where to protect', offering a lack of guidance on the dominant refugee policy challenges of the twenty-first century. Meanwhile, UNHCR is increasingly struggling to fulfil its underlying purpose: to facilitate collective action on protection and solutions for refugees.

Globalization, urbanization, climate change, state fragility, greater opportunities for mobility, the rise of China, the changing nature of conflict, the role of the internet and social media, new technologies, the growth of regionalism, the shift from Cold War bipolarity to unipolarity to multipolarity, to name just a few of the factors, have all radically altered the nature of the forced-displacement challenge, as well as the opportunities available to states to collectively provide protection and solutions. But at no point has there been a thorough reflection on how this radically changed world should shape institutional redesign in the refugee regime.

The inertia may be partly justified through experience. A perennial challenge within the United Nations is the belief that nothing can really change. At least not quickly. No specialized agency has ever disappeared. Reform moments – such as the UN reform process of the early 2000s – yielded disappointingly slow and incremental change. Furthermore, the sheer number of states within the UN General Assembly, and the reality that for most of the UN's history – the Cold War and twenty-first century, at least – its main security body, the Security Council, has been blocked and sclerotic, make the UN reform route appear limited. But this should certainly not be an indelible hindrance to change in the refugee regime.

The gross inadequacies of the inherited system became increasingly apparent. In other areas of international policy, crisis has led to root-and-branch institutional reform. For example, the currency crisis of 1971 led to the end of the fixed-exchange-rate regime. The refugee regime, ossified over several more decades than any other part of the post-war international architecture, is at last under pressure. A Danish professor of law, Thomas Gammeltoft-Hansen, has suggested that European governments are experiencing a 'paradigm crisis' in which for the first time they are starting to recognize that the system may be broken beyond repair.[23]

The political will to reform the system may at last be building. European heads of state have repeatedly met at the highest political levels to try to rebuild the internal and external dimensions of a Common European Asylum System. The UN General Assembly convened its highest-profile meeting ever on refugees on 19 September 2016 and this was followed a day later by a US Presidential Summit on Refugees. Never before have the political aspiration and the inherent need for reform been so significant, and yet across all of these meetings a corresponding policy vision has remained wanting.

To date, the predominant political response to the Syrian refugee crisis has not been a rethink of policy: it has been panic. Prepare for headless chickens.

3

The Panic

Europe's politicians were faced with a global upsurge in displacement, but most evidently an escalating refugee situation due to the continuing violence in Syria. Having inherited a global refugee regime that was incapable of reacting adequately, what they needed was a swift and decisive new approach. Instead, political responses were so inept that they ensured a mounting crisis. Policies have lurched back and forth between the headless heart and the heartless head. In this chapter we recount the stages of this saga.

A central argument of this book is that the series of events we describe need not have led to the terrible outcomes that unfolded with the seeming inevitability of a tragedy. Hence, our story starts not with the first wave of refugees, but with the adoption of policies that created avoidable vulnerabilities. What became, literally, a Greek tragedy, began as a Brussels farce.

MAKING THE TINDER BOX: SCHENGEN

Refugees are defined by flight across a border. But while the rules that define borders are central to refugee policy, refugee policy is not central to the rules that define borders. In 1999, the European Union incorporated border regulations into its legal framework, giving scarcely a thought to the practical implications for the flow of refugees.

The Schengen Area removed all border controls within a vast area of Europe. Though not quite coincident with the EU (it included Norway, which was not in the EU, and excluded Britain and Ireland, which were), it was widely regarded as a flagship political symbol of

European unification: a visible expression of 'ever closer union'. But border controls are not just symbols: they are practical measures. Their removal had two substantive effects, the implications of which would later become fully apparent. One was that anyone (citizen or not) could move between member countries without any scrutiny. The other was that entry to the entire area would be determined by the policies and implementation capacities of each of those countries with an external border. Italy became known as 'Schengen's soft underbelly'.

While the impetus for Schengen was a noble aspiration among political elites for a united Europe, there was an extraordinary disconnection between the will to implement the outcome and the will to make it workable. This vast area was created without either an agreement on common external immigration policies or the creation of a common external border police. An emotive political vision overrode the rather obvious practical requirements without which it exposed the entire area to potential dangers: Europe had made a tinder box.

In order to support Schengen, the European Union tried to create something approximating a shared asylum and immigration policy. Intellectually, it was understood that freedom of movement within the common area would only be sustainable if immigration standards and practices could be harmonized. The Commission gradually negotiated a Common European Asylum System (CEAS) – a series of common criteria for qualification (who is a refugee?), adjudication (how do we determine who is a refugee?), and reception (what rights should asylum-seekers and refugees receive?). The aim was to avoid a 'race to the bottom' in terms of standards, reduce the likelihood of refugees engaging in 'asylum shopping', and ensure no one state ended up with a disproportionate share of refugees because of its having more generous policies.

That was the theory. In practice, the system was dysfunctional from the start. States adopted different asylum standards. Recognition rates for different nationalities, the required duration of residency before asylum-seekers would be allowed to work, and social-security entitlements, for example, all varied markedly across Europe. Governments thereby continued to compete with one another to divert, deter, and deflect unwanted asylum-seekers. Most damaging of all, the removal of internal border controls created a classic weakest-link problem. The entire Schengen Area of 500 million people became as porous as the most open of the countries with external borders. Such a border might be unusually open either because the immigration policies of its government were more generous than those of others, or because in practice its controls were less effective.

While talking the language of harmonization, governments anticipated that it would not work in practice. Realizing that the weakest-link problem potentially exposed them to open borders, the most powerful states took defensive action. A new rule was agreed in 1990, came into force in 1997, and was gradually adapted thereafter through major updates in 2003 and 2013: the Dublin Regulation. It prescribed that the first European country in which an asylum-seeker arrived should either provide permanent haven to them or send them back, according to whether they met the agreed criteria. In effect, the weakest-link problem was to be solved by the rule: if you let them in, you keep them. At the time, frontline countries like Italy and Greece were persuaded to accept these rules because arrival numbers were relatively low and because they believed they had more to gain in other areas of intra-EU bargaining.

Governments with particularly generous welfare systems, such as in Denmark and the Netherlands, were concerned that in the absence of some rule on allocation all those admitted would gravitate to them. But the new rule was hardly an equitable one. As a map of Europe will rapidly reveal, member states were differentially exposed to the arrival of asylum-seekers. Whereas the southern countries had long borders across the Mediterranean from fragile states, and eastern countries bordered the new states of the former USSR, Germany had no external borders whatsoever. In addressing the weakest-link problem, the new rule had done so in a way that also assigned the entire burden of asylum to these frontline countries. Unsurprisingly they complained. The Commission met their complaints through a new fund to compensate them: the European Refugee Fund. Unfortunately for the frontline states, there was never more than a token amount of money in it. Incontrovertibly, a rule had been adopted which favoured the most powerful member countries.

Internal borders having been dismantled, there was evidently the problem of enforcing the Dublin Regulation. A registration system was introduced, feeding into a new Europe-wide database that revealed an asylum-seeker's country of arrival. But as with the common asylum system itself, this depended upon state-by-state compliance. Frontline states sought to cheat the broken system by 'waving through' refugees without recording their details in the European database. The system of registration, intended to enforce the Dublin Regulation, which was itself a response to the presumption that there would be non-compliance with the common asylum policy, lacked an enforcement system. The practice of 'waving through' became the Achilles heel of the system.

Waving through was not the only type of opportunistic practice induced by the Schengen Agreement. The lack of a common migration policy created an unseemly incentive for individual governments to sell the right of entry to the Schengen Area. The opportunity was duly taken. For example, Portugal introduced a scheme whereby for €500k of investment in Portuguese property, anyone could get entitlement for themselves and their children to live in the Area. Wealthy Chinese apparently bought these entitlements so that their children could study in prestigious locations such as Paris. The government of Malta sold the right to settle in the Area at a slightly higher price (€650k). Both have recently been undercut by Hungary, which is offering permanent Schengen residence for €360k. These opportunistic practices were in stark contrast to the noble vision that had motivated Schengen. They were a trivial symptom of the larger problem: fine rhetoric was not a substitute for attention to reality.

Beyond mercenary considerations, some states had generous rules of entry. For example, Spain adopted a rule that anyone arriving on its territory – notably, people on boats from Africa reaching the Canaries – would receive the right to permanent residence after forty days unless expelled. Since there was no capacity for expulsion within such a timeframe, it implied open access to the Schengen Area for anyone able to travel illegally by boat to the Canaries. Ireland had a rule which is estimated to have entitled some 40 million non-Irish people to Irish passports, and hence to residence anywhere in Schengen.

Obviously, a border-free area requires a common external force to police its borders. A real federal state such as the USA has one, but the EU adopted the symbol of borderless passage without the necessary supporting organization. The EC assembled a quasi-volunteer frontier force, Frontex, by drawing on various national forces. But it is a proto-agency that would take many years to build into something equivalent to those of Canada or the USA. Currently, it is tiny and barely serious: as explained to us by an EU official, at Christmas 2015, a time of massive border pressure in Greece from the influx of refugees and migrants, the staff of Frontex simply went home for a week's holiday, leaving their posts unmanned. As a practical matter, this left border policing and migrant processing in the hands of the national administrations of those countries with external borders.

While Frontex fell far short of being equivalent to a national border force such as those of the USA or Britain, its task was an order of magnitude more demanding. Europe borders on two of the world's most conflict-prone regions: the Middle East and North Africa. Further, adjoining each of these troubled regions are other zones of instability: Central Asia, the Sahel, and the Horn of Africa. The gate-keepers for these enormous populations are Turkey, Morocco, Algeria, Tunisia, Libya, Egypt and Syria. The prospects of all of them being continuously cooperative and effective are negligible. The EU tried repeatedly to develop bilateral partnerships and 'neighbourhood policies' in its attempt to develop an 'external dimension' to its asylum and immigration policy. But these frequently fell short, delivering neither managed migration nor the adequate protection of refugees.

This made the weakest-link problem acute because Europe had its very own failing nation-state: Greece, easily reachable from Turkey, but also via Crete from North Africa. In 2011 Greece's then Prime Minister, George Papandreou, had astonished his fellow European heads of government by warning them that the Greek public sector was corrupt to the core. By 2015, with its economy having contracted by a catastrophic 25 per cent, the government in charge of coping with this nightmare, including the reform of deeply flawed public services, was an untested party of the radical left, Syriza. The tinder box was fully prepared, ready for a spark.

THE SPARK

The spark duly came in the form of the poignantly named 'Arab Spring'.[1] A young Tunisian who had a market stall became so frustrated that he set fire to himself and died of his burns. The match struck by Mohamed Bouazizi on 17 December 2010 became the equivalent of the bullet fired by the assassin Gavrilo Princip which killed Archduke Franz Ferdinand and triggered the First World War.

The southern coast of the Mediterranean had long been under the control of a monarchy in Morocco, and three dictators in Tunisia, Egypt and Libya. All had a substantial military capacity, and therefore maintained effective control of their borders. Morocco, Tunisia and Egypt were pro-Western and so naturally cooperative in preventing organized people-smuggling. Libya, under the eccentric regime of Colonel Gaddafi, was ostensibly anti-Western, but needed various forms of European assistance and as a quid pro quo was also effectively suppressing people-smuggling.

Bouazizi's act triggered mass protests, first in Tunisia, and then in the other two dictatorships. All three regimes were swiftly toppled by pro-democracy movements. However, what began as a call for democracy rapidly transmuted into violent religious and ethnic sectarianism. In Tunisia and Egypt elections were won by Islamic parties that found democracy a useful stepping stone to power, but had little interest in building a modern democratic state with checks and balances. In Egypt this triggered a backlash by means of a military coup, returning the state to a repressive autocracy. Fearing the same fate, the Tunisian government gradually softened its Islamic stance and began to share power with other groups. As in Egypt, the society faced a high level of terrorism, but the government managed to retain practical control.

In contrast, despite electing a moderate government, Libya erupted into ethnic violence. As warlords took control of pockets of territory, the Libyan state collapsed, losing control of most of the country, including the capital city. As a minor by-product of this descent into chaos, government control of the coast evaporated: there was no government. This opened the southern coast of the Mediterranean to the people-smuggling business. In a way that was analogous to the external borders of the Schengen Area, control of the southern coast of the Mediterranean posed a weakest-link problem. The people-smugglers just needed a chink in the armour to get into business. Anyone who could reach Libya and had the money was now going to be able to get on a boat for Europe.

Nevertheless, the barriers to reaching Europe illegally remained significant. The most proximate part of Europe for people-smugglers was the tiny island of Lampedusa, which belonged to Italy. But even to reach Lampedusa involved a substantial sea crossing, making it dangerous and expensive. Further, Libya had only a small population and as a result of vast oil resources its people were not living in poverty. Hence, the demand for places on boats from Libyans wanting to reach Europe was going to be modest. Despite this, the people-smugglers knew that they could build a promising business: their potential market lay to the south of Libya, where there was an ocean of poverty – the countries of the Sahel and beyond them the highly populated states of West and Central Africa. The potential market from this vast pool of people was, however, also limited. To get to the coast the physical barrier of the Sahel, and the dangers involved in crossing such a large and lawless area, had to be surmounted. Between the sea passage and traversing the Sahel, both risks and costs were high. The high costs were constraining precisely because the societies south of Libya were so poor. In practice, the people choosing to use the smugglers would be disproportionately risk-taking, namely young men, and disproportionately affluent.

As the people-smuggling industry scaled up, the Italian authorities began to face difficulties. By August of 2011, nearly 50,000 mainly young male immigrants originally from across Africa arrived on the island of Lampedusa from Tunisia and Libya. Italy in 2011 was a foretaste of what was soon to happen in Greece.

THE ROMAN PROLOGUE

Crossing the Mediterranean in small boats is dangerous, and so the first and most appalling consequence of the new exodus was that thousands drowned. In response, the Italian government mounted a rescue operation, *Mare Nostrum*. Once it had rescued them on the open sea, the Italian navy had no choice but to bring the migrants ashore in Italy. Inadvertently, it was providing a free service to the people-smugglers, and this had an evident potential to be gamed. By towing a dinghy packed with migrants out to sea and abandoning it, the people-smugglers could deliver people to Europe more cheaply, and without taking the risk of prosecution involved in trying to reach the Italian shore.

The numbers involved in both people-smuggling and *Mare Nostrum* jointly escalated during 2014, and 100,000 people were rescued from boats and brought to shore by the Italian navy. The *reductio ad absurdum* of *Mare Nostrum* would have been for the Italian navy to run a free ferry service from the coast of Libya to Italy. Instead, in November 2014 the Italian government suspended *Mare Nostrum*: the heartless head replaced the headless heart. Thereafter, due to these intrinsic contradictions, rescue operations were sometimes scaled up, and sometimes scaled down, depending upon public interest. In April 2015 the inevitable catastrophe hit the media. More than 700 people drowned in two days: the most dramatic demonstration of heartlessness that had been seen to date. Panic took over.

Meanwhile, for those who reached Lampedusa, whether directly on boats run by people-smugglers or courtesy of the Italian navy, what befell them? The people crossing were from a range of countries: some refugee-producing, others less obviously so: Eritrea, The Gambia, Senegal, Somalia, Mali, and Nigeria, and there were a growing number of Syrians. Once they arrived on Italian territory, the Dublin Agreement rules required that the Italian government should register all asylum-seekers and thereafter either give them the right to remain in Italy or return them to their country of origin. Either way, the new arrivals did not have the right to move to other Schengen countries. Although the Italian economy was large, it was in no state to absorb an influx of workers: between 2007 and 2015 Italian per capita incomes declined by 11 per cent. Young Italians were emigrating from Italy in droves to find work in Northern Europe, and the young immigrants to Italy often had the same aspirations.

However, whereas young Italians were free to work anywhere in the EU, the rules of the Dublin Agreement meant that people arriving spontaneously from North Africa were not free to go anywhere beyond Italy. Thus, were it to adhere to EU rules, Italy would consequently gradually lose young Italians, who would be replaced by young Africans. While this was not a package of rules likely to appeal to the Italian government, there were two loopholes.

One critical loophole was that since there was no policed border between Italy and the neighbouring Schengen countries of France and Austria, there was no on-the-ground way of enforcing the condition that people crossing from Libya should remain in Italy. In practice, migrants could move anywhere in Schengen. Once in France, Germany or one of the other Schengen countries their prospects would be more limited than those for Italians. They would need to avoid official recognition: once on the bureaucratic radar screen, their registration would be traced and they would be returned to Italy. Hence, they would not, legally, be able to work: to survive, they would be limited to informal self-employment, below-minimum-wage jobs in the service and agricultural sectors, and crime.

The migrants needed to find unregulated work, and by far the least regulated labour market in Europe was in Britain. Not only was it only lightly regulated, but, unlike the rest of Europe, Britain had no national identity card, and no requirement to register habitation. But Britain was not in the Schengen Area and between it and Schengen was the English Channel. This is why an encampment grew alongside the Calais boarding point for the Channel Tunnel: thousands of young migrants waited there to be smuggled into Britain in lorries. As controls were tightened, the people-smuggling spread along the French coast.

While the first loophole depended upon the ingenuity of individual migrants, the second loophole depended upon the behaviour of government officials. Evidently, the Dublin Agreement rules gave the Italian government little incentive to register the migrants. If they were left unregistered, once they had left Italy for a more promising economy, they could not be returned. The official process incorporated into the Dublin Agreement was that all migrants would be fingerprinted at the point of arrival. With the single entry point of Lampedusa this was entirely feasible, but in practice Italian officials were lax in adhering to the regulations. It is doubtful that enforcement was a high priority for the government. Officialdom was assisted in this process by the migrants themselves, many of whom learnt to hamper any process whereby they might be returned to their country of origin by destroying their papers and refusing to reveal where they were from. De facto, such migrants were able to remain wherever they had reached by the time they encountered officialdom.

While the flow of migrants from Libya to Italy eventually became substantial, it took a long time to build up. It did not trigger a crisis until November 2014, with the suspension of *Mare Nostrum* and the ensuing increase in the number of drownings. The scale of the inflow was constrained by the difficulties posed by the natural barriers. Further, although the primary host society was Italy, the migrants spread themselves across the vast Schengen Area: relative to the host population they were a drop in the ocean. The Italian government complained about its disproportionate burden, but other governments saw the Dublin Agreement as an essential defence: without it, the countries of Southern Europe would have very little incentive to control their borders. Even the impact of that drop in the ocean was softened because the migrants were largely confined to working illegally. They stood at traffic lights washing car windows, busked on the metro, and sold flowers in the street. Nor did they have ready access to Europe's generous array of social services. None of this was very threatening to ordinary European citizens.

The initial exodus across the Mediterranean to Italy was an early effect of Bouazizi's self-immolation. Returning to the analogy with Princip's bullet, the period from 2003 (when the updated Dublin Regulation came into force) to 2014 (when its contradictions became unmanageable) was equivalent to the disastrous interval between Princip's shot on 28 June 1914 and the end of July. In each case panic took over: August soon arrived.

THE SPARK SPREADS TO SYRIA

The protests of the Arab Spring did not engulf the entire Middle East. Just as unrest in Morocco never grew to a level that threatened the state, so all the other monarchies of the region remained in place: in Jordan, Saudi Arabia, Dubai, the UAE, Qatar, Kuwait, and Bahrain. Only the last of these experienced serious protests. Evidently, although autocratic, the monarchies of the Middle East had significant on-the-ground legitimacy. The dictatorships were a different matter. Had Saddam Hussein still been ruling Iraq he would probably have faced a major uprising. As it was, Iraq was already in such disorder that there was little left for the Arab Spring to disrupt. The remaining Arab autocracy was Syria. The Assad family had tried to turn itself into a de facto monarchy by passing the succession on to the son of the first autocrat. But monarchy rests upon an entirely different belief system from autocracy, and so Assad II struggled to gain legitimacy beyond his own Alawite minority.

If Ben Ali in Tunisia, if Mubarak in Egypt, if Gaddafi in Libya, why not Assad? More and more people took to the streets. In Tunisia and Egypt the regimes had cracked simply by weight of the numbers on the streets. This did not happen in Syria because, like Gaddafi, the regime tried to tough it out. Given Gaddafi's fate at the hands of the enraged population, this was a decidedly risky strategy. Had the Assad family astutely evaluated their prospects at this moment they would have flown to a political haven where, supported by the fortune they had amassed abroad, they could have maintained their shopaholic lifestyle. Gaddafi's tough-it-out strategy had failed because France and Britain had persuaded a reluctant President Obama to provide air cover for the rebels and freeze the regime's bank accounts. But Syria was perhaps just too close to Iraq. By 2011 American intervention in Iraq had been recognized as disastrous: a 'never again' lesson had been absorbed. President Obama was extolling the strategy of 'leadership from behind', and 'pivoting to Asia'. So, as the Arab Spring began to unravel in Tunisia, Egypt and Libya, the West decided to sit Syria out.

Even without Western military intervention, the Assad regime gradually lost control of territory. But as in the other Arab Spring revolutions, the conflict evolved into highly fractured sectarian and ethnic rivalries. The Sunni wanted to be free of the Alawites; the Islamists wanted to overturn the secular Baathist regime; the Kurds wanted independence from the Arabs; and the Iraqi radical Islamists of ISIS wanted to create a Caliphate that spanned the border. Against them, the Alawites feared that defeat would make them the victims of ethnic cleansing; the Christians feared that an Islamic state would persecute them; and Hezbollah, the regime-supported armed movement that had succeeded in expelling Israel from Lebanon, saw regime preservation as a vital interest. Beyond these groups, the three main regional powers, Iran, Saudi Arabia and Turkey, were each drawn in. What had begun as a democracy protest escalated into an internationalized civil war.

As the regime's military position deteriorated, it resorted to increasing atrocities against the civilian population. President Obama issued a 'red line' against chemical weapons. Assad's forces were sufficiently desperate to cross that line; the international community proved to be sufficiently wary of any involvement for the red line to turn yellow: there was no response. Nevertheless, beset by a wide assortment of armed rebel groups with varying agendas, by the summer of 2015 the regime was sliding into military collapse. Had it continued for another few weeks the interest of the Syrian military would have overwhelmingly been to oust Assad in a coup and reach a deal with the more moderate rebels and the USA to prevent the prospect of far worse. Instead, Russia intervened on the side of the regime with substantial military force that decisively changed the balance of power.

By their nature, armed rebel groups operate outside the constraints of international rules of war. By temperament and desperation, the same was true of the Assad regime. In consequence, the armed groups were brutal not only to each other but to civilians. Sieges and starvation became standard tactics. Between the onset of the conflict in 2011 and 2015 around 10 million people, half of the entire Syrian population, had fled their homes to escape violence. This magnitude of displacement was exceptional even by the dismal standards of civil war. For example, in the other contemporaneous global emergency, the civil war in South Sudan, displacement has affected around a quarter of the population; in Somalia, which has the third-highest proportion of the population displaced, it is just under a quarter. That some of those displaced would seek safety outside Syria's borders was both inevitable and appropriate. Cumulatively, around half of them did so: by 2014, 4 million people had left Syria, being transformed in legal terms from internally displaced people to refugees in the process.

THE SYRIAN REFUGEE CRISIS PHASE I (2011–14): THE HEARTLESS HEAD

Where did these 4 million people go? Syria has a coast and five land borders. The coast is in the Alawite region of the country, firmly under the control of the regime, and so not a route for refugee flight. The land borders are with Turkey, Iraq, Jordan, Israel, and Lebanon. Of these, the border with Israel was heavily fortified by the Israeli army and effectively impassable by refugees. Israel has adopted a strict 'no Syrian refugees' policy, although it has discreetly provided medical assistance at the border, with its army screening the injured on the Syrian side, and hospitals in its border towns offering care. By 2011 Iraq was so beset by violent disorder that it was not a credible haven for refugees, although it did host some camps for Syrian Kurds. Further, eastern Syria, which bordered on Iraq, was only lightly populated and so not a major region of refugee flight. This left Turkey, Jordan and Lebanon as the most feasible destinations.

From the perspective of refuge each had advantages and disadvantages. Like Syria, Jordan and Lebanon have Arab populations and are Arabic speaking. In terms of religion, Jordan and Turkey are best suited, both being predominantly Sunni, whereas Lebanon is a delicate mix of Shia, Sunni, and Christian. In terms of socio-economic absorptive capacity, Turkey was in a class of its own, with both by far the largest population and by far the largest and most rapidly growing economy. In terms of government capacity, both Jordan and Turkey had competent, unified governments that were firmly in control of their territory. In contrast, the structure of the Lebanese government reflected its own long period of civil war, with power delicately shared between different factions. In consequence, it had very little capacity for coherent responses to new challenges.

However, the flight to refuge is not equivalent to normal migration. People flee mass violence as families, not individually. They take as many of their possessions as they can carry, and travelling in large numbers they probably have to resort to informal means of transport. This makes physical proximity more important than other considerations. The country that was most proximate to those parts of Syria which were both heavily populated and affected by conflict was Turkey. In consequence, out of the over 4 million refugees, around half went to Turkey, with roughly a million going to Jordan and a million to Lebanon. Our numbers are rounded off partly because they are constantly changing, but also because many of the numbers are disputed. The flight to refuge is, by its nature, an informal process that is only sporadically documented.

Refugees, being international, become an international responsibility. This responsibility is shared between the first countries in which refugees arrive, which have a direct duty to provide a haven, and all other governments, which collectively have a duty of assistance.

As implied by our discussion above, the capacities of the three haven countries differed considerably. Cumulatively, Turkey received most of the refugees, but in most respects it was best placed to cope with them. It had a competent government, a large and booming economy, the same religion as the refugees, and since Ottoman times it had a tradition of being a multi-ethnic society. Although the influx to Jordan was in absolute terms smaller than that to Turkey, proportionate to its population of just 6.5 million it was far larger. Its economy was much smaller, and less robust. Whereas Turkey was heavily integrated into the global economy, most notably through a trade agreement with the EU, the economy of Jordan was dominated by the public sector, financed by aid and subsidies from the Arab oil economies. Further, while Jordan had a unified and competent government, it rested on the monarchy supported by marital ties to the major clans, which as we have noted was the only system of government in the Middle East to have practical legitimacy. Syrian refugees, coming from a radically different social and political system, could not readily be integrated into this structure. Lebanon was an order of magnitude more stressed by the refugee influx than the other two countries. Its fractured government implied that it had very limited capacity to respond to refugee needs; while its fractured society, with its precarious peace, could potentially be destabilized by a radical change in the balance of the population between the three major religious groups.

These differences in refugee flows and in national capacities suggested that the international response orchestrated by UNHCR would need to be correspondingly differentiated. UNHCR might be most urgently needed in Lebanon given that it hosted over 1 million refugees against the backdrop of a total population of just over 4 million. But weak governance and Lebanon's reluctance to open camps given its past experience of hosting Palestinians since 1948 and its complex relationship with Syria meant that, in practice, the overwhelming majority of Syrians were tolerated and de facto integrated, particularly in the informal economy and impoverished urban areas. Lebanon was therefore a poor fit for UNHCR's standard emergency-driven approach of delivering humanitarian assistance in camps. To all intents and purposes, civil society provided the bulk of the response.

In Turkey, UNHCR's role has also been limited. Less than 10 per cent of the country's Syrian refugees have been in several government-run camps, with UNHCR's role being limited to the delivery of core relief items and support during the winter months. The overwhelming majority of the urban Syrian population have had no contact with UNHCR. Its role has mainly focused on offering targeted support to the most vulnerable 5 per cent through cash assistance, and basic services like counselling and interpretation.[2]

In the event, UNHCR engaged primarily in Jordan. It was directly involved in setting up camps across Jordan, the largest, Za'atari, being close to the Syrian border. To finance its activities, UNHCR appealed to the international community for emergency contributions. As the numbers of refugees accumulated between 2011 and 2015, the need for financing evidently grew. But the emergency-style funding model of UNHCR did not lend itself to the mounting and long-lasting nature of what was required. Donors prefer to make pledges for situations that are new and hence newsworthy. As donors lost interest, contributions began to dwindle. For example, in 2014 the German government halved its contribution. By the spring of 2015 the UNHCR response to the Syrian refugee situation was facing a financial crisis and its modest payments to the refugees in its camps had to be reduced. By that stage, just 35 per cent of the UN's $1.3bn Syrian regional refugee response plan was funded.[3]

Instead, the financial burden increasingly fell upon the governments of the haven countries. As 'middle-income countries', all three hosts were locked out of traditional development assistance opportunities. The Jordanian government financed this by emergency borrowing: as a result, the stock of public debt rose from 70 per cent of GDP in 2011 to around 90 per cent by 2015. It sensed that it was hitting the buffers of the possible. Clutching at straws, the royal think tank invited the two of us to come to Jordan.

In retrospect it is now widely accepted that the failure of the international community to support the haven countries at an appropriate scale and in a timely fashion was both morally shaming and a catastrophic practical mistake. Assessed ethically, we see it as an example of the *heartless head*. Assessed on the conventional public policy metric of costs and benefits, it was not only heartless – it was *headless*: the subsequent costs arising from it have exploded beyond measure.

Evidently, the financing model of UNHCR was not adequate for a protracted and worsening refugee situation such as unfolded in Syria. Yet, more seriously, its model of humanitarian care provided in camps also proved grossly deficient. Even in Jordan, where UNHCR relied most heavily on the camps, they were ignored by a large majority of the refugees.

The fundamental weakness of the UNHCR approach was that it was best suited to the exceptional conditions that had applied in the immediate period before it was established. Like the fable about generals, UNHCR was, literally, fighting the previous war. In the Europe of the late 1940s, with the fighting over, masses of displaced hungry people were trying to return to their homes or reach new ones. Camps were needed to feed them and provide shelter while relatives were traced, and transit arranged. In other words, refugee status was temporary. In contrast, Syrian refugees were not in post-conflict transit: they were waiting for peace to return. In this they were typical of the recent global refugee experience: the usual period of refugee status is now nearly twenty years. This reflects the altered nature of the violence itself. When UNHCR was established, the refugee situation had arisen from an international war, whereas almost all recent refugee situations have arisen due to civil wars. Historically, on average international wars have lasted only six months. In contrast, the average civil war has been much longer, with estimates ranging from seven to fifteen years.

If a family are going to be refugees for over a decade, their priority is not emergency food and shelter. It is to re-establish the threads of normal family life, anchored materially by a capacity of whoever is the breadwinner to earn a living. The camps run by UNHCR met the basic material needs of refugees, but they provided few opportunities to earn a living. Consequently, they left families bereft of autonomy.

The inability of refugees to earn a living within the standard UNHCR approach was not only psychologically diminishing for the refugees, but also highlighted the lack of viability of the financing model. Paying for 4 million refugees to live without work for ten years was manifestly unsustainable. Even at a cost of only $1,000 per refugee per year, which would have implied a drastic reduction in lifestyle relative to Syrian pre-refugee conditions, the bill would have amounted to $40bn. Since the Syrian refugee situation was just one of many, the approach was completely unfeasible. Financially, the only reason it did not break down earlier was itself a devastating critique: refugees overwhelmingly bypassed the camps.

In Jordan around 85 per cent of refugees went to live in cities. Even in the cities, Syrian refugees were not officially permitted to work. But, like many developing countries, Jordan had a large informal economy. In practice, if people were sufficiently desperate, they could work illegally, either as an employee at a wage below the official minimum, or scratching a living in informal self-employment. The same pattern emerged in Turkey: some refugees went to the camps, but most entered the informal urban economy, which abounded with opportunities. In Lebanon, the pattern was yet more dramatic: camps were not established and so the entire refugee influx was absorbed informally. Many refugee households must consequently have experienced a substantial fall in their income as a result of their flight. Often, living standards could be cushioned for a while by depleting assets, but as the conflict persisted this gradually became unsustainable, and many refugees understandably faced mounting anxiety.

In effect, in this phase by far the most useful mechanisms for meeting the needs of the refugee exodus from Syria were the informal economies of the neighbouring countries. They provided the income-earning opportunities which refugees, using their own initiative, grasped: the informal private economy was the lifeboat. In contrast, official policies were constraining. The haven governments prevented all but a handful of refugees from working legally, whereas UNHCR camps were located far away from possible job opportunities.

Necessity is the mother of invention: the next phase built on the ingenuity of refugees.

THE SYRIAN REFUGEE CRISIS PHASE II: THE NEW LAMPEDUSA (NOVEMBER 2014–AUGUST 2015)

By 2014, the 4 million refugees who had fled to the haven countries were safe but poor. In the informal sector their prospects were limited. As the conflict back home escalated it became evident that there would be no early return. Understandably, the more footloose and enterprising among the refugees began to think of ways of improving their prospects. A thousand miles along the Mediterranean coast such a prospect was already on offer, provided by the people-smuggling industry operating out of Libya. As with crossing the Sahara, the journey was risky and expensive, but some young Syrians began to try it.

But reaching the economic opportunities of Northern Europe via a thousand-mile journey along the coast, followed by a long and expensive boat journey to Lampedusa, was wildly inefficient. After *Mare Nostrum* was suspended in November 2014 it also became much more dangerous. After the high-profile tragedies of the mass drownings in April 2015 even the people-smuggling industry must have started to worry that its business model was becoming unviable.

Yet an equivalent European island was just a few miles from where 2 million refugees were already living. Lesbos, a small Greek island just off the coast of Turkey, became the new Lampedusa as people-smugglers spotted the new market opportunity and relocated.

The rules of the Dublin Agreement had limited Lampedusa to being a legal gateway only to Italy. As we discussed above, although the Italian economy was large, it was contracting at an alarming rate and so the prospects of earning a living were poor. This drawback applied far more powerfully to Lesbos than to Lampedusa. According to the same rules, Lesbos would have provided a legal gateway only to Greece.

However, while the Italian economy was contracting, the Greek economy was in free-fall. Whereas the Italian economy contracted by 11 per cent during 2007–15, the Greek shrank by 25 per cent. Formally, Greece was a normal member of the EU: keen on acquiring all the trappings of that status, it had adopted the euro, joined Schengen, and signed the Dublin Agreement. But in practice Greece was a failing state: corrupt, bankrupt, and poor, with the government having fallen into the hands of a new party of the extreme left. As the Greek economy collapsed, so too did its asylum system. In a little-noticed court case of 2011, an Afghan asylum-seeker had challenged the application of the Dublin Agreement to Greece. He had reached Belgium having been first registered in Greece. Following the Dublin rules, the Belgian and Greek authorities duly arranged his return to Greece, where he faced destitution and homelessness.[4] The argument put to the European Court of Human Rights was that Greece was in no position to fulfil its obligations: its government had signed up to something that it could not deliver.

This was not the only European court case of this period that hinged on facing the reality of the Greek situation. Both the German Constitutional Court and the European Court of Justice were agonizing over the same fundamental issue, but in the context of the credibility of Greek commitments to repaying further debt. The European Court of Human Rights took the view that regardless of what the Greek government had signed, it was in no position to live up to its commitments, and so refugees could not be returned by Belgium to Greece. This was the decision of a court, not the policy of European governments: if material circumstances changed, governments could revert to enforcing the Dublin Agreement.

Whether Greece was the only legal destination opened by the Lesbos crossing or the gateway to the Schengen Area was, however, absolutely crucial. If the choice facing enterprising refugees was between working informally in the Turkish economy or in the Greek, it was no contest: Turkey's economy was not only much larger than Greece's, it was one of the most rapidly growing economies in the world.

But since the borderless Schengen Area in practice made it relatively easy for migrants to Italy to evade enforcement of the Dublin Agreement, perhaps it might make it easy for arrivals to Greece? Like Italy, Greece was in Schengen. Perhaps the Greek authorities would emulate the Italian authorities and be lax over fingerprinting those arriving on the boats. Perhaps, given the ramshackle condition of the Greek public sector, islands such as Lesbos would not be equipped with functioning fingerprinting machines and those arriving could swiftly move on towards the border with Macedonia before encountering such a machine. Perhaps, following the ruling of the European Court of Human Rights, the governments of Northern Europe would not try to return people to Greece. Such may well have been the calculations of the first refugees embarking for Lesbos.

Once the people-smuggling industry started to open up the route to Lesbos, it expanded rapidly. Partly, as we have discussed, it offered a huge reduction in both risks and costs relative to the long route via Libya, but this coincided with other changes. The situation in Syria was deteriorating: ISIS had invaded from Iraq and constituted a force of exceptional brutality towards ordinary people. Not only were rebels becoming an order of magnitude more violent, but in August 2013 the increasingly desperate Assad regime had resorted to chemical weapons. This crossed a 'red line' warning that had been issued by President Obama to protect civilians in rebel areas. Yet with military action facing widespread political dissent across Western societies, the red line had proved to be unenforceable. This effectively licensed the regime to use any means to intimidate those civilians it deemed to be its enemies, opening the way for mass barrel-bombing. As their assets depleted, and as the prospect of peace in Syria receded, for many refugees it became time for a change of plan. As one refugee is reported to have said on arriving on Lesbos: 'Syria is finished.'

But perhaps the major reason why the flow of refugees to Lesbos increased so strikingly was that the dynamics of registration were straightforwardly unstable. The more people who chose to cross the sea from Turkey to the proximate Greek islands, the more the Greek border force was overwhelmed. The more overwhelmed the force became, the better the individual refugee's chance of continuing unhindered on to the prosperous economies of Northern Europe. But the better this chance, the stronger the incentive for people to make the crossing. The stronger the incentive, the more people came, further overwhelming the border force.

There was, however, one remaining impediment: whereas Italy had contiguous land borders with other Schengen countries so that migrants could reach virtually the entire Schengen Area without needing to cross a policed border, Greece had no contiguous border with any other Schengen country. To reach the rest of the Schengen Area, it was necessary to pass through a series of small non-EU states in South-East Europe, notably Macedonia and Serbia. The rising number of people trekking from Lesbos on route for Northern Europe needed passage through these countries. Like Greece, they themselves did not offer enticing economic opportunities. Their governments thus had little to lose from allowing the refugees to pass through their territories, as long as their northern borders remained open. But necessarily, the Schengen countries adjacent to these states, Hungary and Austria, had to have a border force checking the papers of those who entered from these non-EU countries.

Hungary, which was the most convenient route, and hence the one initially chosen by most refugees, is a small country that is poor by European standards. Its capacity to absorb an influx of people, whether of those formally seeking asylum, or those simply hoping to find informal work, is limited. Further, by the time enterprising Syrians had reached Hungary, they had travelled a thousand miles from Lesbos. By continuing only 150 miles further they would reach Germany, the largest and fastest-growing economy in Europe. Opportunity beckoned, and so people pressed on. Hence, the influx through Hungary's borders was only an issue of transit, not of permanent settlement.

However, both Hungary and Austria have played a distinctive historical role in Europe. Sometimes individually, and sometimes jointly, for centuries they had self-identified as Europe's bulwark against Islamic conquest. Famously, Vienna had been besieged by the Ottomans and held out. Hungary celebrated its heroic role as a small country resisting the might of the Ottoman Empire. Such histories matter for national identity. Just as the legacy of the French Revolution still lies at the core of French commitment to *liberté*, *égalité* and *fraternité*, and the memory of National Socialism haunts Germans, so Hungarian and Austrian identities are influenced by their past response to Muslims in Europe. Faced with a rapidly mounting and disorderly influx of refugees, many Hungarians fell back psychologically on that historic role.

President Orbán, leading a party of the centre-right, faced pressure from a party of the right which was keen to espouse this role as its cause. A recent analysis by the political scientist Sergi Pardos-Prado finds that across Europe if parties of the centre-right adopt liberal policies on immigration they heavily lose support to parties of the extreme right.[5] Whether for fear of losing power, or because of genuine belief, in June 2015 President Orbán announced that Hungary would build a fence to prevent illegal entry to the European Union through its territory. As the Hungarian authorities constructed this fence, the initial response of refugees was to switch to Croatia. The Croatian authorities promptly directed the refugees to their own border with Hungary. In response, Hungary began to extend its border fence. There were also ugly scenes during which irate and frustrated refugees tried to force their way through the barrier, attacking members of the Hungarian border force with blocks of concrete from a nearby building site, and being met by tear gas and baton charges. In response, the refugee flow moved to Austria as the potential conduit. Austria's initial response was to welcome the new arrivals, knowing that nearly all would soon be in Germany.

By August 2015 thousands of people were arriving at the German border, and Hungarian authorities continued to use a heartless rhetoric. So what should the German authorities do? The question inevitably arrived on the desk of Chancellor Merkel.

THE SYRIAN REFUGEE CRISIS PHASE III: THE HEADLESS HEART (SEPTEMBER 2015–DECEMBER 2015)

On what the German authorities should do with arriving Syrians, the rules of the European Union were clear. Germany had no external EU borders and so anyone arriving in Germany should have already been registered in some other member country. On the principles of the Dublin Agreement they should be returned there. Even if Greece had failed to register them, or was deemed to be unfit for them to be returned there, people could only reach Germany via Hungary or Austria and so should have been registered there. Neither country could credibly be regarded as incapable of providing asylum: neither was in the same league as Greece. Austria was at this stage warmly welcoming refugees who sought asylum, and while the Hungarian authorities were denying transit to Germany, they offered to provide asylum in Hungary itself to those who applied. Had Germany returned refugees to Austria and Hungary the influx may have subsided: neither was as alluring as Germany.

But while the national folk narrative in Hungary was that of the bastion against Islam, that in post-Nazi Germany was of living down the past. This had repeatedly been manifest in German policy. For example, in 2011 when Colonel Gaddafi's threat to hunt down the rebels in their cupboards had prompted the UN Security Council to invoke the right of the international community to intervene militarily to protect Libyan citizens, Germany had shown its opposition to this by abstaining in the Council's vote on the question.[6] This was not due to Germany's superior ability to forecast what would happen, but to the German horror of military action. If bombing had a special meaning in Germany, refugees were even more emotive: Germany had been responsible for creating a refugee exodus, and in the post-war period many Germans had themselves been refugees. In living down the past, welcoming refugees who were arriving at Germany's doorstep fitted the folk narrative.

Chancellor Merkel had initially taken a tough stance on refugees. On German television she had told a young Palestinian refugee that she would not be allowed to remain in Germany: the child had promptly burst into tears, something that had not been well received by viewers. Nor was this the only occasion when Chancellor Merkel had taken a tough stance. In the negotiations with the Greek government during the recent debt crisis in Greece she had been depicted in the Greek press as a latter-day Hitler. That crisis had also confirmed Chancellor Merkel as by far the most powerful politician in Europe. Ostensibly, the responsibility for debt negotiations rested with the European Commission, the European Council, and the European Central Bank, but the head of the new Greek government had flown not to Brussels but to Berlin, and negotiated directly with Chancellor Merkel.

The German national narrative of living down the past and the Chancellor's personal sense of political authority came together in what was soon seen as a sensational decision. In late August 2015, Chancellor Merkel decided that Germany would no longer adhere to the rules of the Dublin Agreement: the refugees reaching Germany would be permitted to remain rather than being sent back to Hungary. It is now clear that this decision was never meant to be made public; it was meant to have been an operational rule for border officials. Consequently, the Chancellor consulted neither her colleagues in the German government nor the Commission and other European leaders before the announcement was made. Inevitably the decision rapidly became an international sensation. In her now famous 'Wir schaffen das' speech, she proclaimed: 'Germany is a strong country – we will manage.'[7] The speech was certainly noble but it was soon to have unintended consequences.

As refugees began to switch from Hungary to transit through Austria, Chancellor Merkel and the Austrian Chancellor jointly announced on 4 September that Austria would provide official transit through to the German border, where refugees would be welcome to seek asylum. The subsequent patterns of movement suggest that this announcement influenced the calculus of migration for three distinct groups of people.

First, for those Syrians who were already refugees in their neighbouring havens, it made onward migration more attractive. Jordan, Lebanon, and Turkey had all imposed greater restrictions on Syrians from October 2014. Many Syrians in the neighbouring countries were struggling to access work and basic services, depleting savings and capital. Sending a family member to Europe offered a lifeline. By the end of July 2015, nearly 375,000 Syrians had already claimed asylum in Europe. Although the movement was already underway, Germany's policy change accelerated the trend: the number had nearly trebled by the end of the year, with Germany the primary destination.[8] However, the barriers of risk and cost remained: the offer of asylum did not come with any means of reaching Germany beyond a bus ride across Austria: it amounted to 'Wir schaffen das . . . provided you can swim'. Had Germany's objective been to provide safe passage, it would surely have also provided humanitarian visas to allow people to fly directly from Bodrum to Frankfurt, rather than risking their lives on rickety boats.[9]

Second, for those Syrians who had remained in Syria, for whatever reason, exit now looked less dismal. Subject to surmounting the barriers, those who left could now look forward to the prospect of new lives in Germany rather than a scratched existence in the informal economies of their neighbours. In August 2015 the military situation of the Assad regime deteriorated further as it lost Palmyra to ISIS. This panicked the Alawite population into the prospect of defeat and mass slaughter, and so some of them decided to leave: refugees from both sides of the conflict headed for Germany.

In September President Putin decided to intervene militarily in support of the Assad regime by heavily bombing the major rebel-held areas. This radically changed the balance of military power, enabling the Assad regime to begin reconquering rebel areas. The offer of a new life in Germany made it considerably more likely that military action against rebel civilians would induce them to leave Syria. Inadvertently, this may have encouraged the Assad regime to intensify the violence. Although this is a strong claim, it is supported by work by Harvard researcher Kelly Greenhill, which shows how dictators frequently use forced emigration as a strategic tool.[10] Facing a Sunni population that as a result of what he had done to it was implacably opposed to him, he may have decided to use his new military strength to encourage Sunni flight: ethnic cleansing became feasible. President Putin had his own reasons for encouraging such an exodus to Germany. Chancellor Merkel had been leading the European imposition of economic sanctions against Russia to penalize the Russian military intervention in eastern Ukraine, and Putin knew that a mass influx of Syrian refugees into Germany would rapidly weaken Chancellor Merkel's political position.

As both Syrian refugees in Turkey and Syrians who had previously decided to remain at home took up the opportunity to cross to Greece, the Greek authorities became yet more overwhelmed: between August and November around half a million Syrians crossed to Lesbos. Whether due to a lack of capacity or to reluctance, only a quarter of these arrivals were fingerprinted by the Greek authorities.

Third, this in turn opened up opportunities for refugees and migrants from around the world. If border forces were unable or unwilling to register and screen extra-legal arrivals, and lacked an effective capacity to return those that were not eligible for asylum, then refugees would not in practice be distinguished from other migrants at the point of arrival. This exposed the Schengen Area to the vastly larger pool of would-be immigrants from poor countries around the world. A breakdown in border controls therefore placed a growing burden on the behind-the-border capacity to send back migrants who were not eligible for asylum. In practice, return faced both practical and legal impediments: if migrants destroy their papers their nationality cannot be established, and many countries are judged not to meet the governance standards required for return.

Turkey bordered Iran, which bordered Afghanistan and Pakistan. In the second half of 2015, around 200,000 Afghans trekked across Iran, Turkey, and the Balkans to reach Northern Europe.[11] From around the world, hopeful migrants flew to Turkey and bought places on boats for Lesbos. The German authorities were themselves unable to manage the number of arrivals: everyone was allowed in, even if they could not be registered, and those that chose to disappear from official view were able to do so. As the migrants trekked through the conflict-damaged countries of South-East Europe, initially the concern of the local population was to speed their passage: a much displayed image shows a sign with an arrow, pointing along the road. Written in English, it said simply 'Germany'. But soon it occurred to local people that if migrants from many different countries could move to Germany, they could do so themselves: why not follow their own signs? By December around 300,000 unregistered migrants were estimated to be living in Germany.[12]

Faced with the rising influx, Chancellor Merkel urged other European countries to take some of those who had arrived in Germany. Since her initial invitation had been given unilaterally, anything beyond moral suasion would be contentious. Nevertheless, the Chancellor asked the Commission to establish a formula for relocating refugees across the EU. For the Commission, the evident need for coordinated action coincided with a natural desire to extend its mandate, and so it obliged. In September, the President of the Commission, Jean-Claude Juncker, outlined the plan: to relocate 160,000 refugees directly from Greece and Italy equitably across EU member states. Thus was created a Schengen legal structure which stripped nationality of significance for citizens of member states, while defining the rights of Syrian refugees by an assigned pseudo-nationality. In arriving at this paradox of removing nationality from nationals, while creating it for non-nationals, the Commission perhaps itself crossed a boundary: between reality and the surreal.

Faced with reluctance on the part of some countries, Chancellor Merkel first threatened reductions in disbursements of structural funds from the EU budget to recalcitrant governments. Since this would have contravened EU rules the threat was not pursued, but that it was made suggested mounting desperation. Instead, the Council took upon itself a historic change of procedure. Hitherto, all contentious Council matters had required unanimity, but in adopting a rule to apportion refugees to other member states, the objections of five governments were overridden. The power of the Chancellor had reached its apex. Nevertheless, the rest of the EU dragged its heels and there was no appetite to implement the relocation deal.[13]

But the Schengen Area effectively became borderless. Anybody who was able to reach Turkey now stood a reasonable chance of reaching Germany and remaining there: some because they would be permitted to do so; some because they could in practice not be returned; some because they could stay below the official radar screen. By the end of 2015 over a million people had arrived in Europe, of whom only around half were Syrian. While the scale of the increase took the authorities by surprise, it could clearly have been anticipated. Young people around the Middle East were linked by social media that generated waves of imitated behaviour. It had fuelled the Arab Spring and now it fuelled the youth exodus.

But there was a yet more powerful factor at work. As the numbers rose and the border chaos deepened, it was evident to anyone not in thrall to their own rhetoric that the situation would not be permitted to continue. Regardless of the generous signs saying 'welcome' held by young Germans at Munich railway station, and regardless of Chancellor Merkel's Obama-style refrain of 'We can do this!', border controls were sure to be reimposed. Would-be migrants around the world could readily tell that it was now or never. In this respect, the stampede of people was analogous to what happens during capital flight: once it starts, the smart thing for each individual is to move as fast as possible.

THE SYRIAN REFUGEE CRISIS PHASE IV: THE RETURN OF THE HEARTLESS HEAD (JANUARY 2016–?)

Within Germany, Chancellor Merkel's decision had meshed with the folk narrative of living down the past. Nor was the influx of people seen as a threat to jobs: the German economy was booming and short of workers. Germans were also understandably unconcerned by the Chancellor's exceptional power vis-à-vis the rest of Europe. But outside Germany it was a different matter.

Only in Sweden was there a remotely comparable folk narrative: having stayed out of both world wars, Sweden carved out a post-war international role as a haven for asylum-seekers. Like Germany it adopted an open door. But even in Sweden the result was a massive popular backlash: a new party of the right became the largest party in the country, and the government, a coalition of the other parties, swiftly reversed policy. In order to defray the cost of the migrants who had reached Sweden the government *halved* its aid budget. In effect, millions of very poor people around the world were going to pay for the Scandinavian-level benefits offered to the thousands fortunate enough to have reached Sweden. But by the end of 2015 Sweden abruptly closed its borders: it shut the door.[14]

This had an immediate knock-on effect. The route to Sweden was through Denmark, where the folk narrative was radically different. Denmark had experienced an unprecedented upsurge in Islamic violence in response to a cartoon in a provincial newspaper. The mutual incomprehension between secular Danes and devout Muslims had left a widespread wariness of further immigration from the Muslim world. Denmark promptly closed its borders and introduced a rule of confiscation of all assets above €1,000 in the possession of refugees. Though widely criticized in the international press, an equivalent policy was promptly adopted by Switzerland.[15]

In Eastern Europe, a strongly Christian culture made some wary of Islam, a prejudice reinforced by folk memory. Poland's 'never again' sentiment was not 'welcome refugees' but 'fear German hegemony'. Being ordered by Chancellor Merkel to accept Syrian refugees whom she had unilaterally invited to Germany played into this fear.

Poland was not exceptional. With many European economies still in recession, and widespread popular wariness of Islam, all other European governments quietly mutinied against the new Commission rule that reassigned refugees to them from Germany. A year after Juncker's relocation plan, less than 5 per cent of the proposed quota had actually been moved. Far from expanding its mandate, the Commission lost legitimacy.

A sad turning point in popular discourse occurred as a result of New Year celebrations in Cologne, when a large group of young Muslim men displayed aggressively misogynistic behaviour towards young unaccompanied women. This would not have made much impact, except that the local authorities, rather than trying to curb the behaviour, tried to suppress its coverage in the media, further exacerbating public anxiety. A similar saga occurred in Sweden, with both incidents opening a new line of discourse: could such a large influx of refugees be integrated into German and Swedish society? 'We can do it!' started to provoke the question: 'How?'

Predictably, even the German government began to discuss quantitative limits, despite the adamant opposition of the Chancellor. Germany's President, a former Lutheran pastor, contradicted her, suggesting that they were both necessary and morally legitimate.

As the prospect of a closure of the German border loomed, the policies of the transit countries changed, just as Denmark had responded to the change of policy in Sweden: none wanted to be caught with refugees on their territory. In Austria, policy was completely reversed and the Chancellor resigned. By the summer, a presidential election revealed the nation to be precisely and catastrophically polarized. By the final round of voting both mainstream parties had been eliminated, leaving the choice between candidates from the Greens on the far left and a party with neo-Nazi roots on the far right. The vote divided 50–50 and the second round – rerun after electoral irregularities – ended in a narrow majority for the Greens. More quietly, controls were reintroduced along many of the borders between Schengen countries: de facto, Schengen had fallen apart.

Faced with this upsurge in popular disquiet, Chancellor Merkel recognized the need for a change of policy. However, she was not prepared to reimpose border controls, and turned to the EU to collectively find an alternative pathway. But one by one each of the EU's main institutions fell into irrelevance. The Parliament was marginalized from the outset. In theory it has shared competence on Justice and Home Affairs issues; in practice, the Council has routinely bypassed it by addressing the crisis under 'emergency measures'. The Commission, under pressure to do something, had spent much of its political capital on getting the unworkable September 2015 relocation deal done and thereafter became sidelined. From that point, it was effectively an intergovernmental game, and the Council was the only EU institution that really mattered.

But among member states, no agreement could be reached on an 'internal solution' to replace the dysfunctional Dublin Agreement. The chosen solution was therefore to 'outsource' border controls to non-EU governments. Initially the objective was to try to close the Western Balkan route by persuading the government of Macedonia to block passage from Greece. But soon the solution came to be seen as persuading the Turkish government to block passage from its ports to Lesbos.

By January, the Turkish Prime Minister was being sweet-talked into toughening exit. But sensing that his Prime Minister was playing a strong hand too gently, President Erdoğan dismissed him and raised the level of Turkish demands. In March, the Commission was in the late stages of negotiating directly with President Erdoğan when a different deal was announced: it had been struck in secret parallel negotiations between President Erdoğan and Chancellor Merkel. To cover the embarrassment, the Commission duly rubber-stamped their agreement.

Its content was that Turkey would indeed tighten controls on exit, cracking down on the people-smugglers. But the crucial Turkish commitment was far more dramatic. Henceforth, anyone making the journey from Turkey to Greece would be returned to Turkey and accepted by the Turkish government. This step, the return to Turkey of anyone making the journey, evidently eliminated the point of making such a journey. In parallel, Merkel had already colluded to close the Balkan route. The combined result was that the Aegean exodus promptly stopped.[16] From the perspective of Chancellor Merkel, the solution had the additional advantage of not requiring any change of policy by Germany itself: anyone reaching Germany's borders would still be welcomed. Consequently, there need be no admission that the earlier policy had been a mistake.

By this time the German debate about capping the inflow had swung heavily in favour of a cap. Chancellor Merkel could not impose one domestically, and so introduced one to the EU-Turkey deal: a 72,000 refugee limit to the number of Syrians that would be resettled to the EU from Turkey.[17] Even with a cap, the policy could still be presented as something approximating an open door. But since people could no longer reach the German border by trekking from Turkey, the open door was moot: the Chancellor had just closed the door that mattered. A relieved German populace was forgiving of this sleight of hand: the folk narrative of welcome need not be called into doubt.

The policy of returning migrants and refugees to Turkey also applied to those currently in Greece. But unlike the policy of returning a future inflow that would not materialize, this posed a substantial practical challenge: how would Europe's cumbersome legal procedure for return be feasible for the many thousands of people currently transiting through Greece, especially in view of the inadequacies of the Greek bureaucracy? The Greek Prime Minister, Alexis Tsipras, who had not been party to the negotiations, was alert to their possible consequence, declaring that Greece was not prepared to be 'a warehouse for human souls'. The word 'warehouse' indicated that Greece was most definitely not prepared to provide haven on its own territory, while 'souls', religious vocabulary not typical of his Marxist ideology, played to the European conscience. It was too late for conscience: those in Greece would be deemed collectively to be returnable to Turkey, which would in turn be deemed a sufficiently decent environment to be a safe destination. To emphasize his power, President Erdoğan announced on the day of the agreement that in Turkey the words 'democracy' and 'human rights' were meaningless. He did not need to resort to the usual diplomatic ambiguities used to mask embarrassments.

In order to get what she needed, Chancellor Merkel had to pay a high price. President Erdoğan recognized that he was dealing with someone whose political survival was at stake, and he had a temperament to ruthlessly exploit his advantage. Partly what President Erdoğan wanted was money. Chancellor Merkel had already agreed to €3bn in an earlier attempt to persuade him to be cooperative. He was now promised a further €6bn. But money was merely the small change of the deal. Its crux was political.

For nearly a century, the thrust of Turkish policy had been to distance itself from its Ottoman past as hegemon in the Middle East. Atatürk had charted a secular, European future. The final step in that process would evidently be membership of the European Union, a step that Europe had been reluctant to countenance. President Erdoğan had steadily distanced himself from this longstanding policy: he saw Turkey as the well-governed Islamic lodestar for a troubled Middle East. But he was also proud. While he did not want Turkey to be European, he most definitely did not want this determined by a rejection of Turkey by Europe. So President Erdoğan insisted on reopening the stalled accession negotiations. While Chancellor Merkel agreed, Erdoğan knew that the accession process was lengthy and so such an offer might well be dismissed by his people as yet another incredible promise. He needed a here-and-now policy change that would be recognized by ordinary Turks as a victory. His demand was for visa-free travel in Schengen for all Turkish citizens. Other European governments baulked at this step, but the Commission itself agreed. At the time of writing it is still officially on track to being implemented, although following a series of terrorist attacks in Turkey, the EU–Turkey deal is precarious and could collapse at any time.

THE BALANCE SHEET TO DATE

The European policies that have shaped the Syrian refugee disaster have lurched between the headless heart and the heartless head. Panic is not too strong a word to describe what happened: each step was a reaction to the unanticipated consequences of previous actions which turned out to be blunders. The cumulative legacy was a series of misfortunes.

While the refugee issue shot to the top of the European agenda, its content was all about Europe rather than about refugees. Which country should accept how many refugees; which country was closing its borders; what should be expected of those refugees in Europe; which European politicians should be taking which decisions? Syrian refugees themselves suffered the neglect of the heartless head. While a small minority reached Germany, the vast majority remained in the neighbouring havens, where they have received little international support. Indeed, the cultural clashes and political polarization which accompanied the influx had the sad consequence of reducing the sympathy of many Europeans for the plight of the displaced. Such sympathy is the key resource on which refugees need to rely. This loss will ultimately make the task of constructing a system which properly responds to refugee needs more difficult.

The European Union has been permanently and radically weakened. Its mechanisms and rules were repeatedly ignored by member states. The authority of the Commission was undermined by its attempt to impose directives on national governments that were seen as illegitimate. The Schengen Area was de facto dismantled. Europe's border controls were outsourced, on humiliating terms, to a non-European state with an authoritarian leader. But, most dramatically, the political representation of the refugee crisis directly contributed to Brexit: the permanent withdrawal from the European Union of one of

Europe's major states. The evidence for this conclusion is stark: 'Leave' campaigners deployed two hard-hitting messages. One was a poster depicting the exodus across South-Eastern Europe and two words: 'Breaking Point'. The other was the slogan 'Take Back Control'. Both communicated the message that the authorities of the European Union had lost control of the borders, something that was difficult to dispute. The message visibly shifted the opinion polls. For leave voters, migration and sovereignty were the most salient issues.[18]

The final legacy of European decisions concerning the refugee crisis may still be in its early stages. In recent months there has been an upsurge in terrorism. The terrorist attacks have focused on France and Belgium, but Germany has also been targeted. The preferred target seems to be young people having fun: a pop concert; a children's roundabout. The attacks are spectacularly barbaric: shortly before these words were being written in rural Brittany, in neighbouring Normandy an 86-year-old priest had his throat cut in front of his congregation. People have become fearful and angry. The attacks are not being perpetrated by refugees. But a widespread public perception has emerged that the upturn in terrorism is connected to Europe's immigration chaos.

Faced with this legacy, Chancellor Merkel has defiantly and bravely declared that Germany will continue to welcome refugees, albeit that it is now somewhat hypothetical. She argued repeatedly on television that 'it was the right thing to do'.[19] While some might interpret this as the familiar reluctance of a politician to admit to a mistake, a more charitable interpretation is that this is the voice of moral courage in the face of a wider systemic failure.

Did Chancellor Merkel do the right thing? We explore this ethical question in the next chapter.

PART II: THE RETHINK

4

Rethinking Ethics: The Duty of Rescue

The plight of ordinary Syrians fleeing violence demands our generosity of spirit. It is not so hard to imagine ourselves in the same plight. Indeed, seventy years ago millions of Germans were themselves refugees displaced by warfare. The Second World War had begun with Poland being occupied by Germany, but ended with it occupied by Russia. Britain was providing a haven for thousands of Poles. A decade or two before that, German Jews were desperately looking for safe haven: many went to Britain and the USA. A decade earlier, Armenians were fleeing Turkish pogroms. Another decade earlier and Russian Jews were fleeing Russian pogroms. Go back three centuries or so and Huguenots were fleeing French pogroms.

You get the picture. Generosity of spirit in response to the need for refuge is not some new demand upon mankind, or an implausible emotion that modernity has to invent from scratch. It is something hardwired into our humanity; revealed again and again when cruel fate has put people in need of it. Without instinctive generosity of spirit, the lives of many millions of our ancestors would have been nastier, more brutish and shorter than they were; and consequently we ourselves might never have been born.

The key difference between us and our ancestors is not that an astonishing new burden is being placed upon us, but that we are much better able to bear it than they were. Our parents and grandparents grew up in a society that was too poor to educate and even to feed all of its children properly. Yet theirs nevertheless managed to accommodate waves of refugees from Russia, Poland and Germany. Generosity of spirit towards refugees is not new. Today, due to 24/7 media, the internet, and broadcast news, we know more about suffering elsewhere than any previous generation, and yet we are turning our backs to it.

But generosity of spirit is not enough: our responses must be grounded in wisdom. The headless heart may lead to outcomes little better than the heartless head. So we need to be a little more specific about what generosity of spirit implies. What should it mean in the context of Syria, and, by extension, what should it mean more widely in the global context of refugees?

Science makes progress through experiments. The natural sciences rely upon lab experiments; medicine and economics progress through randomized controlled trials and natural experiments. None of these approaches are of much use for the present question, but moral philosophy does have its own form of experiment: the *thought* experiment. We can use thought experiments to make progress in teasing out what we should mean by generosity of spirit.

In this chapter we are going to focus on a series of ethical questions. The most immediate of them concerns the initial response to the desperation of people fleeing from violence: what is our moral duty towards refugees? The next ethical question is generated by the desire of many poor people to migrate to Europe, revealed in their willingness to risk their lives in small boats. Do migrants, even if they are not refugees, have a global moral right to migrate to the country of their choice? The final ethical question arises from the arrival of around a million refugees in Germany. What are the moral obligations that follow from this influx, both for Germany and for the refugees?

If you think that this ethical analysis is a waste of time we offer you a challenge. Write down how you would answer these three questions and for each sketch a brief justification. Then read this chapter and think about the arguments. Finally, return to your answers: do your justifications survive what you have learnt from the thought experiments?

In a justly celebrated book, *The Righteous Mind*, Jonathan Haidt shows that people tend to cling on to their moral judgements, wriggling from one fatuous justification to another as each is seen to be wrong.[1] In other words, people are morally lazy. Unfortunately, wisdom is sometimes demanding.

THE DUTY OF RESCUE TOWARDS
REFUGEES

In a famous moral thought experiment, students are asked to imagine themselves alone by a pond into which a child has fallen by accident and is crying for help. As a bystander, you were not responsible for that accident. You are a good swimmer, but is it legitimate for you to ignore that urgent cry because you do not want to damage your clothing? Generosity of spirit quite unambiguously requires that you jump in. Hard luck about your new clothes.

Those Syrians forced to flee their homes by violence are ethically analogous to that drowning child.[2] Like the bystander, we have an unambiguous duty of rescue towards them. This does not follow from some structure of legal rights: like that drowning child, fleeing Syrians are not demanding their rights and threatening to sue you. Nor, like the drowning child, are they blaming you for having caused the problem. A lingering vestige of colonialism is that Western commentators are inclined to explain whatever happens anywhere as being due to Western actions, but Syria was a long-lasting autocracy. It was destabilized by contagion from the Arab Spring, itself an autonomous pro-democracy uprising that started in Tunisia and spread around the Arab world through social media. As the Syrian protest transmuted into sectarian conflict and then to full-scale civil war drawing in regional powers, the West chose not to intervene. Even when the Syrian government resorted to chemical weapons the West stayed out. Occasionally, refugee movements do involve direct Western complicity – Vietnam, Kosovo, and Iraq, for example – but that isn't the case here.

We ground the ethical case for helping refugees in the duty of rescue because it is a moral norm that is widely accepted and it is all that is needed. Wide acceptance is fundamental to any practical prospect of global action. The time when the West could impose the moral values of its elite on everyone else are gone for ever, and in our view this is a cause for celebration. Some commentators in the West have attempted to ground the case for helping refugees in arguments which extend to particular aspects of post-Christian ethics. They urge us to be more morally demanding of ourselves: to be saintly. We are sceptical of such arguments, but acknowledge them here for completeness. One line of argument is that, in a globalized world, all injustice is structurally interconnected.[3] Quite apart from whether this would generate a moral basis for assistance to refugees, it is factually wrong. As an Oxford professor, Matthew Gibney, highlights: 'even in our globalized world, some injustices are simply local',[4] and that is largely the case with Syria. So it does not appear to be a very solid foundation for the duty to help Syrian refugees. Why, then, are you morally obliged to help them?

The first principle of the heart: compassion

Like the drowning child, fleeing Syrians appeal to our common humanity. The instinct they naturally evoke in us is neither the need to obey the law, nor guilt for failing to bomb the Syrian government. It is the raw compassion that is at the bedrock of the human condition. We might think of it as the first principle of the heart. It is not *saintly* to experience such a sense of compassion: it is sociopathic *not* to experience it.

Our duty of rescue to refugees is quite easy to justify morally through a series of steps. We are all part of political communities. These are important because they allow us to live collectively, and to allocate rights and duties. But to function, they generally also have boundaries of membership; they are a bit like – though distinct from – clubs, neighbourhoods, and families.[5] We have 'special obligations' to those within our own political communities, our families, friends, and fellow citizens, but we also have lesser 'general obligations' to others.[6]

Despite this, the boundaries of our moral community go beyond those of our political community, including towards refugees. This is because of our shared common humanity. We are all human beings and hence have some minimal set of shared obligation towards one another as fellow human beings. Again, some Western political theorists are dissatisfied with reliance upon psychology, wanting to deduce duties more grandly from critiques of modernity. We live, they assert, in an interconnected and interdependent world in which our actions have consequences in faraway places.[7] By dint of living in a common system of states, when that system fails for some, we have some shared obligations.[8] The *reductio ad absurdum* of this line of argument would be to assert that everything depends on everything else, deducing that everyone is responsible for everything. While the principle is grandiose, in application it would shrivel to its opposite: with unbounded obligations, nobody would take responsibility for anything.

Several leading political theorists have recognized this weakness and introduced limitations on obligations. They are not as great as the special obligations we have towards family or people in our immediate political community and they have a threshold.[9] For Matthew Gibney states have an obligation to assist refugees when the costs of doing so are low.[10] For Michael Walzer of Princeton University the threshold is cultural preservation.[11] For Seyla Benhabib of Yale University it is the capacity of democratic process to accept inclusion.[12] But the fact that political theorists cannot even agree among themselves upon these supposed boundaries suggests that they will not serve as the basis for wider moral consensus, and so are not a sensible basis for practical global action. Fortunately, we do not need them. The duty of rescue will do the job much less contentiously.

In a famous British case of a child falling into a pond in a park, the frantic mother rushed to two park wardens and begged them to rescue her child. The wardens refused, explaining that they had not been trained for such an emergency; the child drowned. National sentiment quite rightly deemed that the reason given by the wardens was utterly insufficient to justify their decision. Though legally innocent, they were morally guilty.

So what does the duty of rescue oblige us to do? At the minimum, we fish the child out of the pond: that is, we restore a safe environment, free from fear. But let us suppose that while in the pond the child has lost everything: the money she was given by her parents, the food to eat while she was away from home. The extent of our obligation now depends upon what it is feasible for us to do. If we too are penniless then we are condemned to stand shivering together by the side of the pond. But if it is readily within our means, normal compassion should induce us to restore the child to as near to the pre-pond state as possible. We should provide a towel, some money, food, and shelter for the night, while making arrangements to get her back home.

Transposed into refuge, this implies that our duty is to restore circumstances as near to normality as it is practically possible for us to do. Most likely, the person who is now a refugee previously had a home and a means of earning a living, and was part of a community. If we are able to do so, we should aim to restore these basic features of normal life.

The principles of the head: comparative advantage and burden-sharing

Having an obligation, though, does not mean we cannot find ways to intelligently meet such responsibilities. There are better and worse ways in which we can discharge our obligations to refugees. The existing ethics literature on refugees tends to only look at individual states' obligations to offer asylum to a refugee at its borders. It largely misses that, acting together and thoughtfully, there may be ways to meet our underlying obligations more sustainably and at lower cost to ourselves.

Matthew Gibney is one of the few political theorists to recognize this. Faced with an 'if the costs are low' qualification on our obligations to refugees, he suggests that states have the additional responsibility to consider how they can most efficiently discharge this obligation: 'it requires that governments scrutinize their own policies to search for ways that, subject to the political environment they currently face, more protection could be provided to refugees at low cost'.[13]

He expresses concern that under the status quo states have a stronger obligation to refugees at their territorial borders than to those far beyond their borders, and that this leads to at least three ethically problematic outcomes: the unfair distribution of responsibility between states; the misallocation of scarce resources to support bureaucratic asylum systems in rich countries rather than refugees hosted by poor countries; and a bias in favour of refugees who have the means to embark on dangerous journeys to rich countries.[14]

We agree. But while many political theorists debate *whether* we have moral obligations to refugees, few explore *how* this can be most effectively achieved. How can we balance principles of the heart with principles of the head, and discharge our obligations to refugees in an intelligent and sustainable way?

Let's tweak our thought experiment accordingly: you are still by the pond but this time you are not the only person there. This has the potential both to enhance the child's prospects of rescue and to reduce them. The potential for disaster is that each individual might wait for someone else to jump in. Meanwhile the child drowns. Or everyone jumps in and in the resulting confusion nobody manages to find the child in time.

We need some way of coordinating the response. If we can coordinate, the outcome may be much better than reliance upon the solitary bystander: the burden can be shared between us, and if we have different capabilities, each can be harnessed. These are the principles of the head. Partnership involves fair *sharing of burdens*[15] and using the potential of different capabilities to harness the gains from *comparative advantage*.[16] Suppose, for example, that you are jogging and so already in sports gear and evidently fit; the other person is elderly and happens to be carrying a towel. Part of the duty of rescue is for the two of you to get your act together: the head as well as the heart. On this occasion it is not difficult: you shout 'get the towel ready' and jump in. As you bring the child to the bank, he is waiting to lift her out and get her dry.

Transposed to the Syrian refugee crisis, we have arrived at the central moral failing. There were plenty of bystanders around the pond as displaced Syrians fled across the border. Potentially, this could have made it far easier to fulfil the duty. Not only could the burden be widely shared, but the bystanders had different capabilities that complemented each other: the swimmer and the person with the towel. But what actually happened was that first nightmare scenario: everyone stood around waiting for others to act. They stood around not for moments, but for years.

This was a failure of both the heart and the head. Those who chose to free-ride rather than accept a share of the burden suffered from heart failure, those who ignored the scope for comparative advantage suffered from weakness of the head. Since the need was for international coordination, the primary responsibility for failure is with the international agencies tasked with coordination. This takes us back to Chapter 2: the agencies were hopelessly stuck in their silos of 'humanitarian', 'post-conflict', and 'economic development'. The displaced fled across Syria's borders to Turkey, Jordan and Lebanon. The response of UNHCR was camps: the provision of food and shelter based on the needs of the late 1940s. In Jordan around 85 per cent of the refugees ignored the camps; in Turkey it was 90 per cent: what refugees wanted was the autonomy that comes from a job. The World Bank, the world's foremost international aid agency for economic development, simply classified all three haven countries as 'upper-middle income'. As such, they were deemed not to have significant needs for World Bank involvement and so the Bank had no significant programmes or instruments with which to help the refugees who had fled there. Similarly, the pools of international money available for post-conflict recovery could not be used until the Syrian conflict was over.

Meanwhile, the burden of accommodating the refugee influx fell predominantly upon three of the five neighbouring countries. The fourth neighbour, Iraq, provided sanctuary to around 200,000 Syrians in its Kurdish northern region by 2016 but its own growing insecurity made it more of a source country than a destination country for refugees. The fifth neighbour, Israel, was actually occupying Syrian territory. Potentially this territory could have been used as a safe haven for refugees: an opportunity for Israel to claim the moral high ground vis-à-vis Arab governments. For a variety of reasons, the Israeli government did not avail itself of this opportunity.

The three neighbouring countries that became the main havens were all geographically and culturally well-placed to accept the refugee influx. Geographically they were proximate, and so easy to reach, culturally they were similar, all sharing the same religion, and two sharing the same language, as the refugees. But as middle-income countries, they were not well-placed to pick up the bill. Other bystanders had complementary characteristics. The high-income countries defined by membership of the OECD were far less well-placed geographically and culturally, but much better placed to provide the finance: not only were they much richer, but there were far more of them. Their combined GDP completely dwarfed the combined GDP of the neighbouring havens. What rapidly became an unsustainable burden for

Jordan would have been equivalent to a trivial rounding error in the budget of the USA and Europe.

Yet it did not happen. In respect of the Middle East, the USA was in a phase of 'leadership from behind', with policy incapacitated by gridlock between Congress and the Presidency. Not unreasonably, the USA could see the Syrian refugee crisis as primarily a task for Europe. Even by July 2016, by which time Europe had accepted a million refugees while the Republican presidential nominee had proposed banning Muslim immigration to the USA, the moralizing leading articles of the *New York Times* were castigating Europe for its negligence.[17] The multiplicity of countries that constitute Europe had supposedly addressed their coordination problem through the institutions of the EU: the European Commission had Directorates both for humanitarian emergencies and for economic development. Europe could, and should, have picked up much of the bill for the havens. That it failed to do so should become the subject both of soul-searching and of a formal inquiry.

The other bystanders missing in action were the states of the Arabian Gulf. They were, indeed, by far the best placed to act because geography, culture, and finance were all favourably aligned. They could have become what was needed: havens with jobs; and also have financed the three neighbouring havens. When put to the test, generosity to their fellow Sunni Arabs did not stretch very far.

The second principle of the heart: solidarity

These shaming failures suggest a second principle of the heart. Nations not only have radically different advantages, but also radically different international power. There are evident dangers that the international assignment of roles, ostensibly according to principles of comparative advantage, in practice degenerates, as indeed it did. It may lead to the most powerful countries picking up the easiest tasks: the Saudis writing a few cheques. Or, at the other extreme, everyone but the most powerful may free-ride, counting on the leader being the provider of last resort. There was an abundance of free-riding across Europe once Germany stepped forward.

What was missing in this behaviour was *solidarity*. At least symbolically, all participants should be expected to participate in each role. As everyone starts to do everything, the benefits of specializing in whatever is most appropriate will become evident, but a country with an evident advantage in some aspect of the duty of rescue will scale it up in order to justify scaling other contributions down. The rich countries should end up disproportionately taking on the financial burden, but they should begin by also directly accepting some refugees. Analogously, the proximate societies should end up disproportionately performing the haven role, but they should begin by also bearing a modest part of the financial burden: symbolism matters.

Even over the long term, there may be advantages to all states both taking people and contributing funding. There is value in having some symbolic, uniform commitment to admitting people up to at least some minimum threshold. It might well be that such a commitment is an important part of eliciting politically sustainable collective action.[18] There is evidence, for example, that when Northern states are too restrictive towards refugees, this can embolden Southern states to introduce restrictions of their own, thereby undermining international cooperation.[19]

But all of this, crucially, requires a level of solidarity that has been lacking. While the Syrian crisis was building up from 2011, a serious coordinated response to financing the haven countries had to wait until February 2016. It was initiated not by the European Commission or UNHCR, but by an *ad hominem* alliance between the King of Jordan, the Prime Minister of Britain, and the President of the World Bank. The delay was testimony to the limitations of the coordinating institutions supposedly responsible for dealing with the crisis.

The ethical dilemma of high-income countries

Meanwhile, some refugees had spotted an opportunity created inadvertently by the Schengen Area. The evidence that this was a movement of choice rather than a further instance of *force majeure* is that, unlike the flight to refuge, the move to Europe was highly selective. We set this out in Chapter 7. We have already explained why as a system Schengen was so deeply flawed that it was a disaster-in-waiting.[20] With Chancellor Merkel's decision to let refugees remain in Germany rather than return them to Greece, many Syrians found the prospect of moving on to Germany more attractive than staying in Turkey. Both economies were large and growing, but whereas living standards in Turkey were little higher than in Syria, Germany has one of the highest living standards in the world. Most refugees chose to stay where they were, but close to a million became migrants, albeit with refugee status.

This illustrates a dilemma for all high-income countries. An offer of refuge to people from much poorer countries effectively turns refugees into economic migrants, attracted by the prospect of a major improvement in the quality of life: not just compared with the miserable circumstances of being a refugee, but compared with their prior life chances. Evidently, this goes well beyond a duty of rescue, which requires that the life be restored as closely as possible to pre-refuge conditions. The only way that high-income countries can meet the duty of rescue without exceeding it is if they partner with other countries to offer havens that broadly match pre-refuge conditions. The countries that are spatially and culturally proximate provide the locations for the havens, but the rich countries provide the finance and the jobs. Such partnership can potentially better fulfil the requirements of the duty of rescue than any bystander acting alone.

The guiding principles of partnership in meeting the duty of rescue should always be comparative advantage and fair burden-sharing. However, which country has what advantage, and who should be sharing the burden, will vary with the context. The German Jews fleeing Hitler were first and foremost a neighbourhood problem for the rest of Europe. Britain and France were the proximate havens both spatially and culturally. Further, the prospect of safe haven posed no dilemma. Refugees were not being turned into economic migrants: German Jews coming to Britain and France were no better off than they had been in pre-Nazi Germany. Finally, Britain and France were well able to bear the modest financial burden since they were among the richest countries in the world. In effect, Britain and France were to the German Jewish refugee crisis what the Arabian Gulf states have been to the Syrian one: proximate in terms of location, culture, and income, and rich enough to finance any burden themselves.

In the Syrian crisis, instead of partnership based on comparative advantage and fair burden-sharing, there was global neglect followed by a solo act from Germany: the direct offer of safe haven by a high-income country to refugees from a significantly poorer society. While this inevitably went beyond the requirement of the duty of rescue to restore the standard of life, as long as there are no adverse consequences, a reasonable response is simply to say 'so be it'. By offering refuge in their own societies, high-income countries directly demonstrate solidarity with those in need. Refugees get a windfall and good luck to them.

Unfortunately, the German offer to Syrians did have adverse consequences.

Adverse consequences of the headless heart

The most immediate human disaster was that since the offer of refuge in Germany did not come with any legal means of getting there, it resulted in a massive expansion in the people-smuggling industry. The sector is obviously unregulated in respect of safety conditions. Whether a lack of regulation is truly dangerous depends partly upon the intrinsic nature of the activity. Clearly, people-smuggling by small boat across the open sea is intrinsically dangerous. But even such dangerous activities can be reasonably safe without regulation as long as the trade has many repeat transactions: repeat transactions encourage a business to invest in a reputation for safety simply to keep its customers. Disastrously, people-smuggling is dominated by one-off transactions: nobody goes back and forth. Consequently, competition between the people-smugglers can only be on the basis of price, driving costs down at the expense of even minimal concerns for safety.

As the activity expanded, more providers entered the market and price competition drove the cost of a place down from around $6,000 to about $1,500. It was not by chance that boats were overcrowded and sank, but an inevitable consequence of these unregulated market forces and the desperation of the people involved. While the industry was already well-established in the Mediterranean, the massive rise in demand triggered by the invitation from Germany further increased demand for smuggling by criminal syndicates.[21] The industry is estimated to have had a global turnover of around €6bn in 2015.[22]

The suggestion that Merkel's decision to open the borders led to an increase in movement to Germany rests upon an empirical claim. But it is one that is supported by the data. The overall numbers leaving Syria did not increase significantly in the period following 'Wir schaffen das' and the decision to suspend Dublin in late August 2015. However, in September and October three things did happen. More Syrians left Turkey, Lebanon and Jordan to move to Europe. The distribution of Syrians arriving in Germany became a greater proportion of the total arriving in Europe. And the numbers of several non-Syrian migrant populations travelling to Europe via the western Balkans route increased sharply.[23]

Consequently, the expansion in people-smuggling, combined with Europe's political unwillingness to offer safe passage, contributed to thousands of deaths due to drowning. Since almost all of the refugees embarked from Turkey, where they were already in a prospective safe haven, this generous German offer of refuge had deeply ambivalent consequences. Around a million people were tempted to board risky boats, and thousands of lives were lost. In trying, heroically, to meet a duty of rescue, Germany inadvertently created a source of temptation, encouraging more people to embark on dangerous journeys.

A second effect was that as the Greek authorities became overwhelmed, people who were not Syrians were tempted to join the same path to prosperity. Some were refugees from elsewhere, notably Afghanistan, while others were economic migrants from across the world, some were even from middle-income countries such as Morocco. All made their way to Germany. The Syrian government assisted and profited from this process. Desperate for money, with its back to the wall in a process of military collapse, its embassies in the neighbouring havens sold passports at $400 each to all comers. In effect, the legal status of 'refugee' had become sufficiently attractive as a result of the sudden access to Germany that it was up for sale.

The most poignant aspect of this inadvertently opened door was that families in troubled countries around the world seized an opportunity to send their children unaccompanied to Germany. They correctly judged that being under-age, their children, if they could reach Germany, would be taken in by the authorities. Currently, there are around 73,000 such isolated young people in Germany, the likely hope of their parents being that they will soon be old enough to earn money which they will send back home. The ethics of these choices is excruciating. Under-age youths find themselves alone in an utterly unfamiliar society. Often they will be taken under the wing of some responsible person to whom they can relate, but sometimes they will face unsupportable stress. In 2015, 91 per cent of Europe's nearly 100,000 unaccompanied children were male, and over half aged sixteen or seventeen. Research shows that many face psychological distress, remain outside formal education, and are vulnerable to exploitation.[24] As long as rich countries accept unaccompanied minors, some families in poor and troubled societies will choose to send them. That child poverty persists in the twenty-first century is a terrible blight, but this is not a good way of tackling it. Of course, once they are in Europe we have a shared moral obligation towards child protection, but a better approach would have been one that made it unnecessary for desperate parents to send their children to Europe in the first place.

Most of the people who took advantage of the breakdown in border controls were not under-age. They were would-be economic migrants from around the world. This raises a further tangled ethical question: is it reasonable for rich countries to restrict access to these people, or is there a global right to migrate?

IS THERE A RIGHT TO MIGRATE?

The answer to this question could have momentous implications. International surveys have found that nearly 40 per cent of the people living in some poor regions of the world would rather move permanently to rich ones.[25] This is scarcely surprising: the income gap between poor countries and rich ones is truly astounding. Indeed, were the 40 per cent actually able to relocate, it seems quite possible that some of the 60 per cent would follow them. Why would you stay in the Central African Republic if you could live in California, Bavaria or Paris? What keeps people from relocating is legal barriers. Our question is whether these barriers are immoral. Quite a lot turns on the answer.

For some political theorists, the right to move freely across borders is simply a liberal human right. There are four common arguments for a global right to migrate. The first is that borders are arbitrary lines on maps: in the beginning the Earth belonged to everyone. Sometimes God is invoked: God gave the Earth to everyone but mankind created nations. Government-imposed barriers to migration are immoral breaches of the natural right to live anywhere.[26] How does this moral argument stack up?

The 'in the beginning' argument is majestically sweeping. However, it is so sweeping that it would erase not only borders but virtually every other aspect of normal life. Borders, like the governments that they spatially delineate, are 'legal fictions'. So are all the companies in the world, from Apple down to the local shop: most of them are much more recent than governments. All property is also a legal fiction: hence the nineteenth-century anarchist slogan 'property is theft'. Indeed, the 'in the beginning' argument takes us back to the primitive communism of the hunter-gatherer family group, though even then groups defended 'their' territory against 'intruding' groups. Perhaps nobody had adequately explained to them the natural rights of others.

Nations, like companies and property, may be legal 'fictions' but they are enormously important for the existence of modern life. Nation-states create political communities that are useful in allocating rights and duties. They are transformed from fictions to reality by our coordinated behaviour. Apple is real because we all behave as though it is real. Coordinated acceptance of authority enables the typical European government to spend around 40 per cent of the income of the average citizen on the public goods that hugely enhance our lives. Citizenship is itself a legal fiction, defined indeed by borders. The border between France and Germany is no more 'arbitrary' than the demarcation between Citroën and Volkswagen. Not only does it delineate citizenship, but it resolves a different coordination problem: the language through which people communicate with each other. From time to time, borders are changed a little, just as large companies sometimes hive off a part of their business to another company, but that does not invalidate them.

Let's try a different argument. It is that governments have no moral right to prevent people from leaving the country, so that by extension they cannot have a moral right to prevent people from entering it. This argument has to be taken seriously: it has recently been advanced by a senior civil servant in the Migration Secretariat of the European Commission. To an extent it is presumably guiding Commission policy. So how does it stack up?

To take the first part of this proposition, that governments have no moral right to prevent people from emigrating: there are a handful of governments that do not accept this idea, North Korea being the most striking. Eritrea is another: it keeps its young people in the national army for years. Other than for a few people on the Stalinist hard left, such behaviour has little support. It is tantamount to turning a state into a prison. Nevertheless, most people might accept a few exceptions to the moral right to emigrate. Here is a simple thought experiment. A poor society finances a few bright students to study medicine abroad so that they can return as doctors. However, the students, once trained, decide to take up high-paying jobs in the Arabian Gulf or California instead of returning. How do we assess their behaviour? Most likely, while we might accept their legal right not to return, we might judge that they have breached a moral obligation. However, this is only a minor qualification to the general proposition that states do not have the right to impede exit. You might well be able to come up with other thought experiments in which there is some justification for denying someone the right to leave a country, but they are generally either because others will benefit or because the person concerned will benefit. Such exceptions do not amount to a more general refutation of the proposition. In normal circumstances, preventing someone from leaving his or her own country would be morally wrong.

So, given the first part of the proposition, does the second part follow? Can we infer from the moral right to emigrate that there must be a moral right to immigrate?

Again, try a thought experiment. A man leaves his own house, walks down the street and knocks randomly on the door of another house: your house as it happens. He demands the right to live with you. You question his right to do so. He points out that he has the right to leave his own house: you have to agree with him. So it must follow, he says, that he has the right to live in yours. You do not accept this: indeed, you may start to worry that he is a little mad. However, you do ponder whether you have a duty to rescue him. 'Are you safe at home?' you ask. If he isn't safe then *someone* should rescue him, though hopefully not yourself. 'Yes, I'm safe, but it's damp and cold, and pretty unpleasant compared to your house,' he replies. This does not sound very compelling. You conclude that you are off the hook: his right to leave his own house does not confer on him a right to live in yours; nor is there a duty of rescue in this instance.

Now transpose this scene from dingy houses to poor countries. Let's take India and North Korea as examples of radically different situations. Most of the billion-plus people in India would be better off in Europe or North America. The Indian government accepts that it has no moral right to prevent its citizens from emigrating. Does this give Indians the right to choose to migrate to whichever country they prefer? The two types of right are clearly entirely different: the right to leave one place does not confer the right to enter any other place of your choice. Why ever should it? While the two rights superficially sound symmetrical, it is just that: a superficial confusion of categories and an instance of what is sometimes termed 'coarse thinking'.

Now consider North Korea. Unlike India, its government does not accept a right of its citizens to emigrate. This is recognized by most of us as a breach of their human rights. But the fundamental breach of human rights is not that people cannot leave, but what happens to people when they stay. The need for asylum is not created by the denial of exit, but by systematic repression in ordinary life. Suppose that a brave and ingenious North Korean manages to get out: perhaps an athlete performing abroad who has escaped his or her minders. Now the rest of us undoubtedly have a collective duty of rescue.

Precisely the same moral framework now applies that we have previously used for Syrian and Jewish refugees: partnership for comparative advantage and burden-sharing. In the case of the refugee from North Korea the comparative advantage is evident enough: South Korea is proximate both spatially and culturally. It is no longer proximate in respect of income: after half a century of Marxism versus the market economy, the income gap is enormous. Undoubtedly, if North Korea lifted exit controls, a large majority of its population would seek to move to South Korea. At this point there would be a strong case for financial burden-sharing among all high-income countries. But, most likely, the circumstances in which North Korea opened its borders would be those in which the primary international task would be not to welcome refugees, but to build the North Korean economy.

As a matter of logic, a right of exit is void unless there is a corresponding right to enter somewhere else, but this is satisfied as long as there is one viable country of entry. North Koreans are welcome in South Korea; Eritreans are welcome in Ethiopia. The right of entry to somewhere cannot be turned into the right of entry to everywhere.[27]

Overall, the right to emigrate does not seem to be a compelling basis for inferring a global right to immigrate. There is, however, a third common argument: people born into a rich society are lucky: they do not have the moral right to pull up the ladder after them.

Following half a century in which several once poor countries caught up and sometimes overtook the West, prosperous societies are now scattered around the globe. In East Asia, these include Singapore, Japan, South Korea, Hong Kong, and Australia; in Africa: Botswana, Mauritius, and South Africa; in the Middle East: the Arabian Gulf; in Latin America: Chile and Mexico. This global patchwork of prosperity intermingled with poverty will increasingly characterize the next half-century. This is the context in which the ethical question of 'pulling up the ladder' must be posed. Since European discussion of migration from poor countries rapidly becomes entangled with historic guilt over colonialism or racism, it is less confusing for Europeans to think through the ethics of a non-European situation.

Fifty years ago Botswana was dirt poor: landlocked and semi-arid with pitifully inadequate infrastructure. In contrast, Nigeria had a good coastal position, was fertile, and had several major cities. Both discovered a valuable natural resource: Botswana found diamonds, Nigeria found oil. Botswana used this opportunity prudently; Nigeria did not. Today, living standards in Botswana are far higher than in Nigeria: indeed, it offers one of the most pleasant qualities of life in the world. Many people (including Europeans) want to live there. Should Nigerians and the rest of us have the right to do so?

For every Botswanan there are around a hundred Nigerians, so if

Nigerians were free to migrate to Botswana the Botswanans would quite probably become a minority. Were there to be a Nigerian majority in Botswana, government might continue as it is, with arriving Nigerians gratefully recognizing the benefits of Botswanan practices; or conceivably Botswana might come to develop problems resembling those of Nigeria. Having been relaxed about skilled immigration in order to foster development, now that many Botswanans have a good education, the government is refusing to renew residence permits to many foreigners. It has always restricted less-skilled immigration. Being a well-governed prosperous country surrounded by badly governed poor countries, probably the only way it can maintain high living standards is by restricting immigration. It is hard to see this as immoral.

So one reason why there is no global human right to migrate is because it would infringe on the rights of the people living in prosperous societies. While Botswana is a small society facing the possibility of very large immigration, Europe has a large population and so does not face a prospect of immigration on a proportionately equivalent scale. However, the evident fear of uncontrolled immigration apparent among many European citizens need not be due to either racism or ignorance of the likely effects on average income (which are negligible). The individual nation-states of Europe are highly unusual in having built generous welfare systems. The political foundation of these welfare systems is partly the sense of shared national identity between the fortunate and the less fortunate.[28] Recent research has found that, across Europe, those earning an above-median income are less willing to support transfers to those below median income, and the higher the proportion of immigrants and the more salient immigration is as an issue.[29] Migrants do not pose a significant wage threat to indigenous workers, but due to this inadvertent undermining of the instinct to generosity on the part of the better-off, they probably do pose a threat to poorer households. Part of the ethical case for migration controls in Europe is therefore to protect the interest of poorer citizens by sustaining the commitment to social solidarity of their better-off fellow citizens. Furthermore, even if our goal were a more just distribution of global wealth, immigration is a particularly ineffective means to achieve that goal.[30]

The final argument for a global right to migrate is seldom made in public, but is influential in professional economics and hence among some civil servants. It comes from the ethics of 'utilitarian universalism': the greatest good for the greatest number. Many economists are in thrall to this simple ethical framework, but it is not up to the analysis of refugees: the duty of rescue, fundamental not just to thinking about refugees but to AIDS and aid, does not fit into it.[31] Economists have at the back of their minds a simple model in which all restrictions on mobility of either labour or capital cause 'distortions', creating gaps between marginal productivity in one country and another. Free movement of capital and labour maximizes global output and so, with 'appropriate redistribution', 'everyone' could be better off. The beauty of this model is its extreme simplicity. But, of course, there is no mechanism for 'appropriate redistribution'. Richard Baldwin, the foremost scholar of globalization, argues that this has been a deep flaw of public policy. Just as development projects are now routinely required to have an 'environmental-impact assessment' prior to the decision on whether to approve them, he suggests that all steps towards globalization should first have a social-impact assessment to ascertain who might lose and what steps are planned to offset this loss. But, at a deeper level, the movement of goods and services does not require the movement of people: indeed, it is an alternative to it. Even the unrestricted movement of capital is now seen as problematic, and movements of people generate many effects beyond the immediate impact on the labour market.

This logic of radical utilitarianism has been applied to people who cross borders. Most notably, the moral philosophers Peter Singer and Renata Singer set out an 'equal consideration principle'.[32] It argues that we should have equal consideration for the rights of citizens and the rights of those who flee across borders. In other words, the distinctions between our special obligations to citizens and those to non-citizens should collapse. We should treat the stranger in exactly the same way we would our own family members. For Singer and Singer, the implications for public policy are that we should provide access to territory up until the marginal utility of citizens is equal to the marginal utility of those arriving. In other words, we should be obliged to accept people up until our own societies are at the point of breakdown; as the Singers put it, until tolerance, peace and security, and our ecological systems are close to collapse. This, we suggest, is extreme to the point of implausibility, unnecessary in order to meet our moral obligations in a sustainable way, and insulting to the capacity of poor societies to turn themselves round.

We have now thought through four common arguments for a global moral right to migrate. While romantically appealing, they do not survive serious scrutiny. Moderate rates of migration are mutually beneficial, but conferring unlimited rights on would-be migrants would have to confront the powerful moral claims of those in host societies.

The claims of refugees on the rest of us are morally far more powerful than those of economic migrants. They rest not on some dubious global right to migrate, but on the granite-strong duty of rescue, derived ultimately from our core sense of humanity. They have a qualified right to migrate, held insofar as it is necessary in order for them to access a safe haven. Indeed, insofar as the international community is unable to collectively meet the duty of rescue closer to home, onward movement remains a right of last resort. It is time to return to that duty towards Syrian refugees. Our next ethical conundrum is to balance interests among them: refugees are not a homogeneous group of people. Some are attracted by the prospect of succeeding in a high-income society; others, a majority, hope to return to Syria.

THE HUMAN RIGHTS OF THOSE LEFT BEHIND

Germany's generous welcome to Syrian refugees was far more attractive to some than to others: inadvertently, it was highly selective. In part, this is intrinsic to any such offer from a high-income country. German workers are able to earn high incomes because they are educated and have acquired specialist skills through long training. Those immigrants who are already skilled, or at least educated, have the best chance of achieving the high productivity that makes such high pay viable. Consequently, around the world, migration from poor countries to rich ones is more attractive for the skilled and educated than for others.

In the special circumstances of Syria, skill and education were not the only basis for selectivity. The journey in open boats on high seas was risky. Young single males were far more willing to take those risks than middle-aged couples with a dependent family. The photographers of the exodus knew that the most marketable images were of children, so those were the photos that appeared in the media. But in reality most arriving Syrians were single young men as families adopted household-level strategies of sending onwards those most able to find work. Individual photos portray a glimpse of a truth, but collectively, by skewing what is portrayed, they can create a false impression.

The move to Germany was selective by education, gender, and age, but most obviously it was selective by income. Places purchased from a people-smuggler were expensive and so attracted the affluent rather than the most vulnerable.

What can be said about this selectivity of rescue? Most likely, it was inadvertent. Chancellor Merkel did not say, 'Give me your educated, affluent young males.' She would have been upset to learn that this would be the consequence of her generosity of spirit. But it was entirely predictable: somehow, the most powerful position in Europe was briefly controlled by the headless heart. But did the selectivity matter? Evidently, it left the heavy lifting work of rescuing the neediest refugees to others.

The third principle of the heart: need

This suggests a third principle of the heart: the provision of safe haven in high-income countries should be based on need. The self-selection adopted by default as a result of the collapse of European border controls provided for the least needy, not the most. Selection on the basis of need is not esoteric: it is what all high-income societies do in their welfare programmes as a matter of course. The failure to apply this principle in respect of refugees was extraordinarily negligent.

How could selection by need have been implemented? The obvious

way would have been to make this selection in the countries border-
ing on the conflict: it is as people cross the borders from Syria into
these states that they legally become refugees. Selection by need at the
point at which people became refugees would have demonstrated
both solidarity with the proximate haven countries and coherence:
the duty of rescue was being met. Furthermore, the most just way in
which to allocate the opportunity to move onwards to Europe would
have been through organized resettlement places allocated to refugees who either could not have their needs met in the haven countries
or had no prospect of eventually returning home.

With such a process in place there would have been less pressure
from refugees wanting to take matters into their own hands. Had
adequate protection been in place within the neighbouring countries
in the region of origin, the desperate people who resorted to people-
smugglers to come to European shores would have had an alternative.
Those who arrived opportunistically could have been returned without a sense of shame. In the event, as the international responses
lurched from shambles to shambles, refugees reaching Europe were
shipped back to Turkey, but in the most squalid of circumstances.
Return was not a minor component of a coherent European strategy
to fulfil the duty of rescue: it was the centrepiece of 'enough is enough'.

Why selectivity matters

Evidently, German generosity ended up being highly selective. But perhaps we can conclude that Germany had nevertheless done what it
could. The caveat to this comforting conclusion is what happens when
peace is restored in Syria. Conflicts do end: on average people remain
as refugees for around ten years, and conflicts in middle-income countries such as Syria tend to be shorter than average. At the time of
writing, it seems quite possible that Russia and Turkey, the major international powers involved militarily, will reach some rapprochement.
This may presage a return to peace (with or without an overarching
political settlement) in most of the populated part of Syrian territory.

As we discuss in Chapter 7, post-conflict societies are fragile. The
more rapid the economic recovery, the easier it to reduce this fragility.
Much will be at stake, both for the 15 million Syrians who have

stayed in the country and the several million who will return from being refugees in the neighbouring havens. They will need the million or so young, middle-class Syrians in Germany to rebuild the country. The exodus of the young is generally bad news for a poor society. For example, a new study, conducted by the IMF, of the rapid emigration from Eastern Europe concludes that it has reduced the ability of the region to catch up with Western Europe.[33] The migrants themselves benefited, but at the expense of those left behind. In the case of post-conflict countries, the problem is yet more acute. A recent analysis of post-conflict recovery suggests that the loss of educated workers ('human capital' in the ugly jargon of economics) is even more damaging than the physical destruction.[34] Inadvertently, the exodus of young Syrians triggered by Chancellor Merkel's generosity of spirit may have inflicted significant long-term losses on the poor majority of Syrians whose lives will depend upon Syria's long-term prospects. Countries like Laos, for example, have in the past suffered the economic impact of their young and educated refugee populations assimilating abroad rather than returning to the country of origin.[35]

This shifts the question to whether the young Syrians now in Germany will return to Syria once the conflict is over or remain in Germany. The circumstances are not particularly encouraging: affluent families raised the quick finance necessary for transit by selling property at distress prices. Both materially and psychologically, they have perhaps bought places on real boats by burning their metaphorical ones. However, we need to think about this not merely as a forecast, but as an ethical question, because it raises painfully difficult policy choices for the German government.

Again, a thought experiment can help. Take two extremes: in each case a rich country fulfils its duty of rescue by offering refuge to someone from a war-affected poor country. In the first extreme, the month after the refugee arrives the conflict that drove him out ends: peace is restored and it is safe to return. Nevertheless, the refugee decides that living standards are so much higher in the country that has provided refuge that he will stay permanently. Is this an abuse of what was meant by the duty of rescue? In effect, the person has transformed himself from a refugee to an economic migrant. If the host country does not normally grant entry to such economic migrants, would it be within its moral rights to insist on his return? In the second extreme, the conflict continues for half a century before ending. Once it ends, does the host country nevertheless have the moral right to insist on return? These are ethical judgements; how should they be made?

It seems to us that at these extremes the reasonable answers are not difficult. In the former case the would-be immigrant cannot invoke his fleeting status as a refugee to claim the moral right to remain; in the latter case, the prolonged residence as a refugee should give him lifetime rights. Now start changing the numbers: not one month versus fifty years, but two years versus twenty years. There is no convenient cliff face at which the reasonable ethical answer obviously changes, but evidently it must change at some point along the spectrum. Although the 'switch point' will inevitably be somewhat arbitrary, it is nevertheless useful to have a clear rule rather than to make a decision case by case as the situation arises.[36] The advantage of a rule is twofold: all refugees can be treated equally, and all refugees know in advance what to expect. Suppose, for example, that the rule is fixed at five years. Then refugees will follow events in their country of origin and get a sense of how likely return might be. Quite probably, for the first three years they will assume that they are going back. As a result, they will retain their contacts both with their fellow refugees and with their friends and relatives back home. They may save their earnings so as to be better placed for return.

Would such a rule infringe the human rights of the person who was temporarily a refugee? It is fashionable to frame human rights purely at the level of the individual, but the refugee is not the only morally important person who should be taken into account. An implication of what we have just suggested above is that the interests of those left behind in the conflict-affected society should also be considered. It is worth thinking about the ways in which the rights of individual refugees to seek assimilation elsewhere may come into tension with the collective rights of the majority, who will eventually return home. If a privileged few permanently move on, what happens to the majority, who must go home and rebuild their own country?[37]

The benefits to other Syrians of the return to Syria of the skilled refugees currently in Germany pose a further agonizing dilemma for Germany: should integration into German society be the objective?

RIGHTS AND DUTIES OF
INTEGRATION

Clearly, if the Syrians in Germany are helped and encouraged to integrate, they will be less likely to return to Syria. Once the conflict ends, this will disadvantage the 95 per cent of Syrians who are not in Germany. But integration is the best strategy for forging successful lives in Germany, and for avoiding the potential problems to the host society should particular groups develop an oppositional identity, as many Muslims in France and Belgium have felt compelled to do.

Refugees are not migrants: they have not *chosen* to leave their homes. Their homes have become unsafe. Many wish to preserve as many vestiges of normality as possible, and a key aspect of normality is community and culture. Although a large number of refugees are young, aspirational, and cosmopolitan, a significant proportion may well be more likely than most immigrants to prefer to retain community and culture. For such people, enabling them to continue to live collectively may well be the option most consistent with an expectation of eventually returning to Syria.

But, challengingly, this delays the process of integration and may well frustrate it entirely. Once people have been settled in a few large clusters with others like themselves for two or three years, it becomes more difficult to insist that they disperse more evenly across the society. In the event, the German parliament has determined that refugees should be dispersed immediately, with each town taking the same proportion of them. Most likely, the rationale for this was partly the desire to speed up integration, and primarily the need to be seen to spread burden-sharing fairly across Germany. As we have argued, fair sharing of the burden is an important ethical principle, but in this instance it has generated conflicts between the interests of the host society, on the one hand, and those of refugees in Germany and the population of post-conflict Syria, on the other.

Having opted for integration through dispersal, what else might the German government do to assist it? There are a range of policies that might promote integration, though some might be unwelcome to host populations. The minimal policies that need to be imposed on host populations would be rigorous anti-discrimination. However, in many settings discrimination is difficult to determine. Outcomes such as places at universities can become very skewed even without discrimination, and so a notch up would be to prescribe quotas. A notch up from quotas in universities is quotas in schools, most likely achieved by means of bussing. A notch up from that would be quotas in the organizations of civil society. For example, rambling and most activities to do with the countryside have a low rate of participation on the part of ethnic minorities. Potentially, such activities could be put under varying degrees of pressure to attract an integrated pool of participants.

Critical to integration will be employment. But this is not easy to achieve for refugees in Europe. Of 500,000 refugees who arrived in Germany able to work in 2015, just 8 per cent were employed by mid-2016, compared to 66 per cent of the total migrant population. The challenge for Germany has been that as a quality-based export economy and a certificate-based society, the large-scale economic integration of low-productivity refugees is hard. Even given Germany's need for labour to address its skewed demographic distribution of too many old people and not enough young, imparting refugees with the necessary skills and qualifications to address the productivity gap is a major undertaking. Germany's chosen strategy has been to invest in training, particularly to reskill the 70 per cent of arrivals who are aged under thirty in the hope that they can make a long-term contribution. But long-term success remains uncertain: there has been a 10 per cent drop-out rate by Syrians from language classes, significantly because of male refugees refusing to be taught by women.[38] Meanwhile, the rise of the far right threatens the political sustainability of these integration policies.[39]

Again quotas may be useful. The Swiss, a multilingual society, impose quotas on civil service recruitment, with jobs earmarked by language group. Even with their education and skills, many refugees may not be equipped to get over the high productivity hurdle of the German minimum wage and the long apprenticeships that are required by firms as a precondition for employment. Should these hurdles be lowered for refugees: if so by how much and for how long? If not, how is employment to be achieved?

What, if anything, can ethically be expected of the refugees themselves? Around the top of the list is language: without fluency in German, refugees will be unable to integrate into German society. But even here there is a spectrum. Should all refugees be required to attend language classes? Should they be required to succeed? Most controversially, should refugees be expected to participate in attempts to change those aspects of Syrian cultural values that are radically out of step with current German society. For example, should extreme religious attitudes to women, infidels, and apostates be challenged?

A PROVISIONAL CONCLUSION

Our ethical tour has not been comfortable. Where have we arrived? What, echoing Descartes, can we not reasonably doubt?

The granite bedrock of our discussion has been the inescapable nature of our moral duty towards refugees. In meeting that duty we are obliged to use both the heart and the head. Just as the heartless head is cruel, the headless heart is self-indulgent. The lives of refugees are plunged into nightmare: in responding, we owe them both our compassion and our intelligence.

The first principle of the heart is the duty of rescue. That duty is not a catch-all. Refugees are not to be conflated with migrants: the primary objective of migration is to improve the quality of life. The objective of the duty of rescue is not to improve the quality of life relative to the pre-flight situation, but to restore it as near to pre-flight normality as is possible. This is why the second principle of the heart is so important: selection according to need. The needs of refugees will differ: children need schooling, young adults need work, the elderly need care.

Refugee status is defined ethically by involuntary displacement: people who flee their homes because conflict has made them unsafe. Even those who remain within their war-torn society may warrant our help to the extent that we are able to provide it. But for those who have fled their country (and so are also legally refugees rather than internally displaced persons), necessarily the duty is internationalized. But 'internationalized' means that the duty falls on 7 billion people grouped into over 200 countries.

This is where the principle of the head becomes vital. It is that rescue should be done through partnership. Partnership enables gains from both comparative advantage and fair burden-sharing. Partnership requires organized coordination: without it there is a real danger of free-riding as each bystander waits for others to act. This risk of free-riding leads to the third principle of the heart: solidarity. The default option at the onset of a refugee crisis should not be that nobody does anything, but that everybody does everything. Only with this common responsibility will governments recognize the advantages of coordinating on the basis of comparative advantage.

During the Syrian crisis none of this happened. Instead, it was an ethical train crash. As millions of desperate refugees fled across borders to Turkey, Jordan, and Lebanon, the international response was utterly inadequate. The key bystanders – the Gulf States and the OECD countries – failed in the principle of the heart: they did not meet their duty of rescue. And they failed in the principle of the head: they did not coordinate to achieve comparative advantage and burden-sharing. As a result, the level of desperation escalated.

Very belatedly, as we have seen, two distinct groups of leaders launched international efforts. In August 2015, Angela Merkel unilaterally suspended the EU's Dublin Agreement, and then persuaded the European Commission to issue directives for burden-sharing of the resulting influx; the directives were ignored and instead the Schengen process was unilaterally suspended by several governments. In September 2015, David Cameron, the King of Jordan, and Jim Kim of the World Bank convened a global meeting to be held in February 2016 in London, to share the financial burden that had fallen onto the governments of the haven countries, and to create jobs for the refugees in the havens.

Angela Merkel suffered an unprecedented collapse in political support as a result of which she completely reversed her policy, conspiring with the EU and Turkey to close the Balkan and Aegean Sea routes. Sweden underwent a similar transformation. Those Syrian refugees in transit to Germany and Sweden were confined in camps in Greece pending shipment back to Turkey, where, left in limbo with inadequate assistance, some have even frozen to death.[40] The Turkish government was offered €6bn and visa-free access to the EU to accept these returning refugees, and to close its borders so that the flow to Germany would cease at source. As described by a bemused EU official, Europe had outsourced its border controls to Turkey but could not continue to do so for long.[41] Finally, panicked by the spectacle of uncontrolled borders and the prospect of Turkish immigration, the British people voted to leave the EU.

The Syrian refugee crisis was entirely manageable. As we will show, timely application of the heart and the head could have achieved a very different scenario. There need have been no deaths through drowning, no exodus of the skilled to Germany, and perhaps even no Brexit. These catastrophically high costs were attributable to two failures.

The first failure was of international coordination. This was largely due to the inadequacies of the international architecture for refugee policy. But since these inadequacies should have been self-evident, failure was ultimately a sad reflection on global leadership. The second failure was resort to the headless heart. Against the backdrop of free-riding by others, Angela Merkel's well-intentioned intervention and subsequent volte-face have led to ethical dilemmas which may have been entirely avoidable.

5
Rethinking Havens:
Reaching Everyone

Since most refugees, as we've seen, remain in their region of origin, that is where solutions primarily need to be found. While the panic is in Europe, the greatest needs are elsewhere, usually just across the border from conflict and crisis zones. And yet there is a mismatch in terms of attention and resources. We focus on the 10 per cent who reach the developed world but neglect the nearly 90 per cent who stay in developing regions of the world.

For the majority who are concentrated in a relatively small number of host countries in the region of origin, existing models are dysfunctional. The dominant approach has become to create a 'humanitarian silo', physically segregated from the host population and dominated by a model that was designed to deal just with the emergency phase, but has become the only approach, enduring as refugees remain there year after year. The refugee camp is the silo's default haven – usually remote, arid, and dangerous; almost always with strict prohibitions on socio-economic activity.

This approach undermines autonomy and dignity; it erodes human potential by focusing almost exclusively on people's vulnerabilities rather than rebuilding their capacities. Unsurprisingly, many people become disillusioned, and choose to move onwards, whether to urban areas in the host country or risking their lives by crossing oceans.

In this chapter we aim to rethink the humanitarian silo. We recognize that it makes sense to protect most refugees close to home, both because that is where they are and because it is likely to offer by far the most sustainable response at the scale required to address contemporary displacement. However, developing countries are often in need themselves, and we cannot simply let the burden fall largely on countries less able to handle it. A new approach to safe havens that is radically more supportive is urgently needed in order to address this dysfunctional imbalance, and to simultaneously meet the concerns of donors, hosts, and refugees.

WHY CLOSE TO HOME MAKES SENSE FOR MOST

As we have seen, the geographical reality is that the overwhelming majority of the world's refugees are in countries that neighbour conflict and crisis. These 'countries of first asylum' in developing regions today host 86 per cent of all refugees, up from 72 per cent a decade ago. In consequence, it is the countries with the least capacity to host refugees that bear the greatest responsibility. They are the ones that invariably neighbour conflict-ridden or authoritarian states. Although a global total of 21.3 million refugees may sound like a lot, it should be manageable against the backdrop of a global population of over 7 billion. Refugees are just over 0.3 per cent of the world's population. The challenge is not one of absolute numbers but of geographical concentration.

It is in these host countries where most of the world's refugees are that we should concentrate the bulk of our focus and resources. Lebanon, a country smaller than Wales, hosts over a million Syrian refugees, who make up a quarter of its entire population. Between them, Kenya and Uganda also host a million refugees – almost as many as the total number of asylum-seekers to enter all twenty-eight of the EU's member states during 2015, the peak of the 'European refugee crisis'. Until Turkey – host to 2.6 million refugees – recently overtook it, Pakistan had been the world's most significant refugee-hosting country for decades almost entirely because it neighbours Afghanistan. These parts of the world – not Europe – are where the real refugee protection challenges lie.

And in these countries of first asylum the situation is frequently dire. In his book on the Dadaab camps in Kenya, the British author Ben Rawlence writes: 'The term "refugee camp" is misleading. Dadaab was established in 1992 to hold 90,000 refugees fleeing Somalia's civil war. At the beginning of 2016 it is twenty-five years old and nearly half a million strong, an urban area the size of New Orleans, Bristol or Zurich unmarked on any official map.'[1] Al-Shabaab terrorists are active in the camps, young men are susceptible to recruitment by armed groups, violence is endemic, and there is no formal right to work despite food rations being inadequate. Many refugees have been there for at least two decades. The only plausible alternative for Somalis in Kenya is to head to Nairobi, where some can find work or establish informal-sector businesses in the vibrant Eastleigh Estate, where over 100,000 Somalis live. But the trade-off in moving to the city is that in doing so refugees generally have to break the law, abandon all access to formal assistance, and risk round-up and detention during the periods in which there are sporadic police crack-downs on urban Somalis. While extreme, the situation in Kenya is a microcosm of much of the global refugee regime.

When we travelled to Za'atari in Jordan, the situation was not dissimilar for the 83,000 inhabitants. Yes, there were a more vibrant informal market, better rations, and superior basic services, but the underlying model was similar: take your rations, live passively and without work in a remote border area, and we will let you know when peace breaks out and it is time to go home. Farid explained the dilemma this created for his family: 'There is nothing to do here. But we cannot go to the city because there is no support, we have nowhere to live there, and we will not be able to work. My eldest son – he is nineteen years old – has chosen to go back to Syria and take his chances because he could not cope here.'

And yet global public attention and resources have generally focused on a tiny percentage of the world's refugees: either the around 0.5 per cent who receive resettlement to developed countries or the less than 10 per cent who move there spontaneously as asylum-seekers. Those people arriving in Europe or North America are often extremely vulnerable and their lives matter, but so too do the lives of the nearly 90 per cent left behind. Today, the world spends approximately $75bn a year on the 10 per cent of refugees who moved to developed regions and only around $5bn a year on the 90 per cent who remain in developing regions. As we saw in the Introduction, this works out as a ratio of about $135 spent on a refugee in the developed world to every $1 spent on a refugee in the developing world.[2]

Worse, some of the money appropriated for the few who have

reached Europe has been diverted from funds previously earmarked for poor countries. For example, in 2015, Sweden, formerly one of the most generous donors, diverted fully half of its aid budget in this way. An arcane loophole in the OECD rules as to what counts as 'aid' actually enables the Swedish government to continue to count this diverted money in its aid budget, but think about who is really paying for Sweden's refugees. Yet there is also no evidence that those who leave of their own volition are necessarily the most vulnerable. On the contrary, as we document in more detail in Chapter 7, the move to Europe has been highly selective in favour of those who are less needy.

Just because a person has travelled to Europe or elsewhere certainly does not make her or him any less of a refugee. Even if refugees arriving in Europe are statistically more likely to be men, of working age, and educated than those who remain in neighbouring states, the simple fact of their being from a country in which they face serious harm and a threat to their lives makes them refugees and in need of international protection.

It is also important to recognize that refugees arriving in Europe and elsewhere are not just a cost but will also make an economic contribution. As we elaborate in the following chapters, the balance between burden and benefit is a policy choice for host states. Refugees, like anyone else, are used to earning a living. How well they are able to do so depends upon the regulatory environment in which they find themselves. If European policies were designed to enable refugees to be productive, whether as wage employees or entrepreneurs, they need not be a burden and could even be an economic benefit.[3]

However, recognition of this potential contribution cannot plausibly be used as a validation of the status quo. The fact that refugees who come to Europe could make a macroeconomic contribution does not imply that a coherent refugee policy can, or should, be based on a combination of neglect of the many and long-distance spontaneous-arrival asylum for the few. When refugees make an economic contribution, as with other workers the income they generate primarily accrues to the refugees themselves, and to the wider private sector in Europe; it is not reallocated to the global refugee policy pot. Remittances aside, the benefits do very little to help the 90 per cent of refugees still in the region of origin. If refugees can contribute to the GDP of

Where refugees from top 5 countries of origin found asylum | end-2015

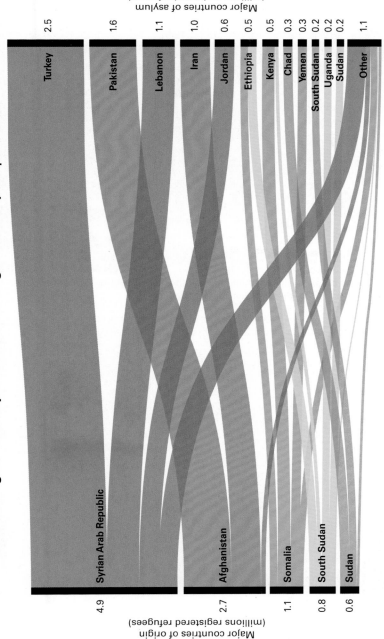

Major countries of origin
(millions registered refugees)

- Syrian Arab Republic — 4.9
- Afghanistan — 2.7
- Somalia — 1.1
- South Sudan — 0.8
- Sudan — 0.6

Major countries of asylum
(millions registered refugees)

- Turkey — 2.5
- Pakistan — 1.6
- Lebanon — 1.1
- Iran — 1.0
- Jordan — 0.6
- Ethiopia — 0.5
- Kenya — 0.5
- Chad — 0.3
- Yemen — 0.3
- South Sudan — 0.2
- Uganda — 0.2
- Sudan — 0.2
- Other — 1.1

Source: UNHCR

Women walk between destroyed buildings in the government-held Jouret al-Shiah neighbourhood of the central Syrian city of Homs.

Syrian children at the recently designed Azraq refugee camp in northern Jordan.

A Syrian family living in urban destitution in an apartment block in Beirut, Lebanon.

Satellite imagery of the Dadaab refugee camps in Kenya, which host nearly 350,000 Somali refugees.

Congolese women selling dried fish and vegetables in the Nyarugusu refugee camp in Tanzania, where refugees have no legal right to work.

The bustling Juru market in Nakivale settlement in Uganda, created in 1958 and home to refugees from Somalia, the Democratic Republic of Congo, and Rwanda.

The Shams-Élysées market street in Za'atari refugee camp in Jordan. Its name is a play on words that combines the old name for Syria with the famous Parisian avenue.

A makeshift bird shop in the home of a Syrian family in the Za'atari refugee camp in Jordan. The camp was created in response to the Syrian civil war and hosts around 83,000 people.

Demou-Kay, a Congolese refugee, running his community radio station in Nakivale settlement in Uganda.

Refugees making biodegradable sanitary pads at a social enterprise in Kyaka II settlement in Uganda.

Refugee and local tailors working alongside one another in Kampala. Uganda is one of the few developing countries that gives refugees the right to work.

A factory in the King Hussein bin Talal Development Area (KHBTDA) in Jordan, one of the economic zones where Syrians are gradually being allowed to work.

Syrian men embark on the perilous journey across the Aegean Sea. Around 8,500 people drowned crossing the Mediterranean in 2015 and 2016.

A woman and child refugee from Syria wait at the border to Austria in Sentilj, Slovenia.

European countries, they can also contribute to the growth of host countries of first asylum: that is where development is really needed.

Our policy-makers are thereby operating a two-tier system for refugees: a boutique model for the 10 per cent who travel successfully to the rich world by whatever means, and a dependency and destitution model for most of the 90 per cent who remain in havens near their country of origin. Of course, those who travel often suffer many hardships on their journey, but the prize they can ultimately attain – a pathway to citizenship in a Western liberal democracy – is of an order of magnitude more desirable than the opportunities and entitlements available to the neglected majority.

Is there any basis on which we should be privileging those who are near rather than those who are far away? Some political theorists like Michael Walzer argue that there can be. He suggests that the salient ethical consideration for whether proximity shapes our obligations hinges upon whether we accept the broader 'acts versus omissions' distinction. He argues that to turn away vulnerable people arriving at our shores is a worse thing than to neglect distant refugees in camps on the other side of the world – because it stems from an act rather than simply an omission.[4]

This argument is not entirely baseless; it maps onto a longstanding debate within moral philosophy, and certainly there are grounds to believe that using violent coercion against vulnerable populations is deeply problematic. But it cannot be a basis for international public policy. From its inception, international refugee policy has rightly aspired to build *global* rules that address *global* needs. The great moral weakness with the proximity-first argument is that it can so readily be gamed. Were proximity just an 'act of God' then it would have real power. But if those people with atypically large resources are able to make themselves proximate, then using it as a criterion for assistance becomes morally negligent. Our help becomes concentrated on those with the least need. And, as we argued in the previous chapter, by rewarding proximity we tempt people into taking risks. If a policy of privileging the proximate lures people to their deaths, we commit not only the sin of omission in neglecting the major need, but a sin of commission. If the underlying purpose of the refugee regime is a duty of rescue and a pathway to autonomy, then the collective challenge should be how we can effectively and efficiently provide those rights to all refugees, rather than a different (and inapt) set of rights for an arbitrarily privileged few.

The right to seek asylum is not the same thing as an absolute right to freedom of movement. Although it has become popular among advocacy organizations and within the liberal filter bubble to see being a refugee as necessarily conferring an unimpeded right to travel, this is neither ethically nor legally credible. Aside from going down a general 'open borders' route, the only refugee-specific argument one could use to justify an exceptional, absolute right to migrate is that because refugees have generally had such a difficult time we might wish to just let them have a 'free pass' in terms of migration. But this ignores that the salient need of a refugee *qua* refugee is protection and a pathway to autonomy; not migration per se.

The refugee's right to migrate is therefore a qualified right. There is no absolute right for a refugee to decide where protection is provided. The right to migrate is justified insofar as it is the means by which refugees can access protection. What are the pertinent rights for refugees *qua* refugees? The overarching one is protection for the duration of risk. But since refuge typically lasts for years, this cannot be sufficient: refugees have a right to expect a pathway to autonomy. The final distinctive right of refugees is that of return or integration elsewhere, depending upon the duration of the conflict. Many conflicts end sufficiently soon for return to be the appropriate aspiration. For those that persist, integration into another society is necessary: people cannot be left in a permanent limbo of isolation. It may well be that a person who happens to be a refugee also has other rights (ethically or legally) that accrue as a result of some other status: 'child', 'migrant', 'human being', or 'private contractor', for example. But these are the broad groups that are salient to *being a refugee*.[5]

Yet too much of the current advocacy strategy is hijacked by a distracting focus on 'the right to migrate' for the minority. Yes, of course, if refugees cannot access the basket of entitlements closer to home then they will – and indeed should be expected to – move onwards in search of those rights. Anybody in a similar situation would consider doing likewise. But the refugee policy challenge should not become diverted by a focus on migration dynamics;

it has to focus on how to provide the relevant basket of rights to refugees in the places where the majority of refugees are actually located.

So the real question is how best can we provide all refugees with the opportunities to which they are entitled as refugees? The place to start should be in refugees' regions of origin for a number of reasons. Above all, we should privilege the region of origin because of geographical fact: it is where the majority of refugees actually are. But protection close to home also has other advantages.

Most obviously, it makes it easier to go home, a theme we take up in Chapter 7. Rather than assimilating in a radically different society or culture, refugees are more likely to preserve ties to the homeland, to retain networks that connect them to their country of origin, and to foresee return as the most likely long-term outcome. Historically, rates of repatriation are far higher from adjacent countries than from those further afield. Indeed, this is already happening in Syria. As towns are being liberated from ISIS, those refugees in the regional havens are returning. As we write, Manbij, a town of 100,000 people in northern Syria, has just been cleared of ISIS and people are already flocking back from across the border in Turkey.[6] Large-scale repatriation from the United States, Canada, Australia, or Europe, on the other hand, is virtually unheard of. With very few exceptions – like returns to Bosnia and Kosovo from immediately neighbouring European countries in the 1990s and early 2000s – a move to a different continent is a pathway to assimilation and permanent integration. It is not a move to ensure protection for the duration of risk.

More surprisingly, it may offer more opportunities for refugees to participate in the economies and societies of their host countries. In four fifths of the world, state borders are the result of the legacies of colonialism. People across borders often have at least as much in common as that which divides them: language, culture, and extended family networks, for example. These trans-boundary ties may offer a basis for temporary participation if the regulatory framework of the host government allows it. This is why many Luvale-speaking Angolans were able to contribute to the economic life of Zambia's Western Province for two decades until going home, why many Syrian Alawites are welcomed in the mainly Alawite south-eastern areas of

Turkey, and why ethnic Somali Ugandans in Kampala privilege employing Somali refugees in their businesses.

Facilitating economic participation further afield is complex, in part because it is placing someone within an entirely different socio-economic culture and regulatory regime. As Achim Dercks, of the Association of German Chambers of Industry and Commerce, put it: 'Someone who comes from Eritrea and says he was an electrician might have repaired a radio or laid a cable there but he might have never seen a fuse box, as we use it in Germany.' It is absolutely not the case that refugees cannot be economically assimilated elsewhere – of course they can be, with patience and political will. It is just that, wherever it is possible, there may be distinct advantages to doing it nearer to home, especially if the aspiration is that most will eventually go home.

Another strong reason for privileging the region of origin is sustainability. The number of people seeking refuge is likely to increase over time. Although not inevitable, the dynamics of conflict, climate change, and state fragility strongly imply that displacement – and survival migration – will be a defining feature of the twenty-first century and beyond. The question is not so much whether it will happen but how we will manage it.

A final reason is that the rich countries are becoming less reliable as places for mass refuge. Liberal democratic states around the world are facing a socio-political crisis. From Europe to the United States to Australia, there has been a polarization of politics. The right has become more right wing, the left more left wing, and the centre ground has been decimated. In particular, parts of Europe have experienced a rise of the far right: from Victor Orbán in Hungary, to Marine Le Pen in France, to Frauke Petry in Germany, to Nigel Farage in the UK, to the massive support for a far-right presidential candidate in the Austrian elections. Meanwhile, the election of Donald Trump as the US President shows that these trends extend beyond Europe. Across the entire political spectrum, there has been a lurch towards nativism, as populist nationalism has become the common currency of democratic politics. Isolated terrorist attacks have been used to repudiate the right to asylum in Europe.

The challenge is to consider ways to address alienation and fear. Politicians now face the dilemma of how to reconcile democracy and refuge in ways that can take majoritarian politics with them. Nearly all of the opinion polls and social-psychology evidence tell us that public concern about asylum is not about numbers per se; it is about a perceived loss of control. [7] This trend casts serious doubt on spontaneous-arrival asylum in developed regions of the world as a viable long-term solution for the majority of the world's refugees. 'Sanctuary Europe' became politically unsustainable in less than a year.

Democracies are deeply concerned about a range of aspects of globalization, including openness to trade and immigration. These are vast, complex, and contradictory matters that will not be easily resolved. Voting patterns in Brexit revealed how polarizing globalization has become.[8] In too many of these debates about globalization, refuge has been drawn in. But thought about properly, it should be disentangled from these divisive debates. Refuge is about shared values and could be reconceived as a unifying issue in Western societies and globally.

But the very embarrassment of the rich world can be leveraged into a solid system of international financing for the first countries of asylum. As we elaborate below, with levels of economic support that are entirely feasible for the high-income countries, being a regional haven can be turned into an attractive opportunity. This is reinforced by the extraordinary repeated concentration of refugees in only ten haven countries. Were even a sliver of the income of high-income countries reliably focused on these havens it would make a large difference to their willingness to host refugees. For example, the combined GDP of the richest five countries in the world is around $40,000bn, and the combined GDP of Jordan, Lebanon, Uganda, Kenya and Pakistan is $450bn. This is a ratio of nearly 100:1, meaning that a transfer of 0.1 per cent of GDP from the rich countries would be equivalent to a gain of 10 per cent of GDP in the host counties.[9]

Further, the same reason that makes the proximate havens particularly suited to refugees makes the refugees particularly suited to the havens. There are often historic ethnic and linguistic overlaps and cultural affinities. And the legal frameworks that apply to their own citizens on employment and certification are usually well-suited to what is required for refugees to earn a living: the regulatory problem is exclusion, not mis-design.

Contrary to the framing put forward by some European politicians, an approach focused on dramatically improving outcomes in regions of origin does not exclude preserving a space for asylum elsewhere. Spontaneous-arrival asylum and resettlement have a valid place in the policy toolbox. But, in contrast to much current thinking, we need to be absolutely clear on their ethical and political purpose.

The preservation of spontaneous-arrival asylum outside the region of origin has two possible justifications. First, as a symbolic commitment to reciprocity: it demonstrates to first countries of asylum that all governments around the world have a duty to open their borders to asylum-seekers. How effective or salient this is, however, is an empirical question. Second, as a last resort: it ensures that if effective protection is not available in another part of the world, a person can move onwards to find it.

Meanwhile, resettlement has two further main functions. It can remove the most vulnerable, whom it would simply be inappropriate to leave in camps and urban areas. Further, it can provide a long-term solution for those unable to go home or locally integrate in the host country after an extended period in exile. However, contrary to the vocal advocacy of a large resettlement and asylum industry in Europe and North America – an industry worth an estimated $100bn per year – these solutions do not represent the principal way in which a sustainable response to the refugee crisis will be found.

THE FAILURE OF THE HUMANITARIAN SILO

The current system for refugees who remain in their region of origin is a disaster. It is premised upon an almost exclusively 'humanitarian' response. A system designed for the emergency phase – to offer an immediate lifeline – ends up enduring year after year, sometimes decade after decade. External provision of food, clothing, and shelter is absolutely essential in the aftermath of having to run for your life. But over time, if it is provided as a substitute for access to jobs, education, and other opportunities, humanitarian aid soon undermines human dignity and autonomy.

Most camps are designed as if they were temporary structures created just for the fleeting emergency phase. Even though many exist for decades, they are almost never planned to last. Consequently, although a great number have been around for years – Nakivale in Uganda opened in 1958 – they have not significantly changed since they were set up. Many may look like cities – Dadaab is the third-largest city in Kenya – but they are certainly not designed as cities. To do so would be to create an aesthetic of permanence that would risk disturbing the convenient fiction of temporariness perpetuated by the host government and the international community. The consequence is that facilities are not built to last: housing, schools, and community facilities are often of an unacceptably low standard, and funded through UNHCR's precarious single-year funding cycle rather than predictable multi-year funding such as it used for development projects.

As a concept, the strength of the camp is that – at its best – it can offer an initial source of stability. It is an efficient way to provide initial assistance to large populations fleeing a crisis. It can offer life-saving support and enable people to regain health, re-establish contact with families, and acquire a minimum level of security. But, over time, if camp life endures for too long it may lead to long-term reliance upon aid, exacerbate vulnerability, and erode people's capacities for independence.

The core problem is that most camps are premised upon a model of segregation; they physically separate refugees from the citizens of the country, frequently in remote border locations. Because many host societies perceive the long-term presence of refugees as a source of competition for scarce resources or a threat to security, politicians are under pressure to minimize their participation in the economic and political life of the host state. They legislate to deny them the right to work and freedom of movement.

The theory is that refugees will soon have access to a 'durable solution' – a pathway to long-term integration within a community. But this has become an elusive fiction: the international community is not managing to end conflicts to allow people to go home; it is not persuading host countries to integrate locally; and resettlement places are a drop in the ocean. Instead people are left in limbo, with generations of refugees being born in camps, growing up in camps, and becoming adults in camps. Around them, they struggle to find role models because their parents have usually been denied hope and opportunity.

To give just one example, Esperance is a refugee from the Democratic Republic of Congo. She fled her home town of Bukavu in 1998 and travelled with her family across Lake Tanganyika to Tanzania. At the time she was fourteen years old. Today, she is thirty-two. Throughout that time, she has lived entirely in the mud-brick-house-lined Nyarugusu refugee camp, where she has subsequently married and given birth to her three children. Based on Tanzania's encampment policy, refugees are obliged to live in camps and are not allowed to travel freely outside them or to engage in formal economic activity. Despite this, Esperance is unable to fully support her family based on the World Food Programme's food rations and so sometimes sells dried fish or other wares in the settlement which she generally purchases from Tanzanian or Congolese fishermen near the entrance to the camp.

During the time Esperance has been there, Nyarugusu's population has occasionally fluctuated. In 2009, with gradual repatriation of some Congolese refugees, Tanzania closed its other nearby camps, consolidating its then entire 100,000 Congolese refugee population into the one camp. In 2015, renewed civil war in Burundi led to 100,000 Burundians arriving in the camp, swelling its population to 160,000, briefly making it the largest single refugee camp in the world. Esperance explained: 'Each year I ask myself if we are better off with this life or risking going home. But I no longer know any life other than the camp. My children were born here.'[10]

The situation is riddled with contradictions. Congolese refugees who arrived during the Second Congo War are in camps while a few miles away thousands of Congolese migrant fishermen line Lake Tanganyika, generally tolerated by the authorities. The refugees have a potential economic contribution to make and work illicitly, and yet the District and Regional Commissioners believe that, politically, encampment is the only tenable option to preserve their local power base. UNHCR has for nearly a decade supported repatriation for the Congolese as the most viable long-term solution and yet, in practice, cycles of violence in South Kivu have made this risky if not impossible for most people.

Despite the inhumanity of this kind of stasis – effectively creating a 'lost generation' – all of the incentives are perversely aligned to preserve the status quo of encampment, not only in Tanzania but around the world. Camps suit host states because they simultaneously appease citizens and attract a dribble of funding through visibility. They suit UNHCR because they bankroll the organization. And they suit donors because they contain a population that might otherwise be a source of instability or move onwards in search of a better life.

Of course, camps vary in form. But even where supposedly innovative camp designs have been tried, the results are equally disastrous, especially if camps continue to deny refugees access to jobs, education, and economic participation. The Azraq refugee camp in Jordan offers a case in point. Opened in 2014, with the personal endorsement of the UN High Commissioner for Refugees, António Guterres, it is one of the first internationally planned and designed refugee camps in the world.[11] In theory, it offered an increasingly self-aware UNHCR an opportunity to put into practice everything it had learned about the pros and cons of different forms of camp design during its sixty-year history.

And yet, despite being planned from scratch as a dream camp, Azraq is a grim place to live. Built on an ex-army base, it is in a remote desert area, twenty kilometres from the nearest town, and temperatures can reach 40°C by day and fall below zero at night. Accommodation is divided into four villages of uniformly distributed shipping container housing, each interspersed with the same, standard key facilities and services – primary schools, sports facilities, and communal areas. The layout is designed to ensure security; with all areas being extremely visible to the Jordanian police's permanent surveillance.

For the camp's 53,000 Syrian refugees there is almost no scope for individual autonomy. There is no market and almost all economic exchange is strictly prohibited. There is a single large supermarket, run by a Jordanian chain, Sameh, which has been granted a monopoly status within the camp. Refugees are provided not with money but with World Food Programme vouchers, which they can only spend on the items that the Sameh supermarket offers for sale. No other businesses or services are allowed to enter the camp. Practically the only form of individuality able to shine through within the otherwise soulless design comes from refugees' own occasional murals and graffiti on the outer walls of their shipping container homes. Mahdi, whom one of us met on a visit in 2015, explained: 'we thought it would be better than this. What can we do here? There is not even a market. Had we known, we would not have come. As soon as we are able to we will try to move to Amman.'[12] UNHCR's model for the future is, in reality, a vision of hell.

Azraq defies almost every basic rule ever learned in urban planning. It is to refugee settlements what Brasilia, Chandigarh, Canberra, and Le Corbusier's *banlieues* are to cities: a well-intentioned, high-modernist catastrophe. As the anthropologist James Scott compellingly argues, to be successful human settlements have to allow scope for organic development; they must allow individuals and communities the autonomy to freely define their own environment.[13] Top-down planning strips away everything that sustains vibrant and inhabitable communities. As with Scott's analysis of cities more generally, one of two outcomes is possible: either people reassert their autonomy or they will wish to leave.

The default logic of the refugee camp can therefore be characterized as a humanitarian silo. Most obviously, they are usually physically segregated, isolating the population from wider participation in local, national, and global socio-economic life: they are deliberate ghettos. Activity is led almost entirely by humanitarian agencies. Even though refugee issues lie at the intersection of a Venn diagram between humanitarianism, economic development, human rights, security, and post-conflict recovery, the response is dominated by a humanitarian logic. The result is an ongoing paternalism and custodianship over people's lives even at a stage when it would make far more sense to embrace a development approach that could restore people's dignity and autonomy over a longer time horizon.

THE NEGLECT OF URBAN REFUGEES

Predictably, people are voting with their feet and shunning refugee camps. Following a wider global trend towards urbanization, most now go to cities, even though host countries discourage it. Over half of the world's refugees now live in urban areas, and in some countries, like Jordan, the propostion is as high as 80 per cent. But in doing so they generally relinquish formal assistance, and yet sometimes do not even have the right to work. Even where access to employment is at least tolerated, refugees face discrimination and exploitation, and are frequently left destitute. From Nairobi to Dar es Salaam, to Istanbul, to Johannesburg, to Bangkok, the situation faced by urban refugees is bleak.

In 2009, UNHCR unveiled its first serious urban-refugee policy.[14] It is a well-crafted document, setting out a comprehensive protection strategy in areas as diverse as registration, community relations, livelihoods, and health and education facilities. However, in reality, it has had little impact on the lives of most urban refugees. The widely held consensus among practitioners is that although it offers a safety net to some of the most vulnerable, implementation of the policy has been patchy.[15] This is in part because the refugee system still lacks a viable operational model for protecting people in cities, which offer such a radically different protection environment compared to camps. Organizations struggle to build working relationships with municipal authorities, to identify vulnerabilities in densely populated areas, and to support livelihoods when refugees' right to work is either prohibited or heavily regulated. In practice, to move to an urban area is usually a choice to go it alone.

Amman hosts 175,000 Syrian refugees. Accompanying UNHCR staff on a home visit in the district of Al-Hashmi Al-Shamali, we met a family of five living in a crowded, damp, and dilapidated two-room apartment that they rent on the private market. The father has diabetes and hypertension and was in such bad health he could not work. This left the eldest son, Saad, as the family's primary breadwinner at the age of just fifteen. Saad had been out of school for four years at that point and earned money by washing cars at a Jordanian-run garage. Working without the government's prohibitively expensive formal work permit, this provided scarcely enough money for the family to survive. They explained that they had originally brought savings from Syria but that these were now depleted, leaving the family increasingly reliant upon *zakat* (charitable giving) through the local mosque. The catch-22 is that urban refugees are expected to help themselves and yet cannot freely access the labour market.

But even though refugees struggle in Amman, UNHCR's operation there is actually one of the better urban operations around the world. In other countries, protection for urban refugees is virtually non-existent. South Africa operates a 'self-settlement' policy for refugees. In practice this means it is one of the only significant refugee-hosting countries in the global South without camps, and the overwhelming majority of refugees are in its big cities. The upside is that, unlike in many countries, refugees are able to work as soon as they arrive. The downside is that neither the government nor international organizations provide any material assistance. And because refugees face discrimination in accessing jobs, education, and housing, and sometimes even sporadic xenophobic violence, many struggle to find viable livelihoods. The country hosts Somali, Congolese, Burundian, Rwandan, and Nigerian refugees, for example. But the struggles of its urban refugees are perhaps best illustrated by the presence of Zimbabweans in the country over the last decade or so.

At the peak of the Zimbabwean refugee influx in 2008, Zimbabweans comprised a quarter of the world's total number of asylum-seekers. Most were in South Africa and most in urban areas, with the largest concentration in Johannesburg. Unwelcome in the townships, huge numbers congregated around the central business district, especially in high-rise buildings around Johannesburg's Braamfontein district. Those who could afford to occupy private apartments did so. For those who could not, options were limited and many therefore ended up homeless. In March 2009, 3,400 Zimbabweans were living in just one church, the Central Methodist Church in downtown Johannesburg, sleeping in church annexes, bible study rooms, and even in the aisles among the pews. Although Zimbabweans courageously organized themselves within the church to offer informal education to children and provided sources of community-led social protection, the South African police repeatedly tried and failed to forcibly remove them from the church. By the time the Central Methodist Church closed its doors to refugees in 2015, it had hosted an estimated 30,000 Zimbabweans over an eight-year period. But the very fact that a church became a sanctuary of last resort to so many is itself a testament to the lack of options available to many urban refugees.

Governments tend to fear large urban-refugee populations. South Africa's initial solution to the mass influx of Zimbabweans was to claim that they were not refugees and to deport them. Jordan would far prefer Syrians to be in camps, because of both worries about terrorist infiltration and competition for jobs and resources. However, forcibly removing large numbers of refugees from the mega-cities of the global South is almost impossible and so most host countries begrudgingly tolerate the presence of urban refugees while doing as little as possible to welcome them, and sometimes as much as possible to deter their arrival.

The humanitarian silo model is increasingly out of touch. It fails against almost any metric. It doesn't help refugees, undermining their autonomy and dignity. It doesn't help host governments, transforming potential contributors into a disempowered and alienated generation in their midst. It doesn't help the international community, leaving people indefinitely dependent upon aid, less capable of ultimately rebuilding their countries of origin, and with onward movement as their only viable route to opportunity.

Demonstrably, this model, inherited from the long-past legacy of the Second World War, is not fit for purpose; and has not been so for several decades. The international architecture of refugee policy has remained unaltered, not because it works, but because its repeated failures have never sufficiently exploded into the headlines. The Syrian refugee crisis has created the first true opportunity for reform, not because of its unique severity, but because at its edges it has spilled over to Europe. Thanks to the European refugee 'crisis' a rethink is at last possible. So what should that rethink be? This book is built around four interrelated proposals. It is time for the first of them.

REFUGEES AS DEVELOPMENT OPPORTUNITY

There is an alternative. And it starts with recognizing that refugees have skills, talents, and aspirations. They are not just passive objects of our pity, but actors constrained by cruel circumstance. They do not have to be an inevitable burden, but instead can help themselves and their communities – if we let them. Imagine if, instead of the humanitarian silo, we could conceive of an approach that could support refugees' autonomy and dignity while simultaneously empowering them to contribute to host communities and the eventual reconstruction of their country of origin. Central to this vision is the idea that refugees do not have to be understood just as a humanitarian issue; they can also be seen as a development issue. Humanitarianism may be appropriate during an emergency phase but beyond that it is counter-productive.

'Development' means many things to many people but it can be broadly understood as an approach that attempts to enhance long-term human welfare, whereas 'humanitarianism' is simply about the short-term alleviation of suffering. The humanitarian toolbox offers food, clothing, and shelter; it focuses exclusively on refugees and their vulnerabilities. The development toolbox offers employment, enterprise, education, healthcare, infrastructure, and governance; it focuses on both refugees and host communities, and it builds upon the capacities of both rather than just addressing vulnerabilities.

As soon as we recognize that the assumption that refugees will go home quickly is a fiction, then it becomes imperative to embrace a development-based approach as early in a refugee crisis as possible. If refugee camps are becoming like cities, then we need an approach that can treat them as such. For the period that refugees are in limbo, we should be creating an enabling environment that nurtures rather than debilitates people's ability to contribute in exile and when they ultimately go home. This should involve all of the things that allow people to thrive and contribute rather than merely survive: education, the right to work, electricity, connectivity, transportation, access to capital. Ideally refugees should be allowed to fully participate in the socio-economic life of the host state. But even when full participation is politically blocked, we should at least be able to reimagine geographical spaces that can empower people, and allow them to become self-reliant pending a longer-term solution.

To achieve this vision, host communities must share in the benefits. Just as we recognize that there are pressures for more sustainable refugee policies in the North, so too this applies in host counties in the South. Host governments – whether democratic or not – are under pressure from their own citizens to ensure refugees do not become a source of competition for scarce resources. Service provision that supports refugees' access to health and education should also benefit surrounding host communities. Jobs and markets that are created to help refugees must also benefit host country nationals. Additional funds should come from the international community in order specifically to support refugee-hosting areas, enabling then to perceive refugees as a potential boon rather than an inevitable burden. Put simply, policies are needed that move host community/refugee relations from a zero sum relationship to a positive sum relationship. Material opportunity needs to be the route through which perceptions and prejudices are altered. If just some of the $135 spent on the 10 per cent for every $1 spent on the 90 per cent could be reallocated, then an alternative vision might be possible.

The international community has a long but neglected history of applying development-based approaches to refugees. This history offers important insights into how we might achieve our alternative vision. The humanitarian silo model is in fact a late arrival to refugee policy: it became very dominant very quickly. Long before the humanitarian silo came to dominate thinking, development-based approaches were the norm for refugees.[16]

One of the earliest examples relates to Greece's refugee policies of the early 1920s. With the collapse of the Ottoman Empire, Greece received a staggering 1.2 million Greek Orthodox Christians who had long been living in what became Turkey. In a Greek host population of only 5.5 million this was a truly massive influx. Greece also received a substantial number of refugees from other former Ottoman countries, including what is now Syria. Greece borrowed money from the League of Nations to manage the mass influx, but rather than resort to camps the country chose a different path. The government established new settlements and townships in historically underdeveloped areas, and tried to identify ways in which the refugees could be both self-sufficient and make an economic contribution to the country. Much as the World Bank might today, the International Labour Organization (ILO) provided additional funding to support a variety of national-development projects capable of simultaneously benefiting refugees and hosts alike.

The outcomes were strikingly positive for refugees, local communities and Greece's national-development strategy. One commentator remarked in 1929: 'The refugees have caused vast changes in rural

Greece. Wastelands have been transformed into orchards, vineyards, grain fields, and tobacco plantations . . . better breeds of livestock are being introduced, and nomadic shepherds are being replaced by stock breeders who raise forage crops on their own land . . . production of almost all kinds of agricultural products has increased enormously since the refugees began to flood the country.' Many of the schemes at the time looked significantly like contemporary 'innovative' ideas for refugee integration. Vocational training, micro-finance, and even skills-matching projects were applied by ILO to support refugees in Greece and then scaled to other parts of the Balkans and the Middle East.

Similar approaches were applied across sub-Saharan Africa during the 1960s. In this era, refugee camps were almost never used and refugees in Africa, fleeing colonial-liberation wars, post-colonial power struggles, or Cold War proxy conflicts were invariably self-settled in rural areas. Their only sources of support generally came from development actors that already happened to be working on agricultural or infrastructural projects for the host community. The personal archive of an Oxfam field director at the time, Tristram Betts,[17] reveals the logistics of many of these approaches. In 1966 he wrote a piece comparing development projects for refugees across Burundi, Uganda, and Tanzania. From road-building to credit unions, to agricultural cooperatives, to integrated provision of health and education services for hosts and refugees, a range of rural-development projects were viewed to be the answer to refugee assistance.

Tristram Betts also highlights the pitfalls of self-reliance. In the case of Rwandans in Burundi, for example, hubris about the viability of self-reliance led to refugees being 'more or less dumped wherever land was made available with local consent, and without prior planning or reference to soil fertility . . . the result has been the establishment of rural slums, partially self-subsistent and with the minimum spirit of initiative'. However, he nevertheless suggested that with careful research and piloting, community development approaches had immense potential 'to inspire among the people a new spirit of initiative'.

These largely forgotten examples aside, UNHCR has led two large-scale regional attempts to promote refugee self-reliance through development: one for Africa in the 1980s and one for Central America in the 1990s. The first was a failure and the second a success, but both are instructive for understanding when and how development-based approaches can work for refugees.

By the end of the 1970s, some 3–4 million refugees were spontaneously settled across Africa. Until that point, it had been generally assumed that most of these people would go home as soon as independence was achieved. However, by 1979 it was clear that the majority of Africa's refugees were in protracted displacement because of intractable Cold War proxy conflicts in countries like Burundi, Chad, Ethiopia, Angola, Uganda, and Zaire. Consequently, African states realized they needed a change in approach. In May 1979 all of the African states met, under the auspices of the Organization of African Unity (OAU), in Arusha. There, they decided that they would call upon the United Nations to request a series of development projects capable of compensating them for the costs of long-term hosting while simultaneously promoting the self-reliance of refugees, pending their eventual repatriation.

This call led UNHCR and the African states to jointly convene the International Conference on Assistance to Refugees in Africa (ICARA I) in April 1981 and a second conference in 1984 (ICARA II). The conferences were mainly donor events, held in Geneva. But unlike today's big refugee conferences, they were entirely focused on development assistance. UNHCR and UNDP (United Nations Development Programme) spent several months working with the African states to compile a list of projects and programmes, which could then be put to prospective donor countries to finance. The submitted projects included rural development, infrastructure such as roads and water systems, and the improvement of education and health facilities for nationals and refugees.

ICARA I unambiguously failed. The main reason was that African states generally put forward project ideas that served their own interests but often had very little to do with supporting solutions for refugees. Donor governments' pledges at the conference fell far short of expectations, both in terms of overall amount and in the politicized ways in which funds were earmarked to support Cold War allies. Donors were frustrated that the projects submitted by African states were of low quality and self-serving. African states were frustrated that donor contributions focused on strategic interests and were also self-serving. UNHCR's approach had been naïve, believing that African states would benevolently submit projects of benefit to refugees and donors would simply fund them.

Three years later, UNHCR tried again, convening ICARA II in July 1984. This time the strategy was modified in deference to realpolitik. Instead of simply hoping for altruistic pledges and goodwill on both sides, UNHCR tried to introduce greater scope for mutually beneficial bargaining. African states, for their part, would provide self-reliance and long-term local integration for refugees, thereby reducing the long-term drain on humanitarian budgets. In exchange, donor governments would provide significant 'additional' development assistance that would also benefit host governments and their citizens. The conceptualization was far superior to the first time round. And it might have worked but for the fact that by 1984 the world became distracted by an emerging crisis: the famine and drought unfolding in Ethiopia and across the Horn of Africa that would both claim the lives of 400,000 people and transform the face of humanitarianism in Africa for ever.[18]

Despite their failure, the ICARA conferences had an intellectual legacy: it was the first moment in history when UNHCR openly embraced what it called a 'refugee aid and development strategy' (RAD). The conferences recognized that rather than simply being a humanitarian issue, refugees could be thought of in terms of international development. Furthermore, they indicated the possibility for a mutually beneficial deal to be done between Northern donors and Southern hosts to promote refugee self-reliance pending access to longer-term solutions, whether repatriation or local integration. Development for refugees could, at least hypothetically, be 'win–win'.

CENTRAL AMERICA'S SUCCESS STORY

It would not be long before UNHCR was able to prove that this could be the case. By the end of the 1980s, as the Cold War drew to a close, longstanding conflicts in countries like Guatemala, El Salvador, and Nicaragua came to an end. In 1987 the governments of the region even signed a peace deal. The legacy of violence was that nearly 2 million people were left displaced, at least 150,000 of them as recognized refugees, but the peace deal opened the possibility for refugees to either go home or be locally integrated. The international community chose an approach that built upon the 'refugee aid and development' ideas pioneered in the ICARA conferences. But this time it got it right.

The International Conference on Central American Refugees (CIREFCA) was jointly convened by UNHCR and UNDP in Guatemala City in July 1989. But in practice it was a process, rather than just a one-off event, and lasted until 1995. The premise of CIREFCA was that an integrated development approach could simultaneously benefit refugees and host communities, and it adapted its approach from country to country, depending notably on whether the state was primarily a country of origin or of asylum and, in the latter case, how tolerant or restrictive that country was towards the socio-economic integration of refugees.

The projects were also notable for the extent to which they facilitated self-sufficiency and local integration. The most obvious case study for successful self-sufficiency was in Mexico, in Campeche and Quintana Roo in the Yucatán Peninsula, where investment in agricultural projects and new schools and hospitals benefited both Mexican hosts and Guatemalan refugees. In Chiapas, self-sufficiency was also encouraged, but a shortage of land was an obstacle to allowing refugees to become equally engaged in agricultural activities. In Campeche and Quintana Roo, local integration and repatriation were promoted simultaneously from 1996, while in Chiapas local integration *followed* repatriation from 1998 onwards. The self-sufficiency and local-integration projects ultimately provided education, health services, access to markets, and sustainable livelihoods. For the Mexican government, the projects were seen as an attractive means to develop the poorest areas of the country, particularly in the Yucatán Peninsula.

CIREFCA also provided local integration for Salvadoran refugees in Belize, particularly in the hitherto underdeveloped Valley of Peace, a region comprising jungle area, with poor roads and poor-quality land. CIREFCA helped to transform the area. By 2003, some 300 refugee families still remained and were integrated alongside the Belizeans of predominantly Maya Quechi ethnicity. The refugees were supported initially with food aid, a fund to build housing, tools, and seeds, and many of the Salvadorans now work in the tourism industry or in local employment, receiving social services alongside the Belizean community.

In total, CIREFCA is estimated to have channelled over $400m in additional resources to the region, and the process has been widely credited with helping to consolidate peace in Central America. The most significant group of donors were the European states who saw sustainable solutions for refugees as a way to guarantee stability for the region, and thereby encourage inter-regional trade. In its immediate aftermath, CIREFCA was generally seen as a success. A General Assembly Resolution in 1993 suggested that CIREFCA 'could serve as a valuable lesson to be applied to other regions of the world'.[19]

And yet, despite its success, CIREFCA has never been replicated. An approach that created opportunities for refugees to be self-reliant while offering development opportunities for underdeveloped regions of their host countries has never subsequently been reproduced on the same scale.

Today, though, there are even greater opportunities for a development-based approach than were available in the 1990s. Globalization offers a variety of ways to bring economic opportunity to people, irrespective of geography. The internet in particular offers the chance to create footloose and highly mobile livelihoods. Value chains can be disaggregated in ways that allow people in one part of the world to contribute on the basis of their particular comparative advantage. New financing opportunities, including crowdfunding, peer-to-peer networks, and mobile money, may offer ways in which even remote communities can be connected to the global economy. Business – from multinational corporations to small and medium-sized enterprises to social enterprise – is engaging with refugee issues more than it has in the past.[20] There is every reason to believe that a development toolbox should offer even greater prospects than was the case even two decades ago.

Creating opportunities for self-reliance is not in itself a long-term solution for refugees, but it is an important step towards all of the main long-term solutions: repatriation, local integration, or resettlement. This is because offering people autonomy and economic opportunity is likely to empower them to better contribute to whichever society into which they are ultimately assimilated. It can make refugees' eventual return more sustainable because they will return with the skills and motivation to rebuild their country of origin. It can make people better equipped to contribute to a new society once resettled. And it can make them a more desirable resettlement prospect because of their ability to find work and live autonomously.

As we learned from ICARA and CIREFCA, making development opportunities available to refugees is not just a technocratic matter: it is also highly political. It relies upon a bargain between donors and hosts premised upon identifying areas of mutual gain. Markets cannot do all of the work by themselves – the right regulations and institutions have to be in place. And for that to be the case, host governments and donors must face the right incentives to move the needle.

OPPORTUNITIES FOR MUTUAL GAIN

The basic deal that needs to be done is to create a 'win–win' outcome that suits both Northern donors and Southern hosts. The reason this is possible is because of inherently interlocking interests. Northern states want primarily to be able to reduce the need for the onward movement of refugees and secondarily to reduce the long-term drain on humanitarian assistance budgets. Southern host states want to reduce the perceived security threat posed by the presence of large numbers of refugees in urban areas and to create development opportunities for their own citizens. Crucially, these interests are complementary, and there is scope to do a deal based on mutual self-interest. If donor states allocate significant resources wisely, host country politicians may be more willing to create enabling environments for refugees during their period in exile. It's a simple application of game theory.

To get there we need to understand the incentives that shape the behaviour of host countries of first asylum. Who are the gatekeepers in national and local politics who will determine the policies that shape refugees' lives and what would they regard as an attractive package? The answers will vary with context, and will depend in part on whether the host country is a democracy: are politicians primarily accountable to electorates or to patronage relationships?

Kenya offers a recent illustration of how hard it is to find this kind of deal. Twice in the last decade the country has threatened to expel its Somali population. In 2011, after a mass influx due to famine and drought swelled its refugee numbers to an all-time high, politicians sought to exploit their presence in the lead-up to elections. In the aftermath of Al-Shabaab terrorist attacks across the region, expulsion sounded appealing to voters. Shuttle diplomacy and concessions by UN leaders brought Kenya back from the brink. Again though in 2016, with national elections on the horizon, politicians threatened to close Dadaab and expel the Somalis. This time they went much further: in an institutionally symbolic gesture the government closed down the country's Department of Refugee Affairs.

Why, in 2016, did the government of Kenya take such a spectacularly inappropriate step? It was because the Kenyan government was not devising its policy in an international vacuum. Like others, Kenya's President Uhuru Kenyatta was a daily observer of the negotiations between Chancellor Merkel and President Erdoğan. From the perspective of haven governments such as Kenya, President Erdoğan was revealing a valuable new insight: by threatening to expel refugees, a haven country could gain unprecedented power. While the German government complained of 'blackmail' it paid up: Erdoğan got a commitment to €6bn. The government of Kenya wanted a similar pay-day. Behind the scenes, it got one. The quid pro quo was that the threat of mass expulsion was not implemented.

Inadvertently, the headless heart has created powerful and disastrous new incentives. Far from being encouraged to see refugees as potential workers able to contribute productively to their host society, governments are learning to see them as quasi-hostages to be mistreated unless kind hearts with deep wallets pay up.[21] This makes comprehensive reform of refugee policy an urgent necessity. The inherited dysfunctional system is no longer in stasis: it is teetering on a precipice of ruthless opportunism.

But Kenya illustrates just how hard it is to persuade Southern host states to offer opportunities for self-reliance. Westerners often forget that host states in the South – especially democracies like Kenya – also face challenges of political sustainability not entirely distinct from those in Europe. Kenyan politicians are extremely reluctant to consider self-reliance or even increased socio-economic participation for refugees. But at times there have been glimmers of hope. For example, despite anti-refugee rhetoric from the Minister of Defence and the Minister of Home Affairs, a new group of elected Kenyan MPs, led by Kenneth Okoth, MP for Kibera, the Nairobi slum area, has begun to educate politicians about refugees and organize visits of MPs to Dadaab. Gradually there are small glimmers of improvement. For example, with support from the World Bank and UNHCR, Kenya has agreed to open a new camp in the Turkana Valley for some of its Sudanese refugees: Kalobeyei. It does not abandon Kenya's encampment policy but it does at least create a different kind of camp with the potential for greater autonomy. In particular, the design involves an area for refugees on one side, and areas of Kenyan nationals on the other. In between is a shared space – with state-of-the-art schools, hospitals, a market, and possibly even scope for limited employment – available to both refugees and host communities. Because of the potential to improve the lives of the local Kenyan hosts, politicians in the relevant political constituency of Turkana West have embraced the project.

Addressing a host country's security and development concerns is not easy, but, if it can be done, the rewards for everyone are potentially great. It can enhance autonomy and dignity for refugees. But it can also have wider implications. Self-reliance can offer a gradual pathway to longer-term solutions. If refugees are equipped during exile to live independently and contribute to the wider society, they will have a far greater chance of contributing when they go home or assimilate elsewhere, and they will be a more attractive prospect for resettlement or local integration in the event that the route home is indefinitely blocked.

Self-reliance can increase the likelihood of sustainable repatriation. This is because it can equip people with the inclination and ability to rebuild their homes, not only from exile but also once they go back. Empowered people are better able to engage in political mobilization to challenge authoritarianism back home, more likely to send back remittances in ways that contribute to peace and development, more likely to return with skills, and more likely to create footloose businesses that can eventually be moved home and support reconstruction. Circumstantial evidence for this exists with the repatriation operations from the 1990s and early 2000s involving groups who did have the chance to work: Rwandans going back from Uganda to run their country after 1994, Mozambicans going back en masse in the first half of the 1990s who played a key role in peace-building and reconstruction, and returning Bosnians in the early 2000s, often after having acquired new skills in Western Europe.

In the event that the pathway home is closed off, temporary self-reliance may still contribute to alternative long-term solutions. Empowering people while they are temporary residents makes them more likely to contribute and demonstrate over time that they represent plausible candidates for longer-term integration. This is how two of the most significant recent examples of refugee naturalization in Africa came about. In Zambia the long-term presence and contribution of Angolans in the Western Province ultimately persuaded the government to offer those who could not go home a pathway to citizenship. Likewise, Tanzania's commitment to offer naturalization to the 162,000 Burundians who had been in the country since 1972 partly came about because many had become de facto self-sufficient since arriving.

Furthermore, countries outside the region are also more likely to be able to sustainably resettle populations that have been empowered while in exile. EU data on the range of countries' motivations for resettlement reveals that, although humanitarian motives are certainly present, some countries also engage in resettlement on economic and labour market grounds. For instance, the data shows that while the UK's resettlement policy has been more selective on the basis of vulnerabilities, that of Romania has been based on likely economic contribution.[22] This suggests that a larger pool of empowered refugees may lead to an increase in the overall number of resettlement places. Furthermore, once resettled, groups who have experienced better levels of economic opportunity ultimately are better able to integrate.

Enhancing opportunities for refugee self-reliance may also reduce the need for onward migration to Europe. The common conflation of refugees with migrants obscures an important difference in their behaviour. Among those wanting to migrate there is a clear hump-shaped relationship: as their incomes rise in their home country they become more likely to migrate. With more money, they are better able to finance the move. Only once incomes in the home country rise substantially does such migration become pointless.[23] But refugees are just a random sample of ordinary people who have been forced to flee from their homes.[24] Like other people, most are not aspiring migrants. They have the humbler aspiration of restoring normality to their lives.[25] Only if the neighbouring havens do not enable this modest goal to be reached are they likely to resort to a further leap into the unknown. In the few studies that have been undertaken on refugees – such as a large Swiss study of the secondary movement of Somali refugees – lack of economic opportunity closer to home is cited as a common reason for onward movement.[26]

Furthermore, when we look at the cycles of movements of Syrians to Europe, we see that most have taken place since 2015, at a time when Syrians in Jordan, Lebanon, and Turkey had largely depleted savings and capital. Without the possibility to access labour markets, many households developed strategies to send a member of the family to Europe in order to earn and remit money to family members who remained closer to home. Gradually, this initial tipping point in movement opened up a network that others believed could facilitate their movement.[27] Had Syrians had greater opportunity closer to home, there are some grounds to believe that many would not have embarked on perilous journeys.

The big idea introduced in this chapter has been that international policy should be providing opportunities for autonomy to refugees in the haven countries which they are most readily able to reach. It is time to turn to how, in practice, this can be done.

6

Rethinking Assistance: Restoring Autonomy

In principle, when refugees flee a crisis they receive initial emergency assistance and are then offered a pathway towards reintegration into normal life. In practice, however, this rarely takes place; a response designed just for the emergency phase all too often endures. Indefinite dependency on aid has gradually become the default long-term response to refugees. The imagined needs of refugees have almost universally been reduced to two basics – food and shelter – and it has become assumed that the most viable way to provide such rights is through camps.

It was not meant to be this way. The refugee regime was originally intended to promote refugees' access to autonomy; almost half of the Refugee Convention focuses on socio-economic rights such as the right to work and freedom of movement. But these rights are simply not implemented, at least not since the global shift towards encampment from the 1980s. With the option to abrogate long-term responsibility to the international humanitarian system, host states have invariably restricted refugees' participation in labour markets. In countries like Kenya and Tanzania the right to work is prohibited. In countries like Ecuador and Jordan it is subject to significant administrative barriers.

The denial of the right to work has had catastrophic consequences for many refugees, leading to a long-term erosion of skills, talents, and aspirations, and often exacerbating a sense of alienation and hopelessness. It has also left refugees less well-placed to contribute to their host states or to eventually rebuild their own societies when they go home.

If our duty is to restore the life of the displaced to as close to normality as possible, restoring autonomy should be high on the agenda. This is especially so given many refugees stay in this limbo for years and decades, as we have seen. One of the most important components of autonomy is the right to earn a living. Being able to participate in labour markets can enable refugees to regain a sense of dignity, enhance their quality of life, and improve their skills. As with all of us, among refugees' highest priority is the ability to work to support themselves, their families, and their communities.

However, not only is the right to work almost universally restricted for refugees by host governments, but the existing refugee protection system also lacks the necessary expertise to change the status quo. Because the refugee system has become a *humanitarian* system, it lacks expertise in development or the tools to guide market-based solutions that can promote autonomy. The general assumption has been that the primary duty is aid delivery rather than the restoration of independence and capacity.

Yet there is nothing antithetical about someone being both a refugee and also a person capable of enjoying socio-economic autonomy. This chapter argues that we need a paradigm shift in how we think about refugees' needs. How can we move from a focus on vulnerabilities towards recognizing and building their capacities? Rather than seeing refugees as an inevitable burden, how can we find ways in which they can be a benefit? Instead of being viewed as just passive victims of humanitarian disaster, how might they be seen as potential agents of development?

But this requires a vision. There have been far too few good examples of refugees being given access to autonomy and jobs. This chapter examines two cases of approaches that *have* helped refugees to help themselves, including through access to the labour market. The examples are taken from Uganda and Jordan, each of which has pioneered de facto 'experiments' in refugee policy that deviate markedly from the dominant norm of long-term humanitarian aid.

THE ECONOMIC LIVES OF REFUGEES

Rarely have economists thought about refugees. The dominant assumption in policy and academic circles has been that refugees are a humanitarian subject, and the study of refugees has been led by lawyers and anthropologists. But, below the radar, refugees around the world lead complex and diverse economic lives. They are consumers, producers, buyers, sellers, borrowers, lenders, and entrepreneurs. Faced with new markets, regulatory contexts, and social networks, they are often highly innovative, coming up with creative ways to support themselves. Even in the most restrictive environments, refugees find ways to engage in economic activity, including in the informal sector.

As people, refugees are not economically different from anyone else. Despite their common media portrayal as vulnerable and poor, there is nothing intrinsic about being a refugee that makes this inevitable. Whether refugees make a positive economic contribution is not only a result of who they are as people, but of our choices – our policies and our political decisions.

The mere fact of their holding a particular protection status should not delude us into believing either that refugees do not have economic lives, or that they are economically homogeneous. Refugees bring diverse skills and talents. Even within the same refugee cohort, they may have vastly different literacy rates, education, wealth, and remittance networks, for instance. The idea that there is – or should be – absolute equality between refugees is a harmful fiction. Being forced to flee mass violence in their localities, refugees are usually a random sample of their country's population. Inevitably, their differences reflect those within their country. Imposing an overriding common status as 'victims' sheds these myriad identities from people.

The only thing that makes the economic lives of refugees distinct from those of citizens or other migrants is the regulation that affects whether they can participate fully in the economy. We know from the Nobel Prize-winning economist Douglass North's work on New Institutional Economics that all markets are shaped by their regulatory environments and wider institutional context.[1] Institutions matter because they perform functions like ensuring property rights, enforceable contracts, and legal frameworks. Without these institutions, markets would not function.

Refugees' economic lives are distinctive because they are often shaped by different regulations from those affecting host state nationals. In restrictive countries, refugees are often denied the right to own certain types of property, their contracts may not be enforced, and there may be restrictions on mobility and the right to work. These kinds of institutional differences create immense challenges for refugees but they do not extinguish economic life. On the contrary, they shape the nature of those economic lives, explaining the emergence of particular forms of informal economic activity: regulatory separation creates opportunities for arbitrage based on the resulting price and wage differences across the two institutional contexts.

This is why even in the most extremely regulated countries like the Dadaab camps in Kenya or the Burmese border camps in Thailand, refugees and nationals frequently interact in informal markets at the boundaries of camps and settlements. Illicit markets for goods, services, and labour spring up even when suppressed. SIM cards, handsets, and World Food Programme food rations are bought and sold. Almost any item or service can still be procured if the price is right. There may be winners from these distortions, notably brokers and intermediaries. Certain forms of economic activity will thrive, including hawking and vending. Some refugees and even more nationals will accumulate capital in these highly regulated refugee situations.

However, as economics demonstrates, barriers that segment a market reduce overall incomes. Preventing refugees from participating in the economy is inefficient. Even a miniature refugee-only economy, kept separate from the national economy in which it is located, will inflict needless losses on both compared to a single integrated economy. This is because the scope for specialization and exchange is reduced. These economic losses will be exacerbated by the effect that heavy regulation has on suppressing normal and productive economic activity. By creating situations in which there are extreme differences in market power between those who control opportunities and desperate individuals who seek them, we are more likely to leave people open to exploitation.

It therefore makes incontrovertible economic sense to move beyond a dual-economy approach and begin to break down arbitrary boundaries to refugees' economic participation. But, as it turns out, many of the barriers to achieving this are political.

UGANDAN EXCEPTIONALISM

Uganda hosts 1.4 million refugees, making it the largest host country in Africa. Its refugees come from a wide variety of unsettled neighbouring countries, including Somalia, South Sudan, the Democratic Republic of Congo, Burundi, Rwanda, Ethiopia, and Eritrea. Furthermore, given the volatile region in which it sits, it has an almost unbroken history of hosting refugees ever since the late 1950s when Rwandan Tutsis first fled revolution and genocide, and arrived at the still-existing Nakivale settlement.

In contrast to its refugee-hosting neighbours like Kenya and Ethiopia, Uganda has taken a radically different approach to refugees. Shunning encampment, it has allowed refugees the right to work and a significant degree of freedom of movement. In rural open settlements, it gives refugees plots of land to cultivate for both subsistence and commercial agriculture, and allows market activity. In cities, it allows refugees to start businesses and seek employment. Uganda is therefore a fascinating and rare success story that sheds light on what is possible when refugees are given basic socio-economic freedoms.

Uganda's openness to refugees goes right back to its independence in 1962. At the time, it hosted not only Rwandans but increasing numbers fleeing colonial liberation and Cold War proxy conflicts. But with a surfeit of available arable land, it decided the best course of action was to let them self-settle in underdeveloped rural settlements where they could contribute to agricultural development. The country's only brief flirtation with encampment came during the 1990s when, faced with a growing influx from Sudan, it created camps in the north of the country.

Between 1999 and 2002, it formalized its historically open approach within a policy known as the Self-Reliance Strategy, establishing a directive that all refugees should receive access to land, the right to work, and freedom of movement. Aside from reflecting practice, this policy change also suited the government's interests. The government had been widely accused of stealing aid money and this was seen as a way in which it could re-establish credibility with the United Nations.

The First Deputy Prime Minister of the country and its Minister for Disaster Preparedness and Refugees, Moses Ali, led the negotiations with the international community. General Ali was at the time the only surviving Cabinet minister from the Idi Amin regime. His power base was in the Nile Valley area that hosted the majority of the Sudanese refugees and he saw the Self-Reliance Strategy as a means to bring resources to the area, in a way that could simultaneously benefit his constituents. Indeed, the self-reliance deal brought new development money, channelled through UNHCR from donors like Sweden, Denmark, and the Netherlands, all keen to reduce their long-term humanitarian aid budget.

More than fifteen years later, Uganda's Self-Reliance Strategy has endured as a relatively unique experiment. It was further formalized within Uganda's 2006 Refugee Act, now regarded as one of the most progressive pieces of refugee legislation in Africa. At times, self-reliance has been criticized for legitimizing the premature withdrawal of food rations. The quality of plots of land distributed to refugees has also become uneven as numbers have increased. And refugees still clearly face challenges, including discrimination and informal barriers to market participation. But compared to the alternatives in neighbouring countries, the model is both a shining beacon of policy innovation and a rare opportunity to understand what happens when refugees are given autonomy.

From a social-science perspective, Uganda therefore offers a form of 'laboratory' in which it is possible to examine the impact of refugee autonomy on both refugees themselves and the wider host communities. Over a three-year period, the Refugee Studies Centre at Oxford University embarked on a participatory, mixed-methods study to explore exactly these questions, based on both qualitative research and a quantitative survey of around 2,000 refugees of different nationalities across urban and rural locations in Uganda. The outcomes of the study reveal the boundaries of what is possible when refugees are given socio-economic autonomy and, crucially, the right to work.[2]

THE IMPACT OF AUTONOMY

Nakivale is Uganda's largest and oldest refugee settlement, with a population of around 70,000. It is quite unlike camps in other parts of the world, serving as an inspiring illustration of what can happen when refugees are given economic freedoms. The settlement is vast and sprawling, covering over 100 square kilometres and divided into seventy-four separate villages that are split across three administrative areas – Base Camp, Juru, and Rubondo – each with a major market. What is extraordinary about Nakivale is that, even with such diverse nationalities living alongside one another – Somalis, Congolese, Rwandans, Burundians, and Ethiopians – it is much like any other successful city. In fact, Nakivale has become one of the most vibrant market centres in the south-west of Uganda.

On market days, Isangano market at the heart of Base Camp is abuzz with intense economic activity. Refugees bring crops, livestock, and textiles to sell. Clothes, electrical items, cooked foods, and alcoholic beverages are available. Many Ugandan nationals come from far and wide to take advantage of the opportunities on offer. Even away from the Isangano market, almost the entire central area of Base Camp is a permanent hive of economic activity. Many homes in New Congo, Little Kigali, or the Somali Village have been converted into some kind of small or medium-sized enterprise – most buying and selling food or garments but others offering the services of a normal city: a Congolese cinema, a Somali transport company providing the main bus service to Kampala, and a popular Ethiopian restaurant can all be found a short walk from one another. Lines of 'boda-boda' motorcycle taxis wait in the area to transport customers and their wares to other parts of the settlement.

The original assumption of the Self-Reliance Strategy was that refugees would engage primarily in farming activities on their allotted plots of land. Certainly, around 50 per cent of the Congolese, Rwandan, and Burundian refugees are farmers. But diversification and specialization have taken place. The 13,000 Somalis in the settlement do not even have an agricultural background and so do not farm at all. Instead they sublet their allocated plots and open small businesses – specialist shops, restaurants, and fast-food stands, for example. Most are modest in scale but – supported with investment from remittances – can grow to become much larger, with some Somalis becoming wholesalers for the throng of small retailers in the community.

Extremely innovative businesses can also be found in the settlement. A young man named Abdi runs a small video games studio. After finding a disused generator and spending seven months repairing it, he began to collect televisions and old PlayStation games consoles. He now charges young refugees a nominal fee to play Fifa World Soccer and other games, ploughing his profits back into gradually expanding the business.

Furthermore, Nakivale's economy is not just an isolated enclave; it is nested within broader trade routes and supply chains. To take an example, across the settlement, many Congolese buy and sell a brightly coloured ceremonial fabric called *bitenge*. A commonly held belief among many of the international community staff is that the fabric simply comes across the border from the Democratic Republic of Congo. But in fact it is imported from warehouses as far afield as China and India. It comes into the vast Owino market in Kampala before being distributed along refugee-run supply chains to cities located close to refugee settlements. In other words, even in the seemingly remote Nakivale settlement refugees are connected to the global economy.

This pattern is repeated. Somali stores in the same settlement sell tins of tuna fish despite the fact that none is available in shops run by host nationals in the surrounding areas. So how and why did it get there? The answer is that there is a high demand for tinned tuna within the Somali community and so, again, there is a Somali-run supply chain that brings tuna fish from Thailand, via Riyadh and Mombasa, into Kampala, and along road networks to the settlement.

Some refugees do better than others. The average household income in Nakivale is around $39 a month; however, there is still some significant variation, with a range from around $15 a month up to a tiny number earning as much as $150 a month. Although nearly all refugees have some residual access to food rations, some have poor-quality plots of land and struggle to make ends meet. Meanwhile a small number of outliers – mainly entrepreneurs – thrive. To take one example, Munyompenza is a Rwandan businessman who has expanded his maize-milling business over many years and now employs several refugees. He has managed to acquire several generators and maize-milling machines, and has built a rainwater storage system to cool his equipment. So successful has he been that at the height of the influx of new Congolese refugees to Uganda in 2013, the World Food Programme was paying Munyompenza to mill maize for the relief operation.

Nakivale is by no means perfect. But it is at least better than almost every other refugee camp in Africa. It offers not only economic prospects but also hope and scope for aspiration. Skills transfer is endemic, with many refugee-run businesses offering informal apprenticeships in areas such as tailoring, construction, or commerce. Young people at least have the chance to aspire. Demou-Kay, for instance, is a young Congolese man who, having arrived with few skills, has managed to find the resources and support within the settlement to set up a community radio station with friends and begin to make documentary films.

Nevertheless, refugees with higher levels of education and fewer dependants are far more likely to choose to move away from the settlements and relocate to Kampala. In the capital, some groups live alongside co-nationals. For example, many Somalis live in Kisenyi, a densely populated and highly entrepreneurial area known as Kampala's 'Little Mogadishu'. Other groups, such as the Congolese and the Rwandans, are more dispersed. Wherever they reside, refugees are able to take advantage of participation in Kampala's vast economy, including the Owino market, the largest marketplace in East Africa.

Entrepreneurship offers the main way in which refugees manage in the city, with large numbers being self-employed. Small-scale vending, hawking, and running small shops are the most common urban livelihood activities. And many businesses are associated with particular nationalities, with Ethiopians focusing on taxi-driving and foreign exchange; the Congolese hawking jewellery and textiles; and Rwandans often running clothes shops. Such clustering of activity, in this instance on the basis of social networks, is a standard aspect of economic efficiency, a theme we pick up again shortly.

Living and working alongside host nationals, refugees can make a positive economic contribution to the national economy. One of the most striking statistics from the study is that in Kampala 21 per cent of refugees run a business that creates jobs, and, of their employees, 40 per cent are citizens of the host country. In other words, refugees are making jobs not just for one another but also for host nationals.

In addition to entrepreneurship, refugees also create social-protection mechanisms for each other. They provide public goods to support vulnerable members of their own communities. In contrast to the settlements where 83 per cent of refugees receive some form of international support, this figure goes down to just 17 per cent in the city. When refugees struggle they rely on their own communities. Under the radar, there are a series of refugee-led, community-based organizations providing services to the most vulnerable despite usually being locked out of formal funding mechanisms. For example, YARID (Young Africans for Integral Development), founded by Congolese refugees in 2008, is an organization run by refugees for refugees. It began by offering sports activities to children and young people, then expanded to provide language training, and now offers a range of vocational training to men and women across different communities.

Beyond formal organizations, examples also abound of informal networks and religious and cultural practices through which refugees respond to community needs. Within the Somali community, for example, *aiuto*s offer a way in which single female-headed households share savings to allow someone to withdraw from the common pool when they hit hard times. Meanwhile, *zakat* offers a way in which the Somali community self-organizes to provide philanthropic support to those in need. And some Ugandan Somali businesses – such as City Oil – privilege co-ethnic refugees in their employment strategies as an act of solidarity.

THRIVE OR SURVIVE?

We should not romanticize refugee life in Uganda, and not every site provides the same opportunities as Nakivale and Kampala. During the outbreak of renewed violence in the Democratic Republic of Congo in 2013, a new large-scale influx of refugees was triggered. Overwhelmed by the initial numbers, the government opened an additional emergency camp in a remote part of western Uganda: the Rwamwanja settlement. Concerned to manage security, the government imposed stricter controls than elsewhere: it insisted that Rwamwanja's 50,000 refugees only build temporary structures and imposed some initial limits on their movements. Most refugees would rather have been elsewhere; as one put it, 'No one chose to come to this camp. We were forced to come to Rwamwanja.'

Nevertheless, given the right to work, something fascinating happened in Rwamwanja. From an initial 'blank slate', a functioning economy began to emerge. A small number of refugees, arriving with little, took their relief supplies and food rations, and began to sell a proportion to access start-up capital. They would exchange maize and food oil given by relief agencies for Ugandan crops like banana and cassava and sell them in the settlement. These entrepreneurs contributed to the rapid development of a modest economy. Small shops were created, a market appeared; gradually Ugandans started to come to the settlement and even settle in the surrounding areas. One Ugandan told us: 'I used to run a small restaurant in Kampala. My friend told me that there are business opportunities in this area . . . so I decided to move here . . . I receive about two hundred customers per day.' Interactions between the surrounding host community and refugees took off. In just a short time, an economy was created from almost nothing, with some Congolese refugees even choosing to relocate from Nakivale to take advantage of the emerging opportunities.

Rwamwanja challenges the prevailing policy assumption that development-based approaches should only be introduced after the emergency phase of a refugee situation. It illustrates that even simply having the right to work at the outset of an influx can dramatically alter the trajectory of a refugee settlement, enabling specialization and diversification to take hold, in a way that creates opportunities for both refugees and host nationals.

Self-reliance does not have uniform effects for everyone. It leads to significant variation in economic outcomes for different refugee households. Some thrive while others merely survive. The Oxford study reveals six main variables that determine variation in refugees' income levels. First, *regulation*: the greater the degree of full participation in the national economy, the better refugees will do. In Uganda a proxy for this is whether someone is in an urban area, a protracted camp, or an emergency camp. The average income for Congolese refugees in Kampala is $120 a month, in Nakivale it is $39, and in Rwamwanja it is $17. Second, *nationality*: controlling for all other variables the mere fact of 'being Somali' tends to increase income by up to 97 per cent compared to being Congolese. Culture makes a difference, and Somalis are known for enterprise, social protection, and remittance sending, for example. Third, *education*: acquiring an additional year of education is associated with a 3 per cent higher average income, and the type of education matters: an additional year of primary education is associated with 1 per cent higher earnings, secondary school 10 per cent, and tertiary education 27 per cent. Finishing primary school is associated with a 30 per cent higher income. Fourth, *occupation*: self-employed non-farmers earn the most and employed farmers the least. Fifth, *gender*: female primary livelihood earners with equivalent levels of education, the same nationality, in Uganda for the same length of time, and in the same location earn up to 15 per cent less than male primary livelihood earners. Sixth, *networks*: a range of indicators suggest that the greater a refugee household's access to wider national and transnational networks, the greater their income levels.[3]

The policy implications flow logically from the data. Several things need to happen if refugees' incomes are to go up and their dependency levels are to go down. The barriers to refugees' participation in the economy need to be reduced. Cultures of self-help and mutual support need to be encouraged: the antithesis of 'victimhood'. Refugee education should be prioritized, all the way through to tertiary education. Economic diversification and entrepreneurship should be supported through improved access to finance and the reform of business regulations that impede or delay activity. Gender policies for refugees should include a greater focus on socio-economic opportunity. Business transactions thrive in networks, but networks need easy connectivity. For example, do refugees have access to banking services?

But for these things to happen around the world will require a radical shift in how we think about and respond to refugees. Host states need to recognize refugees as potential contributors to national development, and offer opportunities for them to participate economically. This requires international organizations to move beyond the humanitarian silo and to prioritize jobs, education, and economic empowerment for refugees. And this in turn needs new forms of partnership that create the incentive structures for host states to allow refugees greater autonomy and the right to work.

JORDAN IS NOT UGANDA

Most refugee-hosting countries are not like Uganda. The Self-Reliance Strategy of the Ugandan government emerged because of very particular circumstances. These include Uganda's surplus of arable land, its long history of offering de facto self-reliance, the incentives offered by the international community, and the one-party state's insulation from domestic electoral pressures. Context matters. Unlike Uganda, most host countries impose restrictions on refugees' right to work.

Different host countries' refugee policies are shaped by their distinctive politics and history. Attempts to create greater economic empowerment for refugees will therefore need to be context-specific. They will need to be based on a clear understanding of the political and economic constraints and opportunities available within a particular host country. How has a country's refugee policy evolved over time? Who are the gatekeepers, and what incentives motivate them? Under what conditions might hosting large numbers of refugees become a benefit for host states? Only when these factors are understood can the levers for policy change be identified.

Here we can turn to the example of Jordan, a country profoundly affected by the Syrian refugee crisis. Jordan's initial response to refugees was far more representative of host countries around the world; the government of Jordan faced much more severe policy constraints than that of Uganda. But it is also a country whose refugee policies matter more to the rest of the world. Bordered by Syria, Iraq, Saudi Arabia, and Israel, Jordan represents a rare island of stability within an insecure region. It has historically shown immense generosity towards refugees, welcoming and integrating Circassians, Armenians, Palestinians, and Iraqis over several decades. UNHCR estimates that it currently hosts over 600,000 Syrian refugees, although the government contests this figure and suggests it may be over 1 million. This is against the backdrop of a population of just 6.5 million.

A minority of the refugees are in camps such as Za'atari, Azraq, and Zarqa, within which they are effectively 'warehoused' with limited economic autonomy and high levels of dependency on international assistance. By contrast, 83 per cent of Jordan's refugees are in urban areas, with the highest number in the capital, Amman, and others in Irbid and Mafraq. They have voted with their feet: while urban refugees have access to higher levels of autonomy, they relinquish access to most forms of international assistance. Furthermore, while most subsist through their interactions with the informal economy, few are able to access formal work permits either because they are prohibitively expensive or because of the restrictive bureaucratic process.

The international response is premised upon the same default logic that characterizes the entire refugee regime. Donors write cheques to support humanitarian relief and host countries of first asylum are expected to provide the territory on which the refugees are hosted. Less than 3 per cent of the total Syrian refugee population has received resettlement to countries outside the region. Like the other neighbouring countries, this places a considerable strain on Jordan. When pushed to offer greater economic participation to refugees, Jordan has generally responded with two big concerns, relating to development and security.

One concern relates to competition for economic resources. In particular, Jordanians are worried about competition for jobs, downward pressure on wages, upward pressure on house prices, and the depletion of natural resources such as the country's scarce water supplies. Although recent studies reveal that Syrian refugees have had a negligible effect on Jordanian labour markets,[4] this may even be because of the controls imposed, and there is still significant concern.

The key concerns, though, relate to national security. The large concentration of Syrians in cities creates a variety of anxieties, not least the problems that could arise with large numbers of young men with limited long-term economic opportunity. The perceived risk has increased as Syrian refugees deplete the savings and capital they initially brought with them. The timing of Jordan's decision to close its border with Syria in September 2014, for example, coincided directly with a spike in ISIS-related displacement from July 2014 onwards, and the fear of radicalization or terrorist infiltration ultimately concerns the Jordanian government more than labour market implications.

The result is a policy characterized by stasis. Most Syrian refugees are in urban areas but are forced to subsist in the informal economy while their children remain out of school. A minority are in camps dependent on international aid. With increasing security concerns, tens of thousands more are trapped on the other side of the Jordan–Syria border in a demilitarized zone called the 'Berm'. Meanwhile, the international community is effectively left 'waiting for Godot', delivering aid while hoping the war in Syria will come to an end. It is hardly surprising that many young Syrians in the country see their only remaining routes to change as onward travel to Europe or returning to Syria to fight.

The policy challenge in Jordan and around the world is how one can address the development and security concerns of the host country while empowering refugees. There are no easy answers. But we believe that there may be a solution that can simultaneously benefit Jordan, enable refugees, and enhance security in the region. And it lies in a particular approach to job creation.

AN ALTERNATIVE APPROACH

Despite the constraints, one still finds pockets of extraordinary resilience and innovation among the Syrian refugee community in Jordan. In the Za'atari refugee camp, home to 83,000 Syrians, there is no right to work and all economic activity is supposed to be highly regulated by the government. But creativity abounds. The bustling main market street known as the Shams-Élysées – a play on words that references the renowned French shopping district and the historic name for Syria – is lined with shops and small businesses. Despite strict access controls at the entrance to the camp, seemingly every product imaginable – from cosmetics to textiles, to pharmaceuticals, to pets – can be purchased from one or other of these small businesses.

Innovation is on display in other ways. All refugee households are given a caravan to live in, seemingly created from a converted shipping container, provided by the boundless generosity of one of a number of Gulf States. Yet many of these caravans are reconverted. They are moved across the camp, become shops that line the Shams-Élysées, or are converted into furniture, for example. The black market construction trade, which smuggles bricks and cement into the camp, also upgrades and extends many of the shipping container homes or allows them to be used for another purpose. Across the camp, one finds endless illustrations of the creativity and entrepreneurship of refugees: urban gardening, striking murals, and community-led journalism, for example.

While some of this informal activity is tolerated, most is formally prohibited and selectively dismantled. The Jordanian police make occasional raids to shut down some forms of business, either because they have become too large or for more vindictive reasons. Meanwhile, irrational contradictions pervade camp life: hundreds of Jordanian teachers are employed at great expense to teach Syrian children according to the Jordanian national curriculum while hundreds of qualified Syrian teachers are left idle. But the suppression and neglect of skills, talents, and aspirations benefit nobody. What if instead refugees were allowed to join the labour market?

In April 2015 we travelled to Jordan. On a visit to Za'atari, we discovered that just a fifteen-minute drive from the camp, there is a Special Economic Zone (SEZ) – an area in which business and trade laws differ from the rest of the country in order to attract trade, investment, and job creation. It is called the King Hussein bin Talal Development Area (KHBTDA). The government had invested £100m into connecting it to the national road network and economic grid. However, despite having a few factories, it was operating well below capacity. It lacked two key things: workers and business investment. What, we wondered, might be the potential if refugees were allowed to work alongside Jordanian nationals in the economic zone? Might this offer a way to simultaneously benefit refugees, contribute to Jordan's own national-development strategy, and incubate the post-conflict recovery in Syria?

Jordan is a middle-income country. As such, one of the key priorities of its national-development strategy is to make the leap to manufacturing. Yet transitioning to manufacturing is hard. Jordan is in a 'middle-income trap': unable to compete with low-income countries on cheap labour and unable to compete with advanced industrialized countries on technology and innovation. Much of the world's manufacturing is today concentrated in China. For example, most of the world's buttons are manufactured in just one city, colloquially known as 'Buttonopolis'. The reason for this is what is known as 'clustering'; economies of scale emerge for access to labour, supply chains, and buyers when manufacturing is geographically concentrated. This makes it challenging – though not impossible – for a country to break into manufacturing. What it requires is a small number of significant firms to relocate their manufacturing operations to Jordan and for a threshold level of infrastructure and clustering to emerge over time.

For a country like Jordan, refugees arguably represent an opportunity to transition to manufacturing. They are a potential source of labour. Syrians, for example, are often skilled and well-educated, and share a common language with Jordanians. Crucially, the international recognition of a regional refugee crisis creates a potential opportunity for the government of Jordan to appeal for the relocation of a number of multinational corporations to Jordan for reasons that partly connect to corporate social responsibility and partly to core business interests. The crisis also offers a basis on which the government could appeal to other governments – in say Europe or North America – to provide trade concessions that improve access to their markets.

A range of external actors might support the creation of such economic zones for refugees. For example, EU trade concessions, which are conditional upon the employment of and right to work for refugees, might be available to businesses operating within the designated areas. Furthermore, one opportunity might lie in Syrian businesses no longer able to operate in Syria, which could be encouraged to relocate to such zones, assuming they were eventually able to return. Among these businesses are multinational corporations such as American Express, Sony Corporation, and Caterpillar, as well as many Syrian companies.

Special Economic Zones often have a bad reputation because of being associated with exploitative low-wage labour. However, there is no reason why the model could not be adapted to ensure respect for human rights and consistency with a set of ethical practices. The core of the idea would be to allow economic zoning that creates geographical spaces within which refugees receive access to a set of entitlements and capabilities. Crucially, the model should not function on the basis of any kind of coercion but offer sufficiently attractive opportunities to attract refugees to choose to work within and live close to these spaces. They should be premised upon possibilities that enhance refugee choice and autonomy.

A key part of this model, we argued, is that it would contribute to post-conflict reconstruction. Ideally, many of the businesses developed within such spaces would be footloose, enabling them to follow refugees back to Syria when the security situation allows, and thereby play a key role in political and economic transition. The model would not depend upon the end of insecurity within Syria but could be premised upon the idea that it is working towards an eventual post-conflict reconstruction rather than feeding into a narrative of 'local integration'. In that sense it would be a model that works directly to enhance refugees' autonomy, to meet Jordan's concerns about national development and regional security, and to support rebuilding in the new Syria.

THE JORDAN COMPACT

These initial ideas have since gained political traction and begun to be implemented. The trigger for international interest came during David Cameron's visit to Jordan and Lebanon in September 2015. His visit to the region immediately followed an outpouring of public support for refugees after the image of a drowned two-year old boy, Aylan Kurdi, went viral after appearing on the front page of newspapers across Europe, leading the UK government to initiate a resettlement scheme for Syrian refugees by providing official transport direct from the haven countries so they need not take their chances with the people-smugglers. While in Amman, Cameron had met King Abdullah, who suggested the idea to him.

This in turn led the UK government to consult on the contours of the idea, and to convene a series of technical discussions within the Department for International Development and bilaterally with the government of Jordan. The UK government explored possibilities for World Bank involvement in financing relevant infrastructure and for EU trade concessions for exports emerging from the economic-zone pilot. In November 2015 we ourselves went public with the idea, with an article aimed at both the public-policy and business communities in the influential American policy journal *Foreign Affairs*. In January 2016 at Davos, the forum for global business, Queen Rania acclimatized CEOs to the idea that corporate social responsibility to refugees did not mean diverting some profits into sending blankets, it meant putting their core skills to use by integrating refugees into global supply chains. In the context of emerging business interest in solutions to the refugee crisis, a range of manufacturing company CEOs began to take notice.

The formal launch of the pilot project came as part of the London pledging conference on Syrian refugees on 4 February 2016. There, both David Cameron and King Abdullah spoke about the pilot, as did CEOs, including, for example, Andy Clarke, CEO of Asda, the UK subsidiary of Walmart. Cameron argued in his opening remarks that in addition to the $11bn in pledges, the 'mould-breaking and creative' contribution of the conference would be to jobs and development in host countries. The idea drew widespread support, with the UK's former Prime Minister, Gordon Brown, for instance, writing on the day of the conference that 'economic zones should be created in Lebanon, Jordan, and Turkey'.[5]

The basic deal on the table – called the 'Jordan Compact' – was that Jordan would receive around $2bn in assistance and investment. In exchange, it would offer up to 200,000 work permits to Syrians. One of the main vehicles for this would be through a series of five new Special Economic Zones in which refugees would be employed alongside nationals, partly building upon existing development areas like the KHBTDA. Over the next few months, the governments of Jordan and the United Kingdom, together with the World Bank, led the negotiation of a partnership to flesh out the details of the Jordan Compact and to carry the pilot forward. The United Kingdom has provided convening power and funding. The World Bank has offered concessional loan-based finance. But the most crucial component has been the unprecedented commitment of the European Union to provide trade concessions for particular products exported from the Special Economic Zones. In particular, it agreed that concessions would be initially offered in the garment sector, an industry in which many Syrians specialized in now destroyed areas like Homs.

In June 2015, President Obama indicated that he wanted to make bringing jobs to haven countries his personal legacy programme. In July the Obama initiative was duly launched: a direct appeal to the CEOs of major American companies to bring jobs to the refugees. At the time of writing it is too early to tell how successful this will be: it is certainly the right aspiration. But where is the money? And where is the supporting trade policy? Perhaps, with the US Congress unwilling to do anything that might hand the President a success, his only room for manoeuvre is to use his oratory to appeal to the charitable instincts of CEOs. But, to emphasize, firms are not charities.

The deal represents a new kind of partnership: one that involves governments and businesses working together; one that cuts across old silos and situates solutions for refugees at the intersection between development, trade, and security. Crucially, it is built upon a recognition that if areas of mutual gain can be identified, hosting refugees can become an opportunity rather than just an inevitable cost. European governments want to address a migration crisis; Jordan wants to make the leap to manufacturing and manage a security nightmare; business is seeking a new investment opportunity, while also trying to restore citizen respect for modern capitalism; refugees want to work; and just about everyone has a stake in the long-term future of Syria. By linking these concerns, the approach offers scope for everyone to benefit and so provides a more realistic possibility of moving the needle for refugees than the past model of pious exhortation.

The pilot has been described as 'one of the most important economic experiments in the world today'. To be successful over the long run the model will need significant business investment. It will have to be run in a way that is ethical and consistent with protection standards, and it will depend upon the creation of new jobs, rather than simply displacing or formalizing existing jobs. But irrespective of the eventual outcome, the model offers a different kind of vision for refugees: one based on empowerment and job creation, even in countries in which politics constrains the available options.

HARNESSING GLOBALIZATION FOR REFUGE: HOW IT WORKS

Globalization can be a menacing and disruptive force, but it can also be a powerful one for good. At its best, it brings opportunities to earn an income to people in places where previously they were largely absent. Refugees, separated from their prior livelihoods and often clinging to the lowest rung of the economic ladder in their host societies, need this power of globalization more than any other group.

But how feasible in practice is it to bring global opportunities to Syrian refugees? Superficially, those that have moved to Germany would appear to be in the best position. But to date this has not been so, according to the German Federal Employment Agency, which reports a less than 10 per cent employment rate for the new arrivals.[6] It is hoped that this will change over time but the employment record so far for Syrian refugees in Germany is undoubtedly unimpressive. This outcome is not surprising given that Germany's distinctive place in global production is entirely ill-suited to refugees from a poor country.

Production for global markets in Germany has specialized in highly skilled tasks that require years of training. The German system of training, envied around the world, integrates the last years of schooling with the early years of employment. Refugees cannot readily be parachuted into this system. Further, reflecting the high average level of skill, Germany's minimum wage is far, far higher than wages in Syria, which reflected average levels of productivity of Syrian workers: per capita incomes in Germany are around twenty times higher than those in pre-conflict Syria. Consequently, inserting Syrian refugees based in Germany into the global economy is going to be difficult. They are more likely to end up in domestic-service positions created for them in the public sector, like the post office. Even here they face difficulties: a refugee who applied for a job cleaning toilets was ultimately rejected by the local Bureau of Employment on the grounds that 'a native-born German could do the same job'.[7] By that criterion, many of the refugees invited to Germany will continue to languish in unemployment.

Connecting the refugees in the regional haven countries is likely to be easier. Paradoxically, Germany's firms may find it easier to generate jobs for refugees in the regional havens than to integrate them into their German-based activity. This is because German firms have pioneered modern globalization. The world's top authority on this recent form of globalization is Richard Baldwin. As he explains, since the 1990s globalization has not been about shifting production to China; it has been about relocating some tasks that are still done within the same firm to cheaper sites.[8] These sites cannot be thousands of miles from the main factory, because production on both sites must be controlled as an integrated process. For example, managers must be able to fly between them in a day. It is not only distance that matters. If the 'foetus' factory is to be linked by an umbilical cord to the parent factory, there must be no regulatory impediments. Trade barriers between the country of the parent and the country of the foetus would be a killer. In the 1990s the preferred sites for German manufacturing firms were in Poland: very close and much cheaper than Germany, and a member of the European Union and so barrier-free. German firms are not alone in this – the same model has been developed by American and Japanese firms – but they are Europe's leading practitioners. American firms have some tasks undertaken in Mexico, Japanese firms offshore some stages to China.

But, as in China itself, as German production shifted to Poland wages rose and so firms started to look a little further afield. During the past decade the preferred location has been Turkey. Turkey is further away than Poland but still the 'near offshore': if refugees can walk it, German managers can certainly fly it. And although Turkey is not in the European Union, it has privileged status for trade purposes. The European Union lets goods produced in Turkey enter duty-free. Turkey has indeed been growing explosively as a result of breaking into global markets for manufactures. To give an example, within the last decade a nowhere town in central Turkey, not even on the coast, has developed into the dominant global centre of production for synthetic carpets.

If German firms can offshore to Turkey, in principle they can do so in all three haven countries. Turkey's big advantage was its privileged market access to Europe. Both Turkey and Jordan have many industrial zones in which refugees could potentially work alongside nationals. This, of course, requires that the governments of the haven countries permit refugees to work in the zones. The international deal to which the government of Jordan agreed at the London conference in February 2016 included a commitment by the Jordanian government to provide work permits for refugees in return for new jobs being created in the zones: hence the vital role that international business can play in bringing dignity to refugees' lives. The government of Jordan committed to 50,000 work permits in the following twelve months. By the end of 2016, it was close to that target: providing around 38,000 new work permits. But the critical issue is whether international business can actually generate enough new jobs.[9] Until now, many of the work permits provided under the pilot have formalized already existing informal sector jobs. Given Jordan's relatively low growth rates of around 2.5% per year, creating new jobs will require significant investment, higher growth rates in key sectors, and an expansion of the industries that are subject to EU trade concessions.

It may seem as though setting up production in a haven country industrial zone would require years of preparation. But global business does not work to such a glacial timescale. In Mexico, an American firm succeeded in going from zero to production in six weeks. Even the relocation of footwear production from China to Ethiopia took only a few months. In a year a lot can happen if CEOs take the issue seriously.

Nor does the generation of jobs for refugees depend entirely, or even primarily, on manufacturing firms opening new factories in the havens. All the main haven countries for Syrians are already middle-income economies with many firms, international and domestic, producing goods that can be supplied to global marketing chains.

The key companies may not be those engaged in global production but in global retailing. For example, Asda investigated the scope for routing some of its orders to the zones in the havens, in return for commitments by suppliers to hire refugees. It found that this was feasible: now some of the products that British consumers are buying in their local Asda stores have been made by refugees.

Globalization can work for Syrian refugees, but can it work at the required scale? The jobs created by foreign firms, both those that establish new production units and those that buy from firms already in the havens, generate other jobs: there is a multiplier. The incomes earned by these new workers get spent on services and food produced domestically. This jobs multiplier varies depending upon the context, but scales up the impact.

International business can make a real difference to the life chances of refugees, but governments can make a decisive difference by catalysing the process. Following the London conference David Cameron brought a whole-of-government approach to making it happen. He appointed a special envoy, Baroness Morris, to bring in the private sector, and Britain's Secretary of State for Business, Sajid Javid, flew with a group of CEOs to Jordan. That is how the Asda deal came about. Other European leaders were too preoccupied with either trying to offload thousands of invited refugees to their neighbours, or resisting European Commission directives ordering them to do so, to focus on generating jobs for the millions of refugees remaining in the havens.

A GLOBAL PROTOTYPE?

It is not necessarily a case of rolling out the Jordanian Special Economic Zone model to all of these host states. Different approaches are needed for different contexts. The key is to shift from a purely humanitarian approach to a development approach, with jobs and education at the core. The challenge is to engage in the creation of development areas in the peripheral and border locations that repeatedly host refugees.

There are other precedents. The Kaesong Industrial Complex in North Korea uses South Korean capital to employ North Korean workers.[10] Zones were set up in Thailand for Burmese refugees and cross-border workers.[11] And what was originally the Bataan Refugee Processing Center in the Philippines was repurposed into an SEZ.[12]

Every approach should involve promoting empowerment through the right to work, the role of public–private partnership, and the recognition that refugees need to be understood as much in terms of development and trade as humanitarianism, and that deals should be based on the principle of mutual gain.

The Ugandan and Jordanian models illustrate potentially quite different approaches. Area development approaches can vary on a spectrum of participation, between 'integration' (the Ugandan model), at one end of the spectrum, and 'incubation' (the Jordanian model) at the other. At one end, refugees gradually gain full socio-economic and political rights alongside host citizens. At the other, 'incubation' creates the geographically delineated areas within which economic opportunity is available. In different contexts these models will vary in their degrees of feasibility and desirability.

While the Jordanian SEZ pilot focuses on a middle-income country, aspiring to increase its manufacturing base, the basic logic of 'development areas' – whether based on integration or incubation – could also be applied to economies that are primarily seeking to build their primary, secondary, or tertiary sectors, attracting relevant forms of investment. Depending on whether one is seeking to promote economic participation in manufacturing, agricultural, or information economies, the model and partnerships required for success will vary.

Refugee protection is not the same as immigration. Its purpose is to provide people with their full set of rights until they are able to go home or be integrated elsewhere. Nevertheless, with creativity this can be done in ways that promote human flourishing and simultaneously benefit host countries by supporting their development strategies, particularly within underdeveloped border areas.

BEYOND REFUGE

This chapter has introduced a commonsense idea that is tragically new to the humanitarian-dominated domain of refugees: refugees need work. As with 'Africa', in modern popular discourse, refugees have been assigned the role of victimhood. While well-intentioned, this demeaning approach is a travesty. As we have shown here, refugees have been subjected to an international regulatory environment in which they are systematically disconnected from economic activity. Our proposal is to upend this regime: global business could be put to work, bringing to refugees the opportunities to thrive.

But the potential of this new approach extends beyond refuge. In the next chapter we show how it can be made to serve a dual purpose: helping to restore stability to countries once the conflicts are over.

7

Rethinking Post-Conflict: Incubating Recovery

Mass violence is not a normal state of affairs. Even in fragile societies, risks are not often crystallized. Mass violence seldom starts, but it always ends. During the dark depths of a conflict it is easy to lose sight of this truth. Like a young Syrian interviewed on the beach at Lesbos, it is tempting to conclude that 'Syria is finished.' Though it will indeed be left a ruin of its former self, Syria is not finished. As Adam Smith observed in 1777, 'there is a great deal of ruin in a nation': he meant that societies can absorb a lot of disaster and yet recover. This chapter is about what we can do to aid that recovery.

More specifically, it is a proposal to break down the silos that have kept policy towards refuge, and policy towards post-conflict reconstruction, sealed off from each other. Post-conflict recovery is difficult: societies are at risk of falling into a trap in which the risk of conflict remains so high that before it can be brought down it recrystallizes. This is what has happened in South Sudan. Smart policies for refuge can make the post-conflict recovery less difficult and so reduce the danger of this trap. They may even accelerate the onset of peace. Furthermore, integrating policies for recovery and refuge can deliver the resource that the displaced most crave while their lives seem on hold: the hope that normal life will be restored.

WHY RECOVERY MATTERS

In the noisy confusion of the exodus to Lesbos it has been easy to lose sight of the long-term goals of refuge. The media have been dominated by the immediate: rescuing people from sinking boats; finding them shelter during a trek across the Balkans; feeding and housing those arriving in Germany; whether the latest terrorist outrage is linked to the refugee influx. To the extent that Europe's media have considered any wider horizons, they have usually focused on Eurocentric concerns: on how the Syrian refugees who have reached Europe can best be integrated; on how the European Commission can devise rules of apportionment among increasingly reluctant host governments.

All the above are peripheral to the core issues of displacement. The displaced have been forced out of their homes by mass violence. During the Syrian conflict, as in most situations of mass violence, a majority of the displaced do not even leave the country: they are *internally* displaced. Having fled to the safer areas of their country, they are of no interest whatsoever to the international media. The journalists and photographers sent to Syria are there to cover the fighting. Your daily diet of images of the Syrian emergency has been dominated by those who have made the crossing to Lesbos, and by these fighters. The less photogenic reality are the 6 million Syrians who are internally displaced, and the 4 million refugees living in the neighbouring havens.

Once this refocus is achieved, it becomes evident why post-conflict recovery matters. The 6 million internally displaced have probably left their homes with the same fear and remorse that induced others to leave for Germany, but their future will not be determined by whether they learn German. It will be determined by how rapidly Syria restores its economy and its communities. The 4 million in the neighbouring havens may decide to forge new lives in their host societies, those in Turkey learning a new language. But most refugees in neighbouring havens aspire to return once peace permits. Even some of those who have reached Europe may find that they prefer to return home rather than reinvent themselves as Europeans, or remain as Syrians-in-Europe while their children absorb a culture not their own.

So one compelling reason for focusing on the post-conflict recovery is that it is what matters to the vast majority of the displaced themselves. The other reason combines humanitarian concern with self-interest: to avert a relapse into mass violence and more instability in the region. Were the future Syrian restoration of peace to relapse into conflict it would be a disaster for Syria, for the region, and for Europe. If securing the peace matters, the question becomes how post-conflict risks can be reduced.

REDUCING POST-CONFLICT RISKS

The internal conflicts that generate mass violence usually revolve around some intractable difference between peoples. The conflict in Syria is so characterized but has been further complicated by becoming internationalized. Today's news, which is typical of its complexity, has three offsetting developments. Putin is meeting with Erdoğan, and if these two powers resolve their differences the likely outcome will be to strengthen the Assad regime: Assad's removal will no longer be a condition for settlement. Offsetting this, the regime's siege of Aleppo has just been broken by a jihadist force that has been boosted by support from Saudi Arabia and Qatar. But, countering that, the USA and the moderate forces opposing the Assad regime may become queasy about supporting a jihadist force whose goal is supremacist Islam. We are a long way from the chimera of a mutually acceptable peace. Peace will be restored, perhaps zone by zone, but it is likely to be messy.

If there is no quick political fix, then the best that can be hoped for is that the risks of relapse decline gradually. This is the usual pattern: the second post-conflict decade is safer than the first, the third safer than the second. Can anything be said about how risks can be made to decline more rapidly? The politics of healing the identity cleavage of 'us' and 'them' is likely to be very gradual, but something can be done. For example, in post-genocide Rwanda, which had inherited an extreme cleavage of identities, the government suppressed all media mention of 'Hutu' and 'Tutsi' and promoted the notion of a common Rwandan identity centred around the struggle for development. New research evidence finds that this is gradually working, with ethnic identities becoming less salient. But the pace at which identities can be changed is glacial, and international actors have little role to play in it. For policies that might work more swiftly and where international actors have a potential role, it is time to turn to the economy.

The pace at which risks come down is certainly associated with the speed with which the economy recovers. So, helping the economy to recover is a reasonable working hypothesis to guide post-conflict policy, both that of post-conflict governments and for the support provided internationally. But what can be done?

Just as the enduring Western image of conflict is bombing, our image of post-conflict reconstruction is of rebuilding the infrastructure. A bridge was blown up; a hospital was bombed – we will rebuild them: 'If we break it, we fix it', as Secretary of State Powell declared after the invasion of Iraq. This image misses the essence of economic recovery from a civil war: it is about organizations, not concrete. More specifically, it is about restoring the capacity of government to perform key economic functions, and inducing firms to hire workers.[1]

Organizations, whether government or private sector, are teams of people who are motivated to harness their skills, and to cooperate with each other, in order to achieve a clear goal. Large organizations have the potential to reap scale economies and so can be remarkably productive. Those organizations that combine size, motivation, skill and cooperation are complex miracles that underpin prosperity. In all poor societies they are scarce, but in post-conflict societies they are desperately scarce: many of those that existed prior to the conflict have been destroyed. This is indeed a difference between the legacy of international warfare and of internal warfare. Not only are international wars usually much shorter than civil wars, but they typically strengthen the capacity of organizations, especially of government. In tearing people apart, civil wars also tear organizations apart.

Rebuilding an organization is primarily about people: recruiting people with the education, skill, and motivation to cooperate and to be productive. It is about restoring human capital more than rebuilding physical infrastructure.

Rebuilding government capacity can be selective, because some functions normally carried out by government can, at least for a while, be contracted out. For example, churches and NGOs may be willing and able to run schools and clinics. But other functions cannot be contracted out: tax collection, courts, the police, and regulation can only be performed by agencies of the state. Otherwise, there is no state; the society has arrived not at peace but at anarchy. Think, for a moment, about the nature of this list of core activities. What characteristics does a tax collector need? And what are those of a court official? Inescapably, the core functions of government require people with tertiary education.

Most jobs are generated not by government, but by firms. The productivity gains generated by modern firms are transformational: they are what lifts a society rapidly out of poverty.

Unfortunately, post-conflict states have very few formal firms, whether domestic or foreign. There is no mystery to this: firms need to finance themselves from their revenues and during a prolonged civil war the economy falls apart. There are no reliable figures on the Syrian economy, but with a quarter of its population having left the country, and the incomes of those remaining having fallen substantially, the domestic revenues of a typical firm must have collapsed. The World Bank estimates that GDP has contracted by up to 19 per cent per year.[2] Many multinational corporations that previously operated in the country have been forced to leave as a result of the violence.[3] So too have many regional businesses, often operating at a much smaller scale.[4]

So, the post-conflict Syrian economy will be chronically short of modern firms. In principle, in most post-conflict economies the fastest way to get more businesses is to bring in established foreign ones. However, understandably they are reluctant to go to post-conflict countries: markets are small, bureaucracies are liable to be dysfunctional and corrupt (exposing the firm to reputational risk), and the country will have acquired a reputation for violence so that insurance may be difficult, and staff may be reluctant to go there. The few formal firms that do venture into post-conflict situations are abnormal: sometimes this is because they are run by predatory crooks who are comfortable in corrupt environments. These are obviously not the sort of enterprise that a post-conflict state needs.

The problem of attracting companies is compounded because many of the private-investment possibilities will be pioneering: the first such activity in the country since peace was restored. As such, there are many 'unknown unknowns' that can only be resolved by trying. In the act of trying, the pioneer investor generates information that is very useful to potential subsequent investors: if the investment is a success it will get copied. This is good for the country, but bad for the pioneer: it is what economists term an 'externality' – a benefit that does not accrue to the firm taking the decision. This is true of all pioneering investment, but post-conflict economies are distinctive because a much higher proportion of investment is pioneering: in advanced economies most investment is routine. Yet even in advanced economies pioneering investment is recognized as socially valuable and subsidized through various mechanisms. For example, Britain has a tax subsidy for investment in start-ups that amounts to around 40 per cent. Clearly, the governments of post-conflict states cannot afford to provide such a subsidy; nor do they have the governance structures that would permit subsidies to be administered with integrity.

We have arrived at a conundrum: post-conflict countries need modern firms, but modern firms do not need post-conflict countries. They simply do not offer good opportunities to enough of the firms that are reputable. Here is the killer evidence. The International Finance Corporation (IFC), despite its evil-sounding name, is an international public agency run collectively by the world's governments. Its purpose is to attract reputable firms to developing countries, which it does primarily by co-investing with firms. So a good indication of what firms earn on the capital they invest in developing countries is the rate of return on the IFC portfolio. Across the entire portfolio of developing countries, the rate of return on IFC investment has been around 4 per cent, which you might regard as respectable rather than predatory. Only a small share of that investment is in states that are in a post-conflict situation or otherwise fragile, but in those economies its return on investment has been *negative*. That is why there are so few modern firms attracted to post-conflict situations. Yet, without them, countries cannot grow out of fragility. The boards of private firms are legally required to manage their enterprises in the interests of shareholders: they can only scale up investment where it is expected to be profitable.

Evidently, there is a major divergence between the global public interest and commercial private interest. It is very much in the global public interest that modern firms set up operations in post-conflict societies. The jobs and tax revenues that they would bring would help to stabilize a fragile situation. But it is very much not in the commercial interest of firms to do so, and their boards are legally required to operate in the interest of their shareholders, and in Germany also in the interest of their employees.

There is an obvious way out of this impasse: international public money should be used to compensate firms for the public benefit that they generate by operating in post-conflict situations. This idea is finally being implemented. Some fifty-four years after aid for very poor countries was first provided through the World Bank, on an experimental basis the governments that control it are going to allow a small amount of aid to be used to attract investment to fragile states. Governments have been so slow because the only two constituencies that pay attention to the World Bank will each be up in arms. The political right regards aid as a waste, or worse. Throwing public money at investments that private money has 'wisely' decided to avoid will be trumpeted as a demonstration of that folly. Meanwhile the political left regards private firms operating in poor societies as evil incarnate. Diverting aid that could be used to put a smile on the face of a child into their coffers will likewise be regarded as emblematic. Faced with these strident voices from the extremes, we can only hope that the centre does not fall apart.

Donor agencies are well aware of the priority of post-conflict situations. There is usually plenty of money for them. The problem is that to date it has been channelled almost entirely through post-conflict governments and Western NGOs. The governments lack the capacity to spend it properly, and the NGOs only use it for their social agendas: the smiling faces. So there is no lack of international public money that could be used to attract reputable firms to revive post-conflict economies. There has just been a lack of ideas, and the courage to implement them.

But while this idea would be useful, we think that there is an even better one. It should also be less controversial.

INCUBATING RECOVERY

This book has four big new ideas. You met the first in Chapter 4: the right ethical focus is the duty to rescue the displaced from the disruption to normal life generated by their flight from home. You met the second in Chapter 5: the best places for safe haven are those that are easy for the displaced to reach, and rich countries should make it financially feasible for these haven countries to take them. You met the third in the previous chapter: the best way to restore normality is for refugees to be able to work, so jobs should be brought to the haven countries. Now it is time for the final idea: the economic support needed for refuge can be used for the dual purpose of incubating the post-conflict recovery. There are several practical aspects to this idea: we will start with a simple extension of bringing jobs to refugees.

If international firms bring economic activities to the haven countries near the conflict, they can potentially set up production in the country once the conflict ends. Nor would this be quixotic: by the time of peace, they would have established an experienced workforce of refugees, most of whom will be keen to return home. By setting up in the post-conflict country, the firm can retain its workforce. Nothing is as simple as it sounds, and so it is now time for some elaboration on the likely obstacles and the ways around them.

For a start, there looks to be an evident flaw. If the grand international plan is that the firms coming to haven countries during a regional conflict should promptly depart once it is over, the governments of haven countries are unlikely to cooperate with it. The core attraction to the governments of haven countries of the plan to attract firms to them is that, by providing a temporary haven for refugees, they gain a permanent benefit. Fortunately, global capitalism does not work like that: it is not a zero-sum game. A successful firm aims to expand. If it has successfully set up production in a haven country, employing both local citizens and refugees, and its refugee workforce wants to return home, it can set up production in the post-conflict country without closing it in the haven.

But the fact that its refugee workforce wishes to return may well not be a sufficient incentive to compensate the firm for the evident risks of setting up in a post-conflict situation. We have discussed those risks above. But we have also discussed how to offset them. Like any other firms willing to establish themselves in the post-conflict economy, those that come with their refugee workforce will need to be compensated with international public money for the public good that they are providing. Firms are not charities: they are not even legally allowed to behave like charities. And so international public policy cannot be premised on the hope that they will do so. But the cost of temporarily subsidizing new jobs in firms coming to post-conflict economies is modest compared with the vast and often failed expenditures on stabilization that have been conventional. The attempt to stabilize Afghanistan is estimated to have cost American taxpayers $3tn to date. What, on standard policies, is going to be the bill for post-conflict Syria? And if stabilization policies fail, what would be the cost of a reversion to regional conflict? Linking refuge to incubation does not have to be free to be a bargain.

Public money to match the public good of generating jobs that stabilize a post-conflict situation is likely to be necessary, but by itself it will not be sufficient. Recall that Turkey succeeded in becoming the 'near offshore' for German firms because goods made in Turkey could be sold in Europe without facing import barriers. The other haven countries, and post-conflict Syria itself, need the same market access that the European Commission has granted to Turkey in order to become part of Europe's near offshore. But this is not complicated: once the European Commission woke up to the issue, market access for Jordan was granted quite rapidly, coming into effect in June 2016. Such trade advantages should become an integral part of the provision of refuge and of support for post-conflict recovery.

While money and privileged market access are both necessary, President Obama's approach of exhorting leading CEOs can also play a critical role. This does not just work by applying moral pressure. Both modern manufacturing and post-conflict recovery are coordination problems: the decision of each firm matters for the decisions of others. In modern manufacturing, many of the scale economies that lower costs occur at the level of the cluster rather than the individual firm. Recognizing the potential for cost-cutting by bringing firms together has been the rationale for the creation of industrial zones, a strategy that has been hugely successful in East Asia. Post-conflict countries face a yet more acute coordination problem. Not only will costs be lower for everyone if several firms set up in the same place, but the jobs that each generates will make the situation less fragile for everyone. If the board of an American corporation is considering the out-of-the-box proposal to set up a subsidiary in a post-conflict country, it will be very reassuring to hear that several other firms are also considering the proposition and that the President and agencies of state, such as the State Department, are enthusiastically behind it.

Another strategy with considerable potential in the Syrian conflict is to provide proximate havens for Syrian firms. Just as people need a haven, so do businesses. The industrial and commercial capital of Syria is Aleppo, much of which has been under the control of opponents of the regime. In response, with Russian military support, Aleppo has been bombed and shelled. As its people flee, firms not only face equivalent risks; they lose their workforce and their market. Some Syrian firms have already rebased to the neighbouring havens. But if government policies supported the process instead of impeding it, more firms would decide to relocate, and fewer firms would close. Of course, if firms left Syria, their workers would find the flight to safety less daunting, so a strategy for firms works for people as well. What practical policies might help? One type of appropriate policy takes us back to what President Obama has been doing. In relocating, firms face a coordination problem: the chances of success are higher the more firms that cluster in the same place. So, running up a flag to indicate that some haven location is explicitly designed to welcome Syrian firms is useful. The location may be an industrial zone, or a large building suitable for service activities. Such flags not only guide firms; they help fleeing families decide where they might be able to get employment.

Beyond a coordinating signal, there are many other facilitating steps that can be taken. Credit facilities financed out of the aid earmarked for post-conflict recovery can enable firms that relocate to pay the rent on premises and purchase inputs while they get established. Beyond credit, the locations can be equipped with appropriate infrastructure: for example, all economic activity requires electricity and connectivity. A haven business zone needs either to be on the national grid or to have its own power supply, and to be easily reachable from a port or an airport. At the most ambitious end of the spectrum of supportive policies, it may be possible in some locations to create a temporary legal and fiscal 'micro-climate' that enables Syrian firms to operate under laws and taxes with which they are familiar. Just as UNHCR has on-the-ground teams at camps to receive, house, and feed refugee households, so business havens should have equivalent teams, obviously with quite different competences.

Preserving businesses during conflict does not tug the heart strings: there will be no photos with the emotive kick of a dead child on a beach. Consequently, it will struggle for political attention. But that does not stop its being vital: the organizational capital of a society is an important asset. Firms are the predominant means by which economic activity is coordinated so as to make it productive. The networks of relationships, cooperation and authority that are their essence take time to put together and are vulnerable to mass violence. The loss of firms is one reason why post-conflict recovery is difficult: they are destroyed during conflict more rapidly than they can be created after the conflict is over. At the macroeconomic level, the pace at which an economy declines relative to its long-term growth rate during conflict is typically around double the speed at which it catches up again after the conflict. In other words, following a seven-year civil war, it typically takes around a further fourteen years to get back on track, although there is a lot of variation around this average. As measured by the loss of GDP, most of the costs of conflict occur after it is over.[5] Syria is not 'finished', but it will take many years even to recover to its unimpressive pre-conflict growth path.

Beyond strategies for international firms and Syrian businesses, incubating the post-conflict economy can encourage enterprise among refugees. At a minimum, those refugees in the camps can be encouraged to establish small businesses. Hair salons, cobbler's, bicycle repair shops, internet cafés: a few camps are already hives of commercial activity. But most are not: UNHCR has not been designed for this to be a central purpose. For example, electricity provided in camps is usually spasmodic but free. The idea that it could be generated commercially and sold to business-users is alien to the humanitarian mission. Similarly, food is typically provided by means of a special currency, handed monthly to households, that can only be redeemed by the household itself in one or two official shops. Food markets, where they exist, do so on the margins of this official charity rather than being recognized as the natural means by which food provision should be organized. In virtually every developing country, cities have teaming informal economies that provide livelihoods for much of the population. A refugee camp should look like a temporary city: for example, the space within the camp should be organized to provide market centres, enabling businesses to cluster.

Given that most refugees ignore the camps and head for the cities, there should also be scope for making it easier for refugee enterprises to function in host cities. For example, tensions between host communities and refugees might be eased if post-conflict funds were used to provide credit for both host and refugee enterprises in a set proportion, with an explicit narrative that refugee enterprises were preparing for return once the conflict was over. That narrative could be made credible by finance ready and waiting to facilitate return. Permanent integration into the host society need not become the objective unless the conflict persists.

Sometimes, however, economic participation is valuable not just for helping refugees, but for strengthening the host country. In the Syrian crisis the country that has proportionately borne the brunt of the burden of reception is Lebanon. Lebanon is itself a fragile state, with a precarious political balance between religious groups. Further, since 2014 it has been hit hard economically by the fall in the oil price: while not itself an oil-producer, it is the business centre for the entire Middle East. So Lebanon needs economic support. Unfortunately, its government is in no state to deploy a large injection of international aid: the money would be dissipated. The alternative is to stimulate the private economy directly and this is particularly feasible because the key Lebanese resource is entrepreneurship: this has been a trading society for millennia. As we discussed in Chapter 6, global companies like Walmart are now starting to source their supplies from businesses in the haven countries. Were there to be a systematic push to source from Lebanon, Lebanese entrepreneurs have the expertise to respond, hiring both their own citizens and refugees. Plugged into global markets, Lebanon's entrepreneurs could drive the job creation that would help stabilize both Lebanon itself and the wider region.

Lebanon is not unique. As we have seen, just ten countries host the majority of the world's refugees. Because these countries, such as Jordan, Thailand, and Pakistan, are in unstable regions, periodically they get an influx of refugees. While each particular influx may be temporary, the need for a viable haven is more enduring. It would therefore be a wise investment for the global community to support 'incubator cities' in the haven countries that could serve each influx of refugees as need arose. An incubator city would need both good physical infrastructure and conducive regulations. As a regulatory haven it is related to an idea of Paul Romer's, now Chief Economist of the World Bank, that he terms 'charter cities'. Evidently, such places would have to be advantageous to the people and governments of the host countries as well as serving the needs of refugees.

Incubator cities would serve a triple purpose. They would be advantageous for the host country, serve the needs of refugees, and prepare the recovery of the post-conflict economy of the country of origin. The way we treat refugees in exile shapes their capacity to contribute to their countries of origin. This in turn has implications for political transition, peace-building, and post-conflict recovery in the country of origin.[6] Such cities need not infringe on national sovereignty, but could be supported on a long-term basis by a consortium of international organizations, multinational corporations, and foundations. While they would take significant investment to establish, by enabling refugees to earn their own living they would be far cheaper than the present regime, while meeting the duty of rescue more consistently and comprehensively.

The young are more likely to leave a conflict-ridden society than their elders, but currently for many of them life is put on hold, which leads to a general loss of what economists call human capital during civil conflicts. Even at the most elementary level of schooling, refugee camps are not adequately equipped. This is partly because of a working rule of UNHCR which stipulates that it is the responsibility of the host country's government to provide schooling for refugees: clearly it has little incentive to do so. Nor do parents necessarily want their children taught according to the curriculum and language of the host. There is evident scope for deploying those refugees who are teachers to teach child refugees. Sometimes this happens, but it is far from being a universal official international practice: rules need to be changed. But the core exodus is of youths in their late teens and early twenties. This exodus provides a massive opportunity for internationally organized training in the skills that will be needed for post-conflict recovery.

One practical example is the need for construction skills. During conflict society is convulsed in destruction: there is little demand for construction work. As a result, the myriad construction skills ossify. In the 1950s a Nobel Laureate in economics demonstrated that an important process of human-capital formation was the straightforward one of 'learning by doing'. During conflict a society collectively engages in its obverse: 'forgetting by not doing'.[7] The very sector in which forgetting is most severe, construction, is the one in most demand once the conflict ends. It often becomes a bottleneck: the costs of reconstruction explode, dissipating the money earmarked for it. Training during refuge can ease this bottleneck: potentially, it can be linked to donor-financed construction projects in haven countries, providing a reward for the host at the same time that it provides an activity for refugees, and gives people a vital post-conflict skill.

Post-conflict societies also need more sophisticated skills: within the civil service, in health care, and in business. Training for these jobs can usually be provided most cost-effectively in the universities of the nearest haven countries. The small minority of refugees fortunate enough to be given these opportunities have a corresponding obligation. Once they are newly equipped with an internationally valuable skill, their private interest is likely to be to remain in the country of training. They will earn far more, and have more comfortable lives, than a post-conflict country can possibly offer them. But young people should not be put into the position of choosing between self-interest and their obligations to their less fortunate compatriots. The international provision of these opportunities should come as a package with the obligation of return should the society revert to peace within a reasonable time-frame. Acceptance of the opportunity should explicitly require acceptance of the obligation. This is not an affront to the human rights of individual refugees, but rather a recognition of the human needs of the many millions of the displaced.

But it's not just that autonomy enables refugees to meaningfully contribute to a durable peace once it is restored. It may even accelerate the onset of that peace. Empowering refugees can enable them to play a role in the political and economic life of the country of origin while in exile.

The flight to refuge from mass violence is sometimes driven by a state's violence against its people, and sometimes by the fragmentation of power into disorder. In each case, the refugee population can potentially play a role in the restoration of peace.

Zimbabwe between 2000 and 2008 is an example of state violence. Faced with brutal repression by the ruling ZANU-PF, the space for viable political opposition within Zimbabwe shrank dramatically, while the economy collapsed into a spectacular hyperinflation and famine. Members of the opposition Movement for Democratic Change and hundreds of thousands of ordinary Zimbabweans went into exile, mainly in neighbouring South Africa. While there, they sought ways to contest Mugabe's rule from abroad. An alphabet-soup of new diaspora organizations flourished in Johannesburg and elsewhere. Occasionally they had triumphs: in 2008 they successfully blockaded a Chinese arms shipment at the port of Durban that had been destined for Harare; they successfully petitioned the South African police to investigate cases of torture by the Zimbabwean government.[8] For the most part, though, the mobilization of the Zimbabwean diaspora was a missed opportunity, exemplified by the low diaspora turnout in Zimbabwe's elections. More could have been done internationally to support effective diaspora organization and pressure.

Syria began as another example of state violence but became a case of fragmentation and disorder. Where no group is able to win, what is needed to restore peace is the willingness to share power. Potentially refugee populations can incubate the habits and structures of the required cooperation. As we will shortly establish, the Syrian refugee population has become an approximation to a random sample of the overall population: Sunnis, Alawites, Christians; Arabs and Kurds; religious and secular – violence did not spare any group. All with the legal status of refugees are currently reduced to the same powerlessness. Potentially, UNHCR could create councils for refugees on which representation was so structured as to ensure participation and veto power for each significant group. The council could manage real resources but to access them they would need to cooperate. Such a council could collectively represent a new refugee voice at peace negotiations. Despite the viperous sectarian hatreds, all refugees share a distinctive experience invaluable at a peace conference: they are the voice of the suffering that violence brings. This is in sharp contrast with what has typically happened to date. For example, the refugees returning to Bosnia found that they had been shut out politically from the carve-up of power among the men with guns.

RETARDING RECOVERY

Above we have introduced the concept of incubation and sketched what a strategy might look like. As an idea it is already gaining traction. The military spotted the potential for this 'non-kinetic' approach to security and we were invited to address a meeting of NATO officials in Bulgaria. This link with the security sector is potentially a valuable source of support for a new approach. The military, better than anyone else, has learnt the limits of hard power in restoring post-conflict societies.

Every concept has its obverse, and the obverse of incubating recovery would be to *retard* it. Clearly, a conscious attempt to retard post-conflict recovery is anomalous, but occasionally strategies have been devised and even implemented. The most famous instance of retarding recovery is what Rome did to Carthage: not only was everything demolished but the fields were ploughed with salt. In its own terms, the strategy was successful. More recently, vindictive French strategists planned to turn post-war Germany back into an agrarian economy incapable of waging warfare: happily, the plan was never implemented. While conscious strategies for retarding recovery have passed into history, international public policy is sometimes so poorly thought through as inadvertently to have this effect.

Sadly, the Syrian refugee crisis is such an instance. The well-meaning invitation to Europe had the unintended consequence of inducing a highly selective exodus of the skilled. In an emblematic gesture of humanity, the Pope visited the Syrian refugee camps and returned to Italy with three refugee families. The press reported the occupations of two of the heads of household: an engineer and a teacher. They are now settled in Italian communities and presumably leading far more hopeful lives than their experience in the camps. Despite the severe Italian recession, the engineer may well be able to find suitable employment there. But engineering skills are also likely to be useful in post-conflict construction: were all the Syrian engineers to move to Europe it would clearly set back recovery. Perhaps, when the conflict ends, the engineer will return home; perhaps, indeed, he will return better equipped with skills and experience than had he remained in a camp. But perhaps he and his family will settle in Italy, and that would be a loss for post-conflict Syria. The skills of the teacher may be less suited to Italy: tuition is obviously in Italian, and the society has an exceptionally low birth rate. As we discussed above, the teacher may not have been able to teach while in the camp. But other Syrian teachers have taken the opportunity to flock to Europe, abandoning Syrian refugee children in the process. For example, in one refugee camp for Syrian Kurds in Iraq, Syrian teachers have left for Germany and elsewhere, leaving teachers from Europe to provide education in the camp.[9]

The exodus of the educated has been systematic. It is also unsurprising: it was both more feasible and more rewarding for them than for their less-educated compatriots. It was more feasible because the educated tend to be from atypically affluent families and so were better placed to raise the cash needed to pay the people-smugglers. It was more rewarding, because the educated are better placed to get a good job, generating much larger financial returns to the investment in migration than those without education. But the most striking aspect of this selective exodus was its scale. In the chaos of the crisis one luxury that was discarded was systematic data-gathering. However, we have surprisingly good data on the educational composition of those who headed for Europe relative to the refugees who remained behind. UNHCR has done systematic data collection on the people who have stayed in the havens, while a field survey of those arriving on the beaches of Lesbos provides a sample of those who left for Europe. To complete the picture we have census data on the educational composition of the overall Syrian population just prior to the conflict. By comparing the three sources, we can see the extent of selectivity.

What emerges is astonishing. The refugee exodus to the neighbouring havens was virtually a random sample of the overall Syrian population. This implies that the flight to safety was due to *force majeure*: it was not a choice – a location becomes unsafe and the people living there have no reasonable option but to get out. Those near borders flee across them: adults and their children, men and women, the young and the old, the educated and the uneducated, the Sunnis, the Alawites – such differences fade into insignificance. In complete contrast, the move to Europe was highly selective. As we have already noted, the people coming to Europe were distinctively affluent. Prior to the conflict average annual income per person in Syria was barely $2,000. With people-smugglers charging $5,000, only the rich could buy a place. But the surveys reveal other dimensions of selectivity. Those moving were largely adult males: at the peak of the flow in September 2015, around 80 per cent were men. Yet the most striking dimension of selectivity is education. Overall, in the Syrian population university education is rare: around one person in thirty. Among those moving to Europe it was normal: at the peak of the flow half of all those reaching Europe had a university degree.[10] Among the remaining half almost all had completed secondary education, compared to only one in eight of the overall population.[11]

This extreme degree of selectivity has two implications. The less important implication concerns categorization. Unlike the flight to refuge, this move was a choice. Those who took it were taking an economic decision to migrate, not reacting to the *force majeure* of violence. The small minority of Syrians, around one in twenty, who moved to Europe had chosen to become migrants.

But the really important implication of selectivity is for the 95 per cent of Syrians who remain in the region: the exodus of the educated to Europe has drained Syria of around *half* of its entire university-educated population.[12] It has also drained around a quarter of the entire stock of people with completed secondary education. This degree of loss of human capital during a conflict is probably without precedent. It risks turning post-conflict Syria into a society with an educational profile now only found in the very poorest countries. It could set the country back for decades.

Even such a massive and selective exodus of the educated need not imply their permanent loss to post-conflict Syria. That depends upon whether the Syrians in Europe choose, are encouraged, or are even permitted to remain. There is no systematic evidence on current intentions. Based on interviews with young Syrians in Germany, the journalist Joshua Hammer reports that most of the Syrians he spoke to said 'they would *never* go back'.[13]

As we discussed in Chapter 4, the current policy of the German government appears to be to encourage integration into German society, which may discourage return. Inadvertently, this adds insult to injury. Having first encouraged the educated to leave their compatriots, the German government is now encouraging them to stay when the conflict ends. Behind the concern for humanity and solidarity, the uncomfortable reality is that the German government has inadvertently denuded a poor country of the capacity it will need in order to rebuild. While not ill-intentioned, there may be a case for regarding some of the actions of the German government as reckless.

Potentially, however, the refugees could be equipped with new skills that they would bring back home. A valuable study of the long-term effects of young people studying abroad and returning home found clear evidence that they brought back not only the skills they had been taught, but political attitudes. The path to democracy in their home societies was accelerated by students who had been in the West and this could evidently be valuable in post-conflict Syria.[14]

Nevertheless, while it is by no means inevitable that the exodus of the educated young will have gutted post-conflict Syria of the very people it will most need, there is a serious risk that this will be the outcome. An inadvertent policy of retarding recovery would be the quintessential instance of the headless heart. International responses to refugee crises cannot get by on being well-intentioned: they need to be smart, too.

8

Rethinking Governance: Institutions That Work

The institutions created to protect the world's refugees are failing. Global governance exists to facilitate international cooperation, and yet with the highest number of refugees in the regime's history, we have the lowest levels of responsibility-sharing. Against its own criteria, the metrics on the performance of the refugee regime are damning: in terms of protection, the top five refugee emergency operations are less than one third funded. In consequence, even basic nutrition, health-care, and education are not provided, while nine out of the ten largest refugee-hosting countries place major restrictions on refugees' right to work;[1] in terms of solutions, fewer than one in thirty refugees currently receive access to resettlement, repatriation or local integration.

Blame for this failure does not lie in any one place. International organization staff often work heroically but with finite resources and blunt tools. Elected politicians struggle to reconcile democracy and globalization in a way that can allow them to argue persuasively for the rights of refugees. Dominant ideas about the links between security, terrorism, and migration shape the politics of asylum. But effective institutions should be able to transcend this political divergence. The very purpose of institutions is to create predictable patterns of collective action among states even when they have divergent preferences and interests. At their most effective, they achieve this because they recognize trade-offs and scope out areas where mutual gains are possible. Within this range, states are better off committing to work together than they would be acting in isolation.

Our institutions are failing because, still frozen in a distant past, they are mismatched to the contemporary reality. The post-Second World War bargain was implicitly based on a set of assumptions about the nature of the refugee problem: its geographic extent was intra-European, and its origin was persecution. The institutions were designed to address that problem: the solution to the failure of collective action was to provide coordinating mechanisms and an incentive for cooperation through a legal guarantee of reciprocity. These assumptions were not stupid: they held at the time, but they do not hold any longer. Today, the refugee problem is global. It is driven not just by persecution, but by conflict and fragility. Legal principles are less salient than politics in shaping outcomes. Globalization presents both different challenges and opportunities. Of course, the norms and organizations that comprise the regime have adapted, but until now they have done so only incrementally. There has never been systematic reflection on what effective refugee governance would look like in the twenty-first century.

This is not to say that everything has to be rejected. Existing structures like the 1951 Convention and UNHCR have a future role. Refugee law remains valuable: it offers an important and foundational set of principles. It influences some states' behaviour towards some refugees some of the time – in part because states recognize the overall structure as offering a semblance of order, and in part because law has deeply embedded historical roots. A United Nations refugee organization has the potential to bring coherence and legitimacy to collective action, not least through its accumulated expert authority. But the current trajectory is manifestly failing. Law and humanitarian assistance offer only part of the solution, and a new overarching vision is urgently needed.

In this chapter we set out what a new architecture would look like, how it might be built, and why it is likely to be resisted by vested interests. We begin from first principles. Going beyond path-dependency, we consider what a rational redesign for the twenty-first century might look like. Our approach is informed by a set of ideas called institutional design, at the intersection of political science, economics, and law.[2] Institutional design did not even exist as a way of thinking at the inception of the refugee regime but it offers a way of establishing the most rational incentive structures needed to maximize the provision of a global public good.

In order to lay out this vision, we ask three questions which logically follow from one another. First, what are the objectives of refugee governance? Second, how should we allocate responsibilities to meet these objectives? Third, what organizational structures are needed to ensure that these responsibilities are met?

RETHINKING OBJECTIVES

So what should be the purpose of refugee governance? All too rarely has this question been clearly answered. The nearest we get is the Statute of UNHCR telling us that its purpose is to provide protection to, and find solutions for, refugees. Other than clarifying that a High Commissioner for Refugees is about *refugees* and not pandas, this hardly offers much precision as to the specific goals and priorities of the regime.

In the absence of clarity of purpose, the institutional architecture has lurched into path-dependency, with most officials unable to imagine an approach that goes beyond reassertion of the status quo ante. Advocacy organizations vehemently defend the supremacy of existing structures, while governments increasingly bypass them in favour of unilateral actions. In consequence, the organizations like UNHCR – in theory the guardian of refugee governance – have become reactive rather than proactive, defending the waning standards of the past rather than offering a bold vision of the future.

Criticism of the status quo is all too easy: it is time to expose our necks. For us, the response to refugees should be informed by two core principles: rescue and autonomy. The duty of rescue entails ensuring that people in distress have rapid access to their most fundamental needs. But as soon as this is achieved – the child is pulled out of the pond – our purpose becomes to restore autonomy. A satisfactory refugee regime should enable people to help themselves and their communities, particularly through jobs and education. From these two overarching priorities, more specific requirements follow. We distinguish five interrelated components.

Any defensible refugee regime must work for the many, not just for a fortunate few. Hence, our first requirement is *sustainability at scale*. Today we are dealing with an expanded group of people.

Refugee numbers are at record levels. Internally displaced persons, who are potential refugees-in-waiting, are also in higher numbers than ever. In addition, there are emerging new drivers of displacement. Climate change, the likelihood of some fat-tail event in a fragile state (suppose that Pakistan rather than Syria had imploded), and generalized violence are leading to increasing levels of flight-for-survival. Some of these people receive recognition under the existing system; many do not. And yet, insofar as they cannot access the basic conditions of human dignity back home, we will also need to find ways to offer them rescue and autonomy. As numbers increase, the challenge of sustainability will become ever greater.

As the migration expert Martin Ruhs has highlighted, around the world immigration policies are frequently characterized by a trade-off between numbers and rights.[3] He shows that as the numbers of low-skilled immigrants increase, so the rights that governments afford them tend to decline. Insofar as this relationship holds for refugees it creates a policy dilemma: should we prioritize a boutique response for the few or a sustainable response for the many? Our answer is unequivocal: we have to have an approach that can be effective for the many: for *all* refugees.

A defensible regime must work for the duration of refuge, which is typically years, not just respond to crisis. Hence, our second requirement is *protection for duration of risk*. We need to take seriously the content of the duty of rescue. Grounded in our common humanity, it requires that if someone is in distress and we have the ability to help at low cost to ourselves, then we must do so. This entails ensuring that they are not sent back to a country in which they face serious harm and that their most fundamental needs are met until they are able to go home.

However, the duty of rescue does not require an unqualified right of migration or immediate assimilation. There is nothing inherent to being a refugee that necessitates unrestricted global mobility or the ability to choose a destination country. The salient feature of being a refugee is the need for protection, not the need to migrate. Migration becomes a qualified right for refugees only insofar as it is a necessary last resort in order to get access to protection. The duty of rescue requires that protection is available to refugees for the duration of the risk of harm.[4] In general, refugee status should be considered as offering temporary protection pending a change in the circumstances back home.

A defensible refugee regime must restore autonomy. Hence, our third requirement is the provision of *development areas*. Refugees should be within enabling environments that encourage them to be self-sufficient as soon as they arrive. Different approaches will be appropriate for different countries. In some it may be possible to adopt Uganda's model of full economic participation; in others it may need to be based on a model closer to Jordan's approach of development zones. But what they have in common is the model of creating development areas in peripheral parts of the country in which both refugees and the host state and society can benefit from the creation of new jobs, new markets, and improved public services. Development areas provide autonomy not by browbeating a government through its courts, but by aligning it with the interests of the host society.

The precise model will vary across economies that are predominantly agricultural, manufacturing or service sector-based. But, irrespectively, the key is to identify border locations in the major repeat refugee-hosting countries, creating long-term development areas where the presence of refugees generates opportunity for the host community. In order to ensure that refugees thrive rather than merely survive, enabling environments will need to offer the right to work, education, connectivity, electricity, and transportation.

While autonomy can be provided almost as soon as a refugee arrives in a development area, it is by its nature provisional. We all sustain ourselves by some narrative of hope, and inevitably in becoming refugees people lose those narratives. Hence, our fourth requirement is that a defensible regime must provide *a route out of limbo*. No refugee should remain indefinitely displaced.

As we discussed in Chapter 4, any cut-off point is going to be arbitrary, but it is still helpful to everyone to have one, and to know what it will be in advance. The one we would suggest is that after a predetermined period somewhere between five and ten years an official international review should be undertaken to determine whether there is a credible prospect that return home will be possible in the foreseeable future. If it determined that there was no such prospect, then those who had already been refugees for longer than the cut-off would be provided with a pathway towards assimilation within another country.[5]

Although the durable solutions of repatriation, local integration, and resettlement have largely been blocked in recent years, there is every reason to believe that the provision of autonomy to refugees through development areas can contribute to opening up these solutions. Empowering people will enable them to engage in rebuilding their own societies both transnationally before they go back and upon their return. It will also make them far more attractive prospects for either local integration or resettlement places.

While repatriation will therefore remain the predominant solution for most, quotas for resettlement places, based on matching with states' preferences, will therefore still be necessary for many of those unable to go home. But resettlement places should be used far more thoughtfully and strategically as a means to take people out of protracted situations at the end of the cut-off period.

Refugees are not migrants, but sometimes they have to move. However, people-smugglers and the temptation to play Russian roulette should play no part in a defensible refugee regime. Hence, our final requirement: *onward movement should be managed*. Refugee governance is not about migration per se; it is about ensuring rescue and autonomy. Nevertheless, to be effective the refugee regime relies upon a functioning migration system. In the context of globalization, refugees – like everyone else – have increasing opportunities for international mobility, and growing numbers are moving trans-continentally.

The only circumstances in which refugees should be embarking on long journeys is when it is the only available means to seek asylum, or they have other good reasons to move independently of the fact they are refugees. If refugees can access rescue and autonomy in a neighbouring country, there should be no protection-related reason to move onwards spontaneously. For those who wish to migrate, alternative migratory channels should be available through embassies and consulates in the host countries of asylum. Being a refugee should not prevent people from also applying for visas in areas such as labour migration, family reunification, or humanitarian visas, for example, if that is what they wish and these options are available.[6]

RETHINKING RESPONSIBILITIES

So how should we achieve these objectives? Who is responsible? The core principles for assigning responsibilities are obvious: burden-sharing and comparative advantage. The duty of rescue requires both a heart that accepts its share of responsibility and a head that identifies the most effective and efficient ways in which states can collectively meet the needs of refugees.

Burden-sharing is crucial in order to achieve reasonable provision of refugee assistance. As with all global public goods, individual states have strong incentives to free-ride on the provision of other states. Precisely because free-riding is such a widespread problem, various ways of addressing it have evolved. Probably the most common is the power of social norms: within a community where norms of sharing are well-understood, few people want to feel that they are a mean bastard, and even fewer want to be regarded as a mean bastard. One of the hidden disasters of the manifest dysfunctionality of the current refugee regime is that few states feel obliged to honour its codes of conduct. If the rules are indefensible, those who comply with them are not particularly good: they are particularly foolish. We should not underestimate the scope for a coherent refugee scheme to self-police. Governments do not want to look bad in front of either their peers or their electorates, and, as human beings, leaders want to be able to sleep at night.

But all new norms pose a coordination problem. If you comply I would feel bad about not complying, but until you do I might as well wait: *so we all wait*. To get things started, it is probably smart for an explicit new regime to specify burden-sharing and to back the new norms with some token penalties. The penalties need to be token, otherwise they will lose credibility: think how many fines the European Commission has waived for breaches of its fiscal rules.[7] Worse, as a celebrated case of a fine for late arrival at an Israeli nursery illustrates, penalties can backfire if they are reinterpreted as the *price* of not adhering to the rule.[8]

On the other hand, this does not mean that all states have to contribute in identical ways. The principle of comparative advantage

suggests that all states can be better off if there is a degree of specialization, with states focusing on making the contributions that they are
relatively best placed to make. Japan, for example, traditionally admits
very few refugees to its territory but makes a significant financial contribution to supporting refugees. Many host countries in the developing
world have the space to host refugees, but could neither afford to
make a financial contribution to support refugees elsewhere, nor
finance refugees on their territory without development assistance.

There is a good case for a baseline of common commitment. It is
probably symbolically valuable that every state should commit to
admitting at least a certain number of refugees onto its territory
through resettlement. This may be necessary to elicit sufficient aggregate provision of asylum around the world.[9] Similarly, every state
should make a minimum token financial contribution. Such acts of
commission symbolize participation. But, generally, divergences in
preferences and capacities offer opportunities for specialization and
exchange, which makes everyone better off than they would be by
acting uniformly.

The principles of burden-sharing and comparative advantage are
therefore crucial for efficiently and effectively meeting all of the
objectives outlined in the section above. But neither one is adequately
recognized under the existing system. There is no established
burden-sharing framework in the refugee regime. And there is no
explicit recognition of the value of an approach based on comparative
advantage.

So what are the best mechanisms for allocating responsibilities
among different countries? There are a number of options for allocating responsibilities: they can be ranged along a spectrum between
law and ad hoc agreements.

The limitations of law

At the moment, the mechanisms in place are predominantly reliant
on law. In theory refugee law creates an absolutely uniform distribution of responsibility: all states have to admit refugees onto their
territory. But refugee law is no longer effective, and is increasingly
ignored by governments. As the European migration policy expert

Liz Collett has suggested, international treaties are rather like fairies: if you stop believing in them they die.[10] Less glibly, this takes us back to the concept of a 'legal fiction' as a device for coordinating behaviour. Where legal fictions work, they do so primarily because people expect others to comply with the rules and so do so themselves. In turn, this expectation is based on a widespread recognition of the legitimacy of the rules. Achieving compliance through penalties alone requires the full apparatus of a repressive state, and the international community is very far from such an entity. Today, the belief in refugee law as sacrosanct is breaking down because of the manifest dysfunctionality of the current refugee regime. The dysfunction does not stem from non-compliance with the rules, but from incoherent objectives and a lack of clear means to achieve them.

Law can be effective. It influences the behaviour of some states towards some refugees some of the time. But as growing non-compliance with refugee law reveals, its influence has limits. A growing number of signatory states from Europe to East Africa to Australasia are increasingly prepared to ignore the 1951 Convention. And as we observed in the Introduction, some of the most generous host countries around the world – every major host country in the Middle East, South-East Asia, and South Asia, for instance – are non-signatories to the 1951 Convention. These observed patterns confirm the political scientist Steve Krasner's observation that states will comply with international law when it aligns with their interests.[11] But when norms and interests come into tension, most states will side with their own interests. And yet pro-refugee rights advocacy and policy-making is dominated by a dogmatic insistence that reciting international law is the most effective way to influence state behaviour.

It is not that international law has no role to play; it certainly does. It is rather that its relevance should be an empirical question rather than an assumption. Under what conditions is international law effective as a mechanism for coordinating responsibilities across states? The reason we should value refugee law is insofar as it continues to guarantee reciprocity and collective action between states. The norms of the refugee regime continue to offer an important minimal-level safeguard for the rights of refugees. They uphold the taboo against returning people to serious harm and offer an authoritative source through which advocates can seek to hold governments accountable for flagrant rights violations.

But we cannot rely on international law alone. In the absence of a global sovereign, adherence to rules becomes reliant upon coordination and legitimacy rather than enforcement. International law still has a role to play, but as a codifier of norms that command widespread acceptance. The foundation for such acceptance is that a proposed refugee regime should be ethically and practically defensible. That is why clarity of objectives and the means of achieving them are essential, and why their absence dooms the current legal regime to widespread non-compliance. A legal regime that meets widespread non-compliance is not just futile but highly damaging. Inadvertently it undermines habits of compliance with other laws.

Hence, the most viable use of law to supplement gaps in the existing legal framework is unlikely to come from the negotiation of new multilateral treaties. Instead, what is often called soft law – the consolidation of existing bodies of law within authoritative non-binding guidelines – offers a particularly useful route through which to clarify states' obligations in areas that may currently be ambiguous but which would be widely recognized as reasonable. For example, as the challenge of internal displacement was recognized during the 1990s, governments did not negotiate a new formal treaty. Instead, a small group of think tanks and governments consolidated existing refugee, human rights, and humanitarian law into a single authoritative document called the *Guiding Principles on the Rights of Internally Displaced Persons*. Today it shapes governments' response to internal displacement, and may offer a precedent that might be used to develop similarly authoritative guidance to states on how they should reciprocally treat people fleeing desperate circumstances that often fall outside most states' interpretations of who is a refugee within international law.

Reframing regionalism

Refugee movements vary across regions. Consequently, part of the history of the refugee regime has been the development of regional regimes adapted to the needs of particular parts of the world. The 1969 OAU Convention, the 1984 Cartagena Declaration, and the series of European Council directives to emerge on asylum after 2004 all created definitions of a refugee that differ slightly from the globally recognized norm. They were adapted to suit the needs of the regions at the time. Furthermore, regional human rights regimes, like the European Convention on Human Rights (ECHR) and the Inter-American Convention on Human Rights (ACHR) have heard cases that adapt the entitlements of refugees and people displaced across borders in accordance with changing circumstances.

The highest-profile experiment in regional policy relating to refugees is obviously the European Union. And, to this point, it has revealed itself a catastrophic failure. The EU's Common European Asylum System (CEAS) emerged as an outcome of the development of a common market. If Europe was to break down its internal borders, it would logically also need a common asylum policy. A whole apparatus emerged to support this, including the series of directives and the Dublin system explained in Chapter 3. The goals were laudable: to avoid an inequitable distribution of responsibility across the EU and a 'race to the bottom' in terms of protection standards for refugees. But, ultimately, the outcomes have been a disaster – leading precisely to unequal distribution of responsibility and beggar-thy-neighbour dynamics across Europe. Faced with the mass influx of the post-2015 European refugee crisis, Germany, Sweden, Hungary, Greece, and Italy took in disproportionately high numbers compared to the other twenty-three member states. And this in turn unleashed deterrence policies – from the seizure of assets to unilateral border closures to drastic cuts in benefits for asylum-seekers – that viciously undercut the spirit of harmonized standards. The Dublin system collapsed, and EU member states were unable to renegotiate a new deal on responsibility-sharing.

It was the failure of the EU's internal asylum policies that led it to focus on developing an external dimension. And the EU–Turkey deal, with all its attendant weaknesses, embarrassments, and unintended consequences, became the default focus of the EU's attempts to create a viable governance mechanism. So what role should regions play in refugee governance? Well, it depends on the particular region in question, and notably the geography of the region and the extent of development of its regional cooperation in other areas.

In the EU's case, its CEAS should evolve in a number of ways. Most obviously, it needs a *refugee* policy rather than just an *asylum* policy. This entails considering its role vis-à-vis refugees in the wider world rather than simply those that arrive in Europe. It requires the full tool-box of trade and development policies, areas in which the EU should excel, to be deployed to enhance the quality of protection in the areas in which most of the world's refugees reside. A relatively minor component of its refugee policy should be a *resettlement* scheme that enables some refugees in protracted situations who no longer have a credible prospect of return to be matched with, and equitably allocated to, particular EU member states. Finally, in response to the chaos of mass spontaneous arrival, it needs a system that manages a prospective influx in a way that does not endanger lives.

One option would be to have common EU reception areas in Greece and Italy where the claims could be assessed. But this would still amount to luring people into the arms of the people-smugglers, inadvertently favouring those who are well-off and irresponsible. A better approach would therefore be to use the EU embassies that are already present in host countries as the route by which applications for asylum and related matters of visas for work and family reunification, and humanitarian visas, could be processed.

Not just in Europe but around the world, regions offer an important level of governance for cooperation on refugees. In the Middle East, South-East Asia, and South Asia, in which most states are non-signatories to the 1951 Convention, the development of regional refugee frameworks could have significant benefits. These are regions that face significant levels of displacement, including due to natural disasters, and at times the challenge of major refugee emergencies. Gradually creating regional standards could enable them to develop common standards, build mutually beneficial cooperation based on the principles of burden-sharing and comparative advantage, and have greater bargaining power to engage with the wider international community on refugee issues.

Reaching global agreement is often a nightmare: the World Trade Organization, which has a rule of unanimity, has not been able to conclude a single trade agreement in its entire history of over two decades. In response, regional trade agreements have become common as a feasible alternative, and the same should be possible for refugee agreements.

Pragmatic partnerships

The post-war United Nations system was based on a particular view of the scope and form of international agreements: that they should be enduring and multilateral. Sometimes these characteristics may be justifiable.

Creating a long-term agreement ensures repeated interaction over time. Unlike single interactions, repeated interactions create 'the shadow of the future' and this encourages states to reciprocate, knowing that if they free-ride now, someone else may free-ride in the future. In game theory, the famous trap known as the Prisoner's Dilemma arises because it is set up as a one-round game; repeated play normally evolves into happier outcomes.

Occasionally, multilateral makes sense. The scope of a problem may be global in nature, and it may involve a pure global public good for which the externalities extend almost equally to every government in the world. This is the case with climate change. Sometimes multilateralism is not just desirable but essential because of a weakest-link problem. For example, the eradication of smallpox was only made possible as a result of universal compliance.

Whether a particular problem requires the full Monty of an enduring global agreement depends upon its specific features. There is nothing axiomatic that makes such an approach generally necessary or even desirable. Rather than being dogmatic about the scope and form of international agreements, the chief criterion for selection should be what works. The underlying purpose of any agreement – legal or otherwise – is to identify areas of 'mutual gain' that make all participating actors better off than they otherwise would be while promoting the objectives of ensuring rescue and autonomy for refugees.

For some policy challenges, there may be more pragmatic ways to ensure collective action than seeking binding agreements among all 195 of the sovereign nation-states that comprise the UN General Assembly. In many contexts and for particular policy issues or particular geographical contexts, agreements at the sub-global level may be more helpful, whether regional, inter-regional, or bilateral. Sometimes, groups that include non-state actors like business and civil society may be more appropriate to address challenges. There is nothing inherently superior to legalization over and above ad hoc agreements. It depends on the nature of the problem one is trying to solve.

Current debates on reforming the refugee regime are stymied by three flawed assumptions about international cooperation: that such a regime must be exclusively about states, that it must be multilateral, and that its sole focus must be humanitarian. These assumptions condemn the efforts of even the best-intentioned participants to failure. In order to address the many gaps left by existing international law they must be transcended.

Beyond the state

In most spheres the world has moved on from state-centric approaches. Protecting refugees is about more than states; it is about the relationship *between* states, markets, and society, all of which have important roles to play. Business is increasingly important in refugee policy. At the global level, a range of foundations and multinational corporations have become actively involved in funding or supporting refugee assistance through sharing products and processes, from the Ikea Foundation's now famous co-development of the flat pack refugee-housing unit with UNHCR to LinkedIn's attempt to engage in jobs-matching for Syrian refugees in Sweden, to the Vodafone Foundation's development of a tablet-based system called 'school-in-a-box' for camp-based refugee education.

But even at a more local level, business matters as a contributing actor. In Uganda, for instance, the Ugandan social entrepreneur Moses Musaazi has developed a product called the Makapad. It is a female sanitary product made from sustainable papyrus leaves. The product is produced in factories located in the Kyaka II refugee settlement that almost exclusively employ refugees. The products are then sold directly to UNHCR to distribute to refugees within the settlements. The business has not only created jobs for many refugees, and provided efficiently produced products for refugees, but has also led to the creation of a sustainable and award-winning business for Musaazi, which he has subsequently worked to scale to the wider Ugandan market.

Civil society also offers an important and neglected contribution, with a role to play in both host and resettlement countries. Earlier we showed how in Uganda the refugee-led community organization YARID has provided a range of forms of social protection within the community, as well as vocational training as a pathway to jobs. It is far from alone. In the same city, the Bondeko Refugee Livelihoods Centre and Hope of Children and Women Victims of Violence (HOCW) are refugee-led organizations supporting their communities. In Nairobi, the Somali-led organization Urban Refugee Community Development Organization (URCDO) provides similar support. These kinds of organizations are largely locked out of the formal structures of global governance. To a lesser extent, national civil-society organizations are also bypassed by the international system. Of the overall $25bn a year humanitarian assistance budget, just 0.2 per cent goes to national civil-society organizations. Such organizations – whether run by refugees or locals – offer major advantages: they are ideally placed, cost-efficient, and knowledgeable first-line responders. The clear implication is that refugee governance needs better ways to engage and partner with local actors; it needs a 'localization' agenda to devolve resources to where they are most efficiently used. Empowering such organizations can come through reallocating a share of the existing global humanitarian budget but also through innovative peer-to-peer support networks that bypass formal international institutions.

For several decades, Canada has operated a private sponsorship model for refugee resettlement. The model allows citizens individually or collectively to propose and take full responsibility for the resettlement of a refugee. They take on responsibilities for resettlement that are usually assumed by the public sector, including proposing the applicant; arranging and paying for travel; meeting the refugee on arrival; providing accommodation, clothing, and household goods; offering orientation relating to local services such as transportation and banking; enrolling children in school; and providing advice relating to employment. The commitment usually lasts for one year or up to whenever a refugee becomes self-sufficient, with refugees who are not self-sufficient after one year going into the social-assistance system.

Since the scheme began in 1978, a total of 250,000 refugees have received support through private sponsorship, comprising one third of the total resettled. Private sponsorship is most commonly offered by a relative or someone with a link to the resettlement country but it can also be offered by families, faith-based organizations, and – increasingly – businesses such as law firms. Each place costs approximately $12,600 per refugee.[12] The documented advantages of the scheme have included channelling public engagement to support refugees, reducing costs to government, allowing family reunification, supporting integration, and providing a viable alternative to irregular migration.

Business and civil society therefore have important contributions to make. As has been noted across many other policy fields, there has been a surge in the role of private authority in global governance, and the refugee regime is no exception. But we should also not romanticize or exaggerate the extent of the contribution. Privatization is certainly not a panacea within refugee governance. Private organizations should be understood as a complement to, rather than a substitute for, the role of the state. Public authority continues to be central to refugee governance both in its own right and also in order to enable an effective and ethical role for private actors.

Markets rely on public institutions to function efficiently. Likewise, in order for private actors to contribute to global refugee governance, international institutions are still needed to create incentives for action, set ethical standards, fill gaps left by the market, ensure coherence, create systems of accountability, and provide the overarching regulatory framework. This role is all the more important in dealing with vulnerable populations such as refugees.

Beyond multilateralism

This complementarity points to the possibility for partnerships between a wide variety of actors. Refugee governance does not simply imply multilateralism. Particular initiatives might be developed by drawing upon the complementary contributions of particular actors.

Public–private collaborations offer a means to draw in government, international organizations, NGOs, business, academia, and civil society to pilot and prototype innovative solutions, and – where appropriate – bring them to scale.

The Jordanian development areas pilot project illustrates the potential of such partnerships. It did not arise because of an initiative of the United Nations or by waiting for the entire multilateral system to act in unison. It emerged from the initiative of a small group of actors with complementary interests and comparative advantages: the Jordanian and British governments, the World Bank, an Amman-based think tank called the WANA Institute, the European Commission, and the initial enthusiasm of some key business actors such as the Ikea Foundation and Asda. A relatively small coalition was able to get the project up and running and gradually bring on board new partners as the project progressed. The example illustrates how public–private partnership may open avenues for the job creation needed to ensure refugees' access to autonomy in exile.

Another example of a creative initiative relates to the idea of using 'preference matching' for refugee resettlement, which was an idea developed by the Nobel-Prize winning economist Alvin Roth.[13] It offers a way in which two parties to a transaction can express their preferences regarding outcomes, and then have them 'matched' so that they are better off than they otherwise would be. Matching can be defined as 'an allocation of resources where both parties to the transaction need to agree to the match in order for it to take place'. It has more commonly been applied to areas such as school choice, kidney exchange, and hospital residency.

Recently, two academics, Will Jones and Alex Teytelboym, explored how matching markets might be applied to refugees.[14] They argued that matching potentially offers a way in which refugees can be consulted about their preferred resettlement destinations, resettlement countries can be consulted on the types of refugees they wish to receive, and refugees and states can be matched. At an international level, here is how the scheme would work for refugees. First, quotas would be determined for the overall number of refugees each country is prepared to resettle under the scheme. Second, a decision would be made about what criteria would be permitted as valid for state or refugee priorities. This would be an ethical and political choice that would need to bear in mind the consequences for third parties. For example, the sort of educational, gender, and income-related selectivity that has inadvertently happened as a result of the Syrian exodus to Germany would be unlikely to meet ethical standards. Third, the scheme elicits the priorities and capacities of both countries (or their sub-regions) and the preferences of refugees. Finally, a centralized process is needed to undertake the match (this might be at a UN level, a regional level, or a national level, for instance).

The scheme offers an example of how creative institutional design can enable both refugees and host countries to be better off than they otherwise would be. Refugees get to express a preference on destination where they often do not. States get to consider the types of refugees they believe they can best integrate – subject of course to any caveats based on ethical considerations.

The idea has already been applied, albeit at the national level. Jones and Teytelboym created a non-profit organization called Refugees' Say as the vehicle through which to build and disseminate the related algorithms. Their first pilot has been a 'local refugee match' within the United Kingdom. Working with the UK government, they have developed a pilot match between refugees and local communities for resettled Syrian refugees.

A variation on multi-stakeholder approaches is the notion of mini-multilateralism, which can be defined as small groups of states, and occasionally other actors, cooperating at a sub-global level. It enables small 'coalitions of the willing' to forge ahead with mutually beneficial collaboration even in the absence of full multilateral consensus. The conceptual logic for that is that certain forms of response to particular refugee challenges may be club goods rather than global public goods. In other words, they may confer costs and benefits on a particular group of states rather than all states.

Some of the most creative governance innovations relating to forced displacement in recent years have taken on this form. For example, between 2013 and 2015, the governments of Norway and Switzerland convened a government-led informal process called the Nansen Initiative to consider ways in which states can address issues relating to cross-border displacement in the context of natural disasters. With a formal route into UN-level institutional change blocked, the main reform route identified by Nansen was to try to work through the regional level, with a series of regional consultations.

Beyond humanitarianism

We need to recognize that refugees are not just, or even predominantly, a humanitarian issue. They lie at the intersection of a range of policy fields: humanitarianism, development, migration, human rights, post-conflict reconstruction, disaster risk reduction, and state-building. The objectives outlined above rely upon solutions that emanate from and cut across issue-areas. Rescue requires a primarily humanitarian response. Autonomy requires a primarily development response. A route out of limbo requires input from post-conflict reconstruction and state-building. Managed onward movement requires migration expertise.

This in turn requires that no refugee organization can simply be a humanitarian agency; it must also have skills and expertise in other areas. Refugee protection cannot simply fall within the mandate of any one organization; it requires input from the World Bank and its private-sector arm, the International Finance Corporation, the United Nations Development Programme (UNDP), the International Organization for Migration (IOM), the Office of the High Commissioner for Human Rights (OHCHR), and the UN Security Council, and many regional actors such as the African Development Bank.

This further suggests that no organization should be allocated a monopoly status relating to refugee protection. Within the United Nations system, refugees are seen primarily as a humanitarian issue, and UNHCR is treated as though it is the lead agency on refugees, being the anointed gatekeeper through which all other actors aspiring to work with refugees must pass. Yet refugees cannot simply be seen as a 'UNHCR issue'.

RETHINKING ORGANIZATIONS

An effective lead refugee agency is desperately needed to ensure collective action. New agreements are needed that equitably and efficiently allocate responsibilities among states and non-state actors. Some of these may be of a legal character, others will be more ad hoc. Our proposed system requires a facilitator capable of supporting a range of functions, including agenda-setting, negotiation, implementation, monitoring, and enforcement. Building on what already exists may make sense. But our model would require a very different kind of UNHCR, as well as input from organizations with increasingly relevant competences like the World Bank.

The primary purpose of international organizations is to facilitate collective action. The current UNHCR is effective at fulfilling some of the downstream functions of collective action: it has become an operational agency and it is good at humanitarian aid delivery. But it has become desperately weak in other areas. It follows rather than leads the political agenda. It offers legal advice to governments but is often simply ignored. And it manages the misery of protracted refugee situations rather than doing the political deals to end them.

An agency is needed that can become the broker, facilitating new agreements between governments. Rather than being reactive to the inclinations of the lowest-common-denominator states, or an inert guardian of an anachronistic regime, such an agency needs to be proactively setting the agenda. It should be strategically deploying its expert and moral authority to lead states to outcomes that can be simultaneously 'win–win' for donors, hosts, and refugees. It should become the organization that leads from the front, capable of matching a vision of the future to a finely attuned understanding of the changing nature of global, national, and local politics.

This ability to be a facilitator requires such an organization to rethink its relationship to politics. Too often its statutory 'non-political character', originally conceived to distance UNHCR from Cold War ideologies, has been misconstrued as implying that they should not be politically engaged. There are few things more political than arguing for the entitlements and opportunities of non-citizens. To be effective, an agency has to understand the political context of its work and be capable of channelling power and interests into better outcomes for refugees.

All of the pillars of our reimagined refugee regime require an agency that is an effective facilitator. They necessitate an organization willing and able to engage with policy trade-offs and to identify areas of mutual gain. Our vision for development areas to be provided in all the major repeat-host countries around the world needs political deals to be done across North–South lines, and with public and private actors. Ensuring that people can have a route out of limbo requires intelligent bargaining with state and non-state actors.

For it to fulfil this role, UNHCR would need to retool. It is currently overloaded with lawyers and operational technocrats. This inclines it towards playing two functions: offering legal guidance to states – to take or leave – and operational humanitarian delivery, mainly in refugee camps. While these functions will continue to matter, they are ultimately not the most important ones. Today, politics and economics are the factors determining outcomes for refugees, and yet UNHCR has extremely limited professional competence in these areas.[15] While the organization claims to be gradually changing – to embrace a development-based approach, for example – its human and monetary resources remain overwhelmingly focused on increasingly outmoded functions.

A reformed UNHCR should do more by doing less. Its key functions should be political facilitation and expert authority. Were it to get these two right it could wind down the function that currently consumes most of its attention: humanitarian aid delivery. UNHCR does not need to monopolize the refugee space; it can and should share the refugee mandate with other official agencies, and cooperate with NGOs, civil-society organizations, refugees themselves, and businesses.

UNHCR's greatest past successes came when it played the role of an effective facilitator. During the Indochinese Comprehensive Plan of Action and CIREFCA processes of the late 1980s and early 1990s that we discussed in earlier chapters, it played a political facilitation role, proactively setting the agenda. Working collaboratively with other agencies, including development, migration, and security actors, it established dedicated analytical capacity. It was also no coincidence that at the time it had recently promoted and nurtured a small but talented group of staff, which included Sergio Vieira de Mello, Leonardo Franco, Kofi Annan, Shashi Tharoor, Erika Feller, and Irene Khan, all of whom went on to very senior international leadership positions.[16]

Amazingly, amid increasingly intense public debate on the ongoing relevance of the 1951 Convention, UNHCR has largely escaped scrutiny. It is critical that we have a UN refugee agency that works, even if its ultimate role is relatively limited. The importance of getting a treaty is more debatable because it's unclear how much we need law, but effective organizations are indispensable. UNHCR's core donor states would stand to gain enormously from the organization's reform. They would have nothing to fear from its becoming more proactive and politically engaged. Rather, all states would gain from having organizations that are better adapted to the needs of the twenty-first century, and can achieve more effective outcomes with fewer resources.

THE REFORM PROCESS

So how can we get from where we are to where we need to be? We are well aware that there will be obstacles and objections. Institutions always resist change. An entrenched status quo based on decades of path-dependency inevitably builds in a series of vested interests. Inertia to change is to some extent normal. Many lawyers depend for their livelihoods, and their sense of purpose, on viewing refugee protection through an exclusively legal prism. Humanitarian professionals have a strong interest in preserving the centrality of care and maintenance to the refugee regime. No organization wishes to relinquish power by opening up to a greater role for others. But all of these sources of resistance will need to be confronted.

Ultimately, the only place where change can begin is with the initiative of the big donor governments: he who pays the piper calls the tune. The biggest funders to the refugee regime are the United States, Japan, Canada, Australia, and the European states, and they are the ones who have the capacity to ask for meaningful change. Common action may be impeded by differences in their politics as regards refugees. Attitudes in Canada, for example, are very different from those in Australia. But they can now be presumed to share recognition that the current system has failed.

What has been missing has been a realistic alternative. We have not provided a blueprint and this has been deliberate. Change does not occur by organizations gratefully adopting the plans of others. We have tried to do something more modest: set out the objectives that a defensible system should have, and the basic means by which these objectives could be achieved.

There are a range of mechanisms for accelerating institutional reform. Global commissions have a mixed track record. From the Brundtland Commission to the Commission on Global Governance, to the Global Commission on International Migration, quasi-autonomous panels appointed by the UN Secretary-General have sometimes come up with interesting and sensible recommendations for change but at other times created paper reports for politicians to ignore. Meanwhile, state-led informal initiatives with clear mandates have often offered a better route for change, as the examples of the Brookings–Bern Project that led to the development of internally displaced person governance and the Nansen Initiative on disaster-induced displacement illustrate.[17]

The United Nations has initiated a formal reform process. On 19 September 2016 it convened a High-Level Meeting on Refugees and Migrants at the margins of the UN General Assembly. At the meeting, 193 member states committed to a declaration, which included some important ideas: refugee camps should be the exception, all refugee children should have a right to an education, and refugees are a shared global responsibility. The meeting also committed states to work over a two-year period on two further Global Compacts to supplement the refugee system: one on refugees and the other on safe, orderly, and regular migration.[18] It remains to be seen whether these rhetorical and paper-based commitments will ultimately change the behaviour of governments. But, regardless, what has been missing from the UN process is a transformative vision for the future of refuge, or a strategic plan for how to effect change on the ground. Now that the former High Commissioner has been promoted to be the Secretary-General, he is in an ideal position to learn from the deficiencies of his former agency and lead radical change.

Our proposed approach places the emphasis on pragmatic operational changes on the ground rather than the negotiation of lofty, abstract principles. Ours is a call for prototypes that create new ways to ensure rescue, autonomy, and a route out of limbo for refugees. It is designed to adapt to specific contexts, with the focus on the countries that host the overwhelming majority of the world's refugees. Our plan can be implemented gradually and this gives it the advantage of being able to begin in those parts of the world where actors are willing to engage, and then gradually gain momentum towards wider institutional reform based on iterative learning. In short, encourage agencies to pilot an approach based on development areas in particular regional havens, modify it through learning-by-doing, and then try to replicate it more widely. The ambition should be transformative but the starting point pragmatic.

PART III: HISTORY, THE REMAKE

9

Back to the Future

In Part I we set out the tragedy of the Syrian refugee crisis from its antecedents in the creation of institutions to its denouement in the deportation of refugees from Greece. In Part II we set out a new approach to global refugee policy, one anchored not in camps, court decisions, and panic, but in needs and how they could best be met. In this final chapter we face that approach with three questions. We look back, indulging in a fantasy of counterfactual history. Had our approach been in place in 2011, how would the Syrian crisis have been likely to evolve? Then we look forward, and consider whether our approach can travel, and what it might look like if implemented in, say, Kenya. Finally, we tackle head on some of the possible obstacles lying in the path of building consensus around the approach.

THE SYRIAN REFUGEE CRISIS REPLAYED

What became the Syrian refugee crisis was determined by just four critical decisions. The first was indeed barely a decision at all: it was a sin of omission. As refugees poured across the borders into the neighbouring countries seeking safe haven, the major donors largely sat on their hands. The three governments of the regional havens were left to cope with a huge refugee influx with utterly inadequate international support. As we have seen, the government of Jordan received refugees amounting to at least a tenth of its population: the equivalent influx to Germany would have been 8 million. Even the influx of half a million has led the German government to complain bitterly that other European governments are not shouldering enough of the burden. While this failure to fund was predominantly the passive response of inertia, at times it went beyond a sin of omission. In 2014 the German government did revisit its funding decision for UNHCR in Jordan: it halved its contribution.

Unsurprisingly, the governments of the neighbouring havens became increasingly restive as the numbers continued to mount. Jordan closed its borders to further refugees; Turkey opened its coastal borders so that the refugees who had already arrived could leave by means of the people-smugglers. Unsurprisingly, some refugees started to do so.

This led inexorably to the second critical decision: that of Chancellor Merkel to unilaterally repudiate the Dublin Agreement whereby refugees would be returned to the first EU country of arrival. This had three inadvertent consequences. The immediate one was that through the huge ensuing expansion in the people-smuggling business, thousands of people drowned. Tempted to risk their lives, these people would otherwise have remained in the regional havens. The delayed consequence was that the large and sudden influx into Germany and Sweden rapidly changed sentiment from benevolent welcome to resentment and fear.

The change in Swedish sentiment led the Swedish government to reverse its open-door policy, closing its border to refugees, leading the Danish government to do the same. For good measure, the Swedish government decided to switch half of its aid budget from support for poor countries to support for the refugees who had arrived in Sweden. The change of German sentiment had a more far-reaching effect. It triggered a third critical decision, also that of Chancellor Merkel. The thousands of refugees in transit to Germany would be denied admission and would instead be returned to Turkey. To get a truculent Turkish president to agree to accept returning refugees, Chancellor Merkel committed to a somewhat embarrassing package, of which €6bn of financing was the least controversial component. This had the unintended consequence of alerting the governments of other countries which were providing regional haven that they could use their refugee populations as a bargaining chip. As we have seen, an early successful opportunistic use of refugees as hostages was by the government of Kenya.

The unilateral suspension of the Dublin Agreement and the package secretly negotiated between Chancellor Merkel and President Erdoğan faced the European Commission with its own decision point. The Commission could either push back against them or endorse them. It chose to endorse them. It further chose to reinforce them by instigating a rule for reallocating the refugees already en route to Germany to other member countries. The governments of some member countries voted against this proposal, and accepted practice was to adopt such proposals only once there was unanimity. For the first time, the Commission decided to abandon this practice.

This had a third unintended consequence. Britain was already in the late stages of a referendum on whether to remain in the EU. The perceived mismanagement of the refugee crisis by the Commission, and the perceived dominance of its decisions by Germany, were recognized as gift-horses by the Leave campaigners. Their final mass poster, under the banner 'Breaking Point', was of people flocking towards the German border, and its final slogan was 'Take Back Control'. Subsequent analysis of the vote suggests that this was decisive: the key decisions of the refugee crisis inadvertently resulted in the people of one of the largest member countries of the European Union deciding to leave it.

The final unintended consequence of these critical decisions is that as far as can be determined, around half of all Syrians with a university education are now in Europe. Syria has been gutted of the people who will be needed to rebuild its institutions and economy. The recovery of a future post-conflict Syrian society has been retarded.

There, in one page, is a modern tragedy. The inadvertent outcomes: drownings, refugees reimagined as hostages, Brexit, and the prospect of heightened post-conflict fragility. And for what? Four million refugees remain without proper opportunities in the regional havens. Meanwhile, less than a million of the most qualified are kept idle in Europe, costing $135 for every $1 provided to those in the havens. Is any politician seriously going to defend what has happened?

A tragedy is a sequence of events that unfold inexorably to a terrible end, but for which there is some 'if only' that, had decisions been different, would have averted it. It is time to remake history.

As Syria descended into mass violence, and the displaced headed across the borders, a reinvigorated UNHCR, together with a newly mandated World Bank, would have brought into action its standard approach. Generous funding would have been assured because the model of 'crisis – shake the tin' would have been replaced by the regular contributions that had funded disaster insurance.[1] Much of Europe's contribution may well have been organized by, and channelled through, the European Commission.

As a result, the immediate care of refugees would not have burdened regional governments. This emergency response would have rapidly evolved to a further standard phase: the development areas. The governments of the haven countries would already have known about the opportunities that this could bring and may well have competed with each other to attract international firms and the relocation of Syrian businesses. They would not have closed their borders to refugees, nor opened their coasts to people-smugglers, because either act would constitute a fundamental breach of the agreed package.

With the prospect of employment in clusters where many of the workers were Syrian, many of those internally displaced within Syria would have chosen to become refugees. As Syria began to empty of its population this may even have increased the pressure on the various factions to reach a settlement. If so, this would be an attractive unintended consequence rather than an objective.

Some young Syrians would still have dreamed of Europe. Such people would be able to apply for resettlement to Europe, but only while in the development areas. The numbers accepted for resettlement would be determined by what each government was willing to offer, subject to an agreed symbolic minimum. Subject to this, some selection criteria would be allowed as legitimate. In addition alternative migration channels would be available through embassies and consulates. Anyone arriving on Europe's coasts courtesy of people-smugglers would be treated humanely, but – unless unable to access the necessary rights and opportunities nearer to home, or at particular risk – sent back to a functioning development area.

Finally, once peace returned to Syria, which it most surely will, most Syrians in the regional havens would return home: they were never voluntary migrants. However, were the conflict to have persisted for many years, some of those living in the havens would have forged new ties that made them want to stay. Others might seek resettlement elsewhere. They would have the right to do so.

OTHER CRISES AROUND THE WORLD

So having replayed the past for Syria, what might the future look like if our ideas were implemented elsewhere? To illustrate how they might have a transformative effect in other places, let's turn to Kenya.

As we saw in Chapter 5, Kenya represents a 'hard case' for our approach. Since the arrival of hundreds of thousands of Somali refugees and many South Sudanese since the early 1990s, its refugee policy has been almost diametrically opposed to our own model. The government has adopted an encampment policy, insisting that refugees remain in camps, and denying them the right to work. It has also insisted on abrogating all responsibility for refugees to international humanitarian agencies. These agencies have obliged, providing inadequate but indefinite assistance. One outcome has been the Dadaab camps – a collection of the most inhumane and intractable camps in the world, where many Somalis have lived without the most basic socio-economic freedoms for up to two decades.

The government has been persistently intransigent to any proposal to move beyond encampment and the result has been long-term humanitarian dependency. But as we further saw in Chapter 5, the situation got even worse in 2016 when the government threatened to expel all Somali refugees and to close its Department of Refugee Affairs.

But it does not have to be this way. Even in Kenya, we believe that our approach has something to offer. A close look at Kenya's refugee politics suggests that, with the right carrots and sticks, almost anything is possible. Even in 2016, the government has occupied almost every conceivable position on the spectrum. Yes, it threatened to expel almost the entire Somali refugee population. But it also came back from the brink, accepting a new deal on burden-sharing quietly offered by European donor states. Far less known, it has also embarked on a small-scale experiment to pilot refugee self-reliance in the newly opened Kalobeyei camp in the Turkana Valley region. At the time of writing, only a few thousand South Sudanese are in the camp but, unlike those in Dadaab, they have basic economic freedoms. The variety of these political positions suggests the malleability of the government when presented with the right package of international support.

Like our Jordanian example, Kenya could benefit from trade concessions. Unlike some developing countries its exports do not have unconditional access to European markets. It is eligible for concessions under the US government's African Growth and Opportunity Act (AGOA) but is not eligible for the EU's Everything But Arms (EBA) framework for Least Developed Countries. Indeed, at the time of writing, Kenya is explicitly under threat from the Trade Directorate of the European Commission of imminently losing its easy access to Europe's markets. This means that it could benefit from a 'carve out' for access to EU markets. Just as the EU has given Jordan's economic zones for refugees concessionary access to the garment sector, so too it could offer concessions in areas like agriculture, garments, and textiles to Kenya.

With the right trade concessions in place, business investment could be attracted to Kenya. The country already receives significant foreign direct investment and offers highly desirable infrastructure for business. But businesses keen to engage with refugees in Kenya have so far been put off from doing so by the inauspicious regulatory environment. Without the right to work, businesses cannot meaningfully engage. But the potential is there, from agriculture, to agro-processing, to manufacturing. Furthermore, if refugees could be relocated away from the remote, arid border areas of the North-Eastern Province, where Dadaab is based, the economic opportunities for all would be even greater. Mombasa, and the surrounding area, for instance – the area where many Somalis originally settled soon after arrival in 1991 – could offer opportunities.

Just as we discussed for Syria, supporting the human capital of Somalis in exile may offer a route to incubate the eventual reconstruction of one of the most archetypal fragile states. Somalia has undergone wave after wave of failed and abortive peace-building and repatriation. Part of the challenge is the 'Somali paradox': Somalis are among the most entrepreneurial and economically successful communities in exile but have a highly dysfunctional society back home. One reason for this difference is that the attributes for entrepreneurship are at the individual and family level while the attributes needed for successful governance lie at the social level. The competitive dynamics across families and kinship groups that encourage economic success abroad need to be complemented by the cooperative dynamics required for effective governance.

Here, greater freedom in exile may help. Just as we discussed in Chapter 7, incubation in the safe-haven country may directly shape behaviour following return. For instance, economic autonomy and political self-governance, especially when these allow people to work effectively across kinship groups, may help incubate the cooperative behaviours needed to rebuild governance back home.

With remarkable speed, our approach is indeed being taken up by a range of actors new to the refugee scene. In September 2016, President Obama convened a side meeting of the UN General Assembly at which a number of governments made pledges to change their refugee policies. In October, the Board of the World Bank approved a $300m loan on highly concessional terms for Jordan to re-equip industrial zones. This implemented a deal that the World Bank had brokered with the government, providing employment for 120,000 Syrian refugees. The Board also authorized a similar loan to Lebanon, the deal being to bring 300,000 Syrian children into schooling. These were the first loans that the World Bank had ever made concerning refugees. The new mandate was enthusiastically endorsed by the representatives of developed and developing countries alike. Other agencies are also taking up what is being termed 'the Jordan model'. DFID, the British development agency, has just brokered a deal with the government of Ethiopia and the European Commission to provide $500m of funding for a new industrial zone that will provide 100,000 jobs, many for refugees.[2] Angela Merkel is sufficiently enthusiastic about it for her, as we write, to be on a visit to Ethiopia to support the project. Theresa May is also planning a visit. Civil society is innovating as well. Both Refugee Cities, a new NGO, and the McKinsey Global Institute are drawing on private-sector expertise in establishing commercially viable industrial zones to bring jobs at scale to the haven countries.

CLARIFYING OUR APPROACH

We have not set out to solve every problem in the world. Instead, our focus has been clearly delineated: to come up with a workable system that can sustainably offer sanctuary to the world's refugees. Our challenge has been to identify an approach that can offer rescue, autonomy, and a pathway out of limbo to all refugees, not just a minority, while working within the constraints of the contemporary world.

At the heart of our approach is the creation of safe havens in the countries in the developing world that neighbour conflict and crisis. This is because it is where the overwhelming majority of refugees are, because remaining there creates the greatest likelihood that people will ultimately go back and rebuild their own countries, and because it offers a far more efficient and sustainable way to allocate scarce resources.

But safe havens cannot continue to be structured in the way they are today. The current camp-based humanitarian assistance model is failing and benefits nobody. It is inhumane and out of touch with the contemporary world. Understandably, people leave. The current model needs to be replaced with one that places the emphasis on autonomy and employment. If people can help themselves and their families, not only will they benefit but they will be better able to contribute to their host societies and to rebuild their own societies when they go home.

There is a spectrum of models of economic participation that will be differently relevant to different safe-haven countries. Uganda has allowed its nearly half a million refugees almost full participation in the economic life of the country. But not every country can adopt the Ugandan model. Jordan is embarking on an alternative route to offer jobs in economic zones. Different approaches will work for different contexts but the common theme is incubating people's capacities through economic empowerment.

To unlock this approach, new forms of partnerships are needed. Donors have to be prepared to commit the resources needed to address haven countries' concerns relating to refugees' right to work. They need to open up their markets in order to entice businesses to invest. Business investment has a central role to play. And new organizational models are needed in order to economically and politically facilitate these partnerships.

We believe that the model can provide autonomy and dignity to refugees, serve as a development opportunity for haven countries, and contribute to post-conflict reconstruction in countries like Syria. But what we have laid out is an approach, not a blueprint. There is still much to be worked out, and the evidence of effectiveness will be determined through piloting and prototyping. In order to assist with that, it's worthwhile for us to engage with some potential sources of criticism. Let's briefly look at three common objections.

What about the people who cannot go home? No refugee should be expected to remain indefinitely in limbo. At some given cut-off point, if there is no realistic prospect of an eventual return home, then an alternative pathway to assimilation in a new society should be offered. As we have suggested, this is where resettlement should be directed. At a prearranged cut-off point, which might be between five and ten years, if a designated independent body determines that no solution is in sight, then resettlement to a third country should be made available.

Does the approach prevent people migrating? Our goal is not to prevent people from moving. If people wish to be migrants, then alternative avenues, including labour migration and family reunification, may be adopted. But for refugees – as refugees – the need is for rescue and autonomy, not migration. Of course, they should have a right to move insofar as it necessary to access a viable safe haven within which this need is guaranteed. But, beyond that, migration is incidental to refuge. If we provide adequate safe haven closer to home, there are good grounds to believe refugees will be less likely to resort to smuggling networks and embark on dangerous journeys: unlike most other migrants, refugees have left because of desperation not aspiration. Importantly, though, the cart cannot come before the horse: if European governments are serious about reducing onward movement they must first invest in increasing economic opportunities in the safe-haven countries.

How can we prevent economic exploitation? Some people are concerned about the idea of creating employment opportunities for refugees because they believe that they risk exploitation by powerful corporations. Yet, when we listen to refugees, most simply want the opportunity to work, to support themselves and their families. The key is to ensure that the option to work is voluntary and that employment practices meet basic standards. Given the combination of international-organization oversight, media scrutiny, and the reputational concerns of large corporations, the risk of abuse is remote. Exploitation and abuse seem far more likely under the status quo whereby refugees work illicitly in the informal sector with no recourse to law or public scrutiny. Our approach is one that seeks to increase opportunities and choices for refugees, not to impose additional constraints.

REMAKING THE FUTURE

If politicians are not willing to defend what has actually happened, they face a choice. The default option is for them to hunker down and turn their attention to something completely different. The refugees have stopped coming to Europe: out of sight, out of mind. We know where this leads: to the inevitable mishandling of the next unanticipated crisis. Algeria? Kabul? Ukraine? Neither we nor anyone else can predict. But should global strategy simply be to count on there being no further refugee surges? Would any politician seriously defend such an approach?

So the approach that has been in place for decades has demonstrably failed, and we need another one. The alternative to the politics of the ostrich is to embrace change. Our politicians now need to pay sufficient attention to rethinking refugee policy for it to actually get changed. That change cannot be cosmetic.

In this book we have tried to formulate an alternative, using both our hearts and our heads. We are well aware of the gulf between ideas and actions. Getting from the pages of a book to actions that make a difference at scale for refugees will depend upon champions who overcome the inertia, self-interest, and cynicism by which the status quo has been preserved. Only in moments of crisis can changes to the international system be made, and so the scale of the challenge should not be discouraging but galvanizing. We hand over to you.

References

INTRODUCTION

1. This ratio is a broad estimate extrapolated from the Cologne Institute for Economic Research's estimate of the public-sector resource allocation to refugees in Germany and UNHCR's Annual Budget data on resource allocation to support refugees in host countries of first asylum. The Cologne Institute estimates that federal expenditure in Germany on 1 million refugees in 2016–17 will be $54.3bn. Meanwhile, in the same year, UNHCR will have an annual budget of around $6.5bn for a refugee population of concern of 16.1m (although in practice only a proportion of this funding is focused on refugees). This gives a ratio of 135:1. This ratio comes with three caveats: (i) these numbers are estimates based on limited available data; (ii) they include only costs incurred through public expenditure and do not account for the benefits or returns from refugees' economic contributions; (iii) they do not by themselves imply that the funding could or should simply be reallocated. We include them to show how relatively little money is supporting protection in the main safe-haven countries. See, for example, Russia Today, 'Asylum Seekers to Cost Germany €50bn within 2 Years – Forecast' (1 February 2016), https://www.rt.com/news/330869-germany-migrants-50bn-cost.

1. GLOBAL DISORDER

1. Although 21.3 million is the highest figure reported by UNHCR in any year since the Second World War, the way it has calculated its 'refugee' numbers has changed. The headline figure now includes the approximately 5 million Palestinian refugees, which were excluded from UNHCR's previous peak figure of 17.5 million during the Bosnia crisis in 1992. See, for example, the *Economist*, 'Daily Chart: The World's Refugee Crisis: Past and Present', http://www.economist.com/blogs/graphicdetail/2016/05/daily-chart-21.

2. These data are the latest available for 2015, published by UNHCR. See UNHCR, *Global Trends: Forced Displacement in 2015* (Geneva, 2016: UNHCR).

3. Leo Tolstoy's *Anna Karenina* begins: 'Happy families are all alike; every unhappy family is unhappy in its own way.'

4. Mary Kaldor, *New and Old Wars: Organized Violence in a Global Era* (Cambridge, 2012: Polity Press).

5. See Paul Collier and Anke Hoeffler, 'Do Elections Matter for Economic Performance?', *Oxford Bulletin of Economics and Statistics*, 77/1 (2015): 1–21.

6. Nicolas Berman, Mathieu Couttenier, Dominic Rohner, and Mathias Thoenig, *This Mine is Mine!*, OxCarre Working Paper 141 (2014), http://www.oxcarre.ox.ac.uk/files/OxCarreRP2014141.pdf.

7. Maddalena Agnoli, Lisa Chauvet, Paul Collier, Anke Hoeffler, and Sultan Mehmood, 'Democracy's Achilles Heel: Structural Causes of Flawed Elections and Their Consequences for Citizen Trust', unpublished paper, CSAE.

8. See Paul Collier, 'The Institutional and Psychological Foundations of Natural Resource Policies', *Journal of Development Studies* (forthcoming).

9. See P. Cirillo and N. N. Taleb, 'On the Statistical Properties and Tail Risk of Violent Conflicts', *Physica A: Statistical Mechanics and its Applications*, 452 (2016): 29–45.

10. See, for example, Ian Bremmer and Preston Keat, *The Fat Tail: The Power of Political Knowledge in an Uncertain World* (New York, 2010: Oxford University Press).

11. By 'honeypot' country, we mean a high-income economy, defined by the World Bank as one with a GNP/capita above $12,475 in 2015.

12. Calculated in terms of the aggregate total of the number of refugees hosted for each year across the period 1975–2015, excluding the Palestinians, whose situation is somewhat distinctive because of their quasi-permanent presence.

2. THE TIME-WARP

1. Claudena Skran, *Refugees in Inter-War Europe: The Emergence of a Regime* (Oxford, 1995: Oxford University Press); Phil Orchard, *A Right to Flee: Refugees, States, and the Construction of International Cooperation* (Cambridge, 2014: Cambridge University Press).

2. For analysis of the *Travaux préparatoires* of the 1951 Convention, see, for example, Andreas Zimmermann (ed.), *The 1951 Convention Relating to the Status of Refugees and Its 1967 Protocol: A Commentary* (Oxford, 2011: Oxford University Press); Paul Weis, *The Refugee Con-*

vention, 1951: The Travaux préparatoires Analysed (Cambridge, 1995: Cambridge University Press).

3. For a history of the refugee regime, see Alexander Betts, Gil Loescher, and James Milner, *UNHCR: The Politics and Practice of Refugee Protection*, 2nd edn (Abingdon, 2012: Routledge).

4. See, for example, Gil Loescher, *UNHCR and World Politics: A Perilous Path* (Oxford, 2001: Oxford University Press).

5. For example, other than these definitional adjustments, both the African and Latin American regional agreements otherwise simply adopt the 1951 Convention framework. Moreover, even in many of the African signatory countries to the OAU Convention, the 1951 'persecution'-focused definition is regularly used instead of the the wider 'serious disturbances to public order' definition.

6. This argument is made expecially effectively by James Milner in relation to Africa. James Milner, *Refugees, the State and the Politics of Asylum in Africa* (Basingstoke, 2009: Palgrave Macmillan).

7. Alexander Betts, *Survival Migration: Failed Governance and the Crisis of Displacement* (Ithaca, 2013: Cornell University Press).

8. Matthew Price, *Rethinking Asylum: History, Purpose, and Limits* (Cambridge, 2009: Cambridge University Press).

9. Alex has also grounded this idea in the related ethical concept of 'basic rights' in Betts, *Survival Migration*.

10. Serious physical harm would still be subject to interpretation. We would argue that it would include arbitrary deprivations of liberty as well as forms of psychological as well as merely physiological harm. It would thereby include most of the circumstances currently recognized as falling within the scope of 'persecution' but would be far less ambivalent about flight from conflict, natural disaster, and state fragility, for example.

11. The reasonable person standard is used in legal systems around the world. While it poses the challenge to define 'whose standard of reasonableness matters?', it allows for interpretive discretion and adaptation to contemporary circumstances.

12. Betts, *Survival Migration*.

13. Data on refugee recognition rates in Europe is published through Eurostat and by ECRE. For discussion, see EurActiv, 'Asylum Systems in Europe Remain Disparate', 22 September 2015, https://www.euractiv.com/section/justice-home-affairs/news/asylum-systems-in-europe-remain-disparate.

14. A suasion game is a game-theoretical situation that has been used to describe international cooperation problems in which the two layers have asymmetrical power. For application to the refugee regime,

see Alexander Betts, 'North–South Cooperation in the Refugee Regime: The Role of Linkages', *Global Governance*, 14/2, 2008, 157–78.

15. Alexander Betts, *Protection by Persuasion: International Cooperation in the Refugee Regime* (Ithaca, 2009: Cornell University Press).

16. For an overview of the Indochinese CPA see, for example, W. Courtland Robinson, *Terms of Refuge: The Indochinese Exodus and the International Response* (London, 1998: Zed Books).

17. See, for example, Milner, *Refugees, the State and the Politics of Asylum in Africa.*

18. This was the language used in a campaign against 'refugee warehousing' by the US Committee for Refugees and Immigrants in 2004.

19. Loescher, *The UNHCR and World Politics.*

20. Nina Hall, *Displacement, Development, and Climate Change: International Organizations Moving beyond Their Mandates* (Abingdon, 2016: Routledge).

21. These ideas were offered by Sarah Cliffe in a presentation at the Open Society Foundation in New York on 7 April 2016.

22. UNHCR 2014, 'Policy on Alternatives to Camps', (Genera: UNHCR), http://unhcr.org/uk/protection/statelessness/5422b8f09/unhcr-policy-alternatives-camps.html.

23. Thomas Gammeltoft-Hansen, paper presented at 'Rethinking the Global Refugee Protection System' conference, SUNY Global Center, New York City, 6 July 2016.

3. THE PANIC

1. Of course, the rumblings of the migrant crisis were in motion before 2011. For example, in 2006 the focus had been on movement from West Africa to Spain via the Canary Islands. Meanwhile, the movement of people from Libya to Lampedusa had been longstanding, albeit on a smaller scale and with less media and political attention.

2. UNHCR, 'Global Focus, UNHCR Operations Worldwide: Turkey' (2015), http://reporting.unhcr.org/node/2544.

3. *Guardian*, 'UN Agencies "Broke and Failing" in Face of Ever-Growing Refugee Crisis', 6 September 2015, https://www.theguardian.com/world/2015/sep/06/refugee-crisis-un-agencies-broke-failing.

4. The Case of M.S.S. v Belgium and Greece, ECtHR 2011. Application No. 30696/09.

5. Sergi Pardos-Prado, 'How Can Mainstream Parties Prevent Niche Party Success? Center-Right Parties and the Immigration Issue', *The Journal of Politics*, 77/2 (2015): 352–67.

6. *Guardian*, 'Libya No-Fly Resolution Reveals Global Split in UN', 18 March 2011, https://www.theguardian.com/world/2011/mar/18/libya-no-fly-resolution-split.

7. BBC, 'Migrant Crisis: Merkel Warns of EU "Failure"', 31 August 2015, http://www.bbc.co.uk/news/world-europe-34108224.

8. The data shows that while Syrians had already been coming to Europe in ever-increasing numbers since the summer of 2014, the peak arrival months in Europe were September and October. The number of Syrians seeking asylum in Europe was 77,692 for August; by October it had more than doubled to 159,226 for the month, with the majority going to Germany. At the end of July, the cumulative total of Syrian asylum-seekers in Europe stood at 372,105 and by the end of the year it was 903,545. http://data.unhcr.org/syrianrefugees/asylum.php.

9. Alexander Betts, 'Let Refugees Fly to Europe', *New York Times*, 24 September 2015.

10. Kelly Greenhill, *Weapons of Mass Migration: Forced Displacement, Coercion, and Foreign Policy* (Ithaca, 2010: Cornell University Press.)

11. For an excellent analysis of the data, see Pew Research Center, 'Number of Refugees to Europe Surges to Record 1.3 Million in 2015', http://www.pewglobal.org/2016/08/02/number-of-refugees-to-europe-surges-to-record-1-3-million-in-2015.

12. *The Times*, 'Germany's 300,000 "Lost" Refugees', 6 December 2015.

13. *Guardian*, 'EU Met Only 5% of Target for Relocating Refugees from Greece and Italy', 6 December 2016.

14. See, for example, James Traub, 'The Death of the Most Generous Nation on Earth', *Foreign Policy*, 10 February 2016, http://foreignpolicy.com/2016/02/10/the-death-of-the-most-generous-nation-on-earth-sweden-syria-refugee-europe.

15. *Guardian*, 'Switzerland Seizing Assets from Refugees to Cover Costs', 15 January 2016.

16. Empirically, it is worth noting that the numbers of people crossing the Aegean Sea had already begun to fall from January 2016, partly because of winter but also because Merkel collaborated with the EU to close the Balkan route and because Turkey had already begun to implement mobility controls at Germany's behest.

17. *Guardian*, 'EU-Turkey Deal to Return Refugees From Greece Comes into Force', 18 March 2016, https://www.theguardian.com/world/2016/mar/18/refugees-will-be-sent-back-across-aegean-in-eu-turkey-deal.

18. See for example, Kirby Swales, 'Understanding the Leave Vote' (London, 2016: National Centre for Social Research).

19. *Politico*, 'Merkel: Welcoming Refugees "Right Thing to Do"', 13 November 2015, http://www.politico.eu/article/merkel-welcoming-refugees-right-thing-to-do.

4. RETHINKING ETHICS

1. Jonathan Haidt, *The Righteous Mind: Why Good People are Divided by Politics and Religion* (New York, 2012: Vintage).
2. For applications of the duty of rescue to aid see Paul Collier, 'The Ethics of International Aid', in *The Oxford Handbook of International Political Theory*, eds. Chris Brown and Robyn Eckersley (Oxford, 2017: Oxford University Press).
3. Thomas Pogge, *World Poverty and Human Rights*, 2nd edn (Cambridge, 2008: Polity).
4. Matthew Gibney, *The Ethics and Politics of Asylum* (Cambridge, 2004: Cambridge University Press), p. 235.
5. Michael Walzer, *Spheres of Justice: A Defence of Pluralism and Equality* (Oxford, 1983: Martin Robertson).
6. Samuel Scheffler, 'Relationships and Responsibilities', *Philosophy and Public Affairs* 26/3 (1997): 189–209.
7. Kimberley Hutchings, *Global Ethics* (Cambridge, 2010: Polity), pp. 122–4.
8. Hannah Arendt, *The Origins of Totalitarianism* (London, 1986: André Deutsch); Emma Haddad, *The Refugee in International Society: Between Sovereigns* (Cambridge, 2008: Cambridge University Press).
9. Thomas Nagel, *Equality and Partiality* (Oxford, 1991: Oxford University Press).
10. Gibney, *Ethics and Politics of Asylum*.
11. Walzer, *Spheres of Justice*.
12. Seyla Benhabib, *The Rights of Others: Aliens, Residents, and Citizens* (Cambridge, 2004: Cambridge University Press).
13. Gibney, *Ethics and Politics of Asylum*, p. 236.
14. Ibid., p. 240.
15. Matthew Gibney argues that a just distribution of responsibility between states is an important normative goal both for its own sake and as a means to enhance the collective capacity of states to enable refugees to flourish. See Matthew Gibney, 'Refugees and Justice between States', *European Journal of Political Theory*, 14/4 (2015): 448–63.
16. James Hathaway and Alexander Neve have used the concept of 'common-but-differentiated responsibility-sharing' to suggest the value of comparative advantage in enabling states to collectively reduce the

aggregate cost of providing protection to refugees. See James Hathaway and R. Alexander Neve, 'Making International Refugee Law Relevant Again: A Proposal for Collectivized and Solution-Oriented Protection', *Harvard Human Rights Journal*, 10 (1997): 115–211.

17. *The New York Times*, 'Europe's Continuing Shame', 23 July 2016, p. 8.

18. James Hathaway, 'Why Refugee Law Still Matters', *Melbourne Journal of International Law*, 8/1 (2007): 89–103.

19. Karen Hargrave and Sara Pantuliano, 'Closing Borders: The Ripple Effects of Australian and European Refugee Policy', Policy Brief No. 66, (London, 2016: Overseas Development Institute), https://www.odi.org/sites/odi.org.uk/files/resource-documents/10868.pdf.

20. Refer back to Chapter 3.

21. See, for example, Ruud Koopmans, 'How to Make Europe's Immigration Policies More Efficient and More Humane', *Migration and Citizenship: Newsletter of the American Political Science Association*, 4/2 (2016): 55–9; and for debate on the empirical legacy of 'Wir schaffen das', see also Cathryn Costello, 'Europe's Refugee and Immigration Policies – Obligation, Discretion, Cooperation and Freeriding', *Migration and Citizenship: Newsletter of the American Political Science Association*, 4/2 (2016): 59–66, and Georg Menz, 'Europe's Odd Migration Policy Choices', *Migration and Citizenship: Newsletter of the American Political Science Association*, 4/2 (2016): 51–5.

22. See, for example, Clár Ní Chonghaile, 'People Smuggling: How It Works, Who Benefits and How It Can be Stopped', *Guardian*, 31 July 2015.

23. For an alternative view, see Thomas Spijkerboer, 'Fact Check: Did "Wir Schaffen Das" Lead to Uncontrolled Mass Migration?', Guest Blog, 28 September 2016, Oxford University Faculty of Law, https://www.law.ox.ac.uk/research-subject-groups/centre-criminology/centreborder-criminologies/blog/2016/09/fact-check-did-.

24. See, for example, Save the Children, 'Children on the Move in Europe: Save the Children's Response to the Deepening Child Refugee and Migrant Crisis in Europe', 26 July 2016, https://savethechildreninternational.exposure.co/children-on-the-move-in-europe. Other relevant data can be found on Eurostat, ec.europa.eu/eurostat/documents/2995521/7244677/3-02052016-AP-EN.pdf.

25. Gallup's 2007–9 surveys conducted in 135 countries found that around 700 million adults (or 16 per cent of the world's adult population) would like to migrate permanently if they had the opportunity. In sub-Saharan Africa this rose to 38 per cent of the adult population. Gallup, '700 Million Worldwide Desire to Migrate Permanently',

2 November 2009, http://www.gallup.com/poll/124028/700-million-worldwide-desire-migrate-permanently.aspx.

26. Of the authors who argue that there is a human right to migrate, stemming from basic liberal values, the most compelling arguments are offered by, for example: Kieran Oberman, 'Immigration as a Human Right', in *Migration in Political Theory: The Ethics of Movement and Membership*, eds. Sarah Fine and Lea Ypi (Oxford, 2016: Oxford University Press), and Joseph Carens, *The Ethics of Immigration* (Oxford, 2013: Oxford University Press).

27. See David Miller, *Strangers in Our Midst: The Political Philosophy of Immigration* (Cambridge, Mass., 2016: Harvard University Press).

28. David Rueda, 'Dualization, Crisis and the Welfare State', *Socio-Economic Review* 12/2 (2014): 381–407.

29. Sergi Pardos-Prado, 'How Can Mainstream Parties Prevent Niche Party Success? Center-Right Parties and the Immigration Issue', *The Journal of Politics*, 77/2 (2015): 352–67.

30. Brian Barry, 'The Quest for Consistency: A Sceptical View', in B. Barry and R. Goodin (eds.), *Free Movement: Ethical Issues in the Transnational Migration of People and of Money* (Hemel Hempstead, 1992: Harvester Wheatsheaf).

31. See Paul Collier, World Development (on AIDS) (2017).

32. Peter Singer and Renata Singer, 'The Ethics of Refugee Policy', in Mark Gibney (ed.), *Open Borders? Closed Societies? The Ethical and Political Issues* (Westport, 1988: Greenwood Press).

33. Ruben Atoyan et al., 'Emigration and Its Economic Impact on Eastern Europe', IMF Staff Discussion Note, July 2016, https://www.imf.org/external/pubs/ft/sdn/2016/sdn1607.pdf.

34. Martin Barber, *Blinded by Humanity: Inside the UN's Humanitarian Operations* (London, 2014: I.B. Tauris).

35. Seernels et al., 2014.

36. James Hathaway has also suggested this 'switch point' is about five years, on the grounds that social psychologists generally agree that this is about the time at which assimilation sets in in any case, and return becomes more difficult.

37. The underlying dilemma is about whether individual migrants from a particular society should share collective responsibility for their own soctieties, or whether their own individual freedom should be privileged. See, for example, Kieran Oberman, 'Can Brain Drain Justify Immigration Restrictions?', *Ethics*, 123/3 (2013): 427–55.

38. Presentation by Wolfgang Müller, Managing Director for European Affairs of the Bundesagentur für Arbeit, St Anne's College, Oxford, 7 September 2016.

39. *Guardian*, 'European Countries Mistreating Refugees in Cold Weather, Says UN', 13 January 2017.

40. As of September 2016, the far-right Alternative für Deutschland (AfD) had gained representation in ten of sixteen German state parliaments.

41. *Financial Times*, 19 July 2016.

5. RETHINKING HAVENS

1. Ben Rawlence, *City of Thorns: Nine Lives in the World's Largest Refugee Camp* (London, 2016: Portobello Books), p. 2.

2. This ratio is a broad estimate extrapolated from the Cologne Institute for Economic Research's estimate of the public-sector resource allocation to refugees in Germany and UNHCR's Annual Budget data on resource allocation to support refugees in host countries of first asylum.

3. Estimates of the impact of refugees on the European economy vary across a vast range. At one end of the spectrum, Philippe Legrain argues that refugees could boost Europe's GDP by up to 0.23 per cent per year by 2020 if the right policies are adopted. At the other end of the spectrum, Bernd Raffelhüschen suggests that each refugee is likely to cost Germany an average of €450,000.

4. Michael Walzer, *Spheres of Justice: A Defence of Pluralism and Equality* (Oxford, 1983: Martin Robertson).

5. In the jargon of economics, one might consider the optimization problem within the refugee regime as how to deliver rescue, autonomy, and a route out of limbo to all refugees at the lowest overall cost.

6. *Financial Times*, 'Refugees flock back to Syrian town as ISIS flees', 15 August 2016.

7. For example, Ipsos Mori showed that in September 2016 around 51 per cent of Europeans across twelve countries had a great deal of or some sympathy for Syrian refugees. However, there were significant concerns about allowing them into the country – relating mainly to national security, costs to government, and pressure on national welfare systems – with only 17 per cent suggesting they had no such concerns. See Ipsos Mori, 'Public Attitudes towards Refugees in Europe', September 2016, https://www.ipsos-mori.com/researchpublications/researcharchive/3786/Public-attitudes-towards-refugees-in-Europe.aspx.

Meanwhile, a recent study by Bansak et al. suggests that Europeans are more likely to support refugees when it is based on fair and orderly responsibility-sharing. See: Kirk Bansak, Jens Hainmueller, and Dominik Hangartner, 'Aristotelian Equality and International Cooperation:

Europeans Prefer a Proportional Asylum Regime', 2016, Stanford–Zurich Immigration Policy Lab Working Paper No. 16. https://ssrn.com/abstract=2843697 orhttp://dx.doi.org/10.2139/ssrn.2843697.

8. In the Brexit vote, sovereignty and migration were the two most salient issues for Leave voters, while the economy mattered most to Remain voters. In the US presidential elections, according to data from the Pew Research Center, terrorism, immigration, and trade ranked second, third, and ninth in terms of salience for Trump supporters. Meanwhile, the importance of immigration had increased significantly since the 2012 presidential election, rising from 47 per cent of Republicans believing it 'very important' to 77 per cent, and from 37 to 65 per cent among Democrats. http://www.people-press.org/2016/07/07/4-top-voting-issues-in-2016-election.

9. IMF World Economic Outlook (WEO), April 2016.

10. Interview by Alexander Betts during a visit in Nyarugusu refugee camp on 16 September 2009. Name of interviewee changed to safeguard anonymity.

11. UNHCR, 'UNHCR Chief Guterres Meets Refugees at Jordan's Azraq Camp', 3 May 2014, http://www.unhcr.org/news/latest/2014/5/5365368c9/unhcr-chief-guterres-meets-refugees-jordans-azraq-camp.html.

12. Alexander Betts visited Azraq in November 2015 on an official UNHCR visit. Name of interviewee anonymized.

13. James Scott, *Seeing Like a State: How Certain Schemes to Improve the Human Condition Have Failed* (New Haven, 1998: Yale University Press).

14. UNHCR, *UNHCR Policy on Refugee Protection and Solutions in Urban Areas* (Geneva, 2009: UNHCR).

15. Jeff Crisp and MaryBeth Morand, 'Better Late Than Never? The Evolution and Implementation of UNHCR's Urban Refugee Policy', seminar presentation, Refugee Studies Centre, Oxford, 6 May 2015.

16. Evan Easton-Calabria, 'From Bottom-Up to Top-Down: The "Pre-History" of Refugee Livelihoods Assistance from 1919 to 1979', *Journal of Refugee Studies*, 15 April 2015.

17. Despite having the same surname as Alex, Tristram Betts is completely unrelated.

18. For more details on ICARA I and II, see Alexander Betts, *Protection by Persuasion: International Cooperation in the Refugee Regime* (Ithaca, 2009: Cornell University Press).

19. For more details on CIREFCA, see Alexander Betts, ibid.

20. For an analysis of the role of business in relation to refugees, see, for example, Alexander Betts et al., *Refugee Economies: Forced*

Displacement and Development (Oxford, 2017: Oxford University Press), Chapter 9.

21. For analysis of the manipulation of refugee sending for foreign-policy purposes, see, for example, Kelly Greenhill, *Weapons of Mass Migration: Forced Displacement, Coercion, and Foreign Policy* (Ithaca, 2010: Cornell University Press).

22. See, for example, Will Jones and Alex Teytelboym, 'The Refugee Match', presentation at the CMS conference on 'Rethinking the Global Refugee System Protection', New York, 6 July 2016.

23. Hein de Haas, 'Turning the Tide? Why Development Will Not Stop Migration', *Development and Change*, 38/5 (2007): 819–41.

24. Most of the social-science literature on the determinants of irregular migration to Europe does not disaggregate refugees and migrants. See, for example, Katie Kuschminder, Julia De Bresser, and Melissa Siegel, 'Irregular Migration Routes to Europe and Factors Influencing Migrants' Destination Choices' (Maastricht, 2015: Maastricht Graduate School of Governance).

25. When Canada launched its plan to resettle 25,000 Syrian refugees in a matter of months in late 2015, over 100,000 text messages were sent to refugees in Lebanon and Jordan asking if they wanted to be resettled to Canada. 70 per cent of respondents said 'no', either because they wanted to remain close to Syria, because of narrow definitions of family, because of a desire to remain in a familiar cultural context, or due to a lack of information about conditions in Canada.

26. Swiss Forum for Migration, 'Movements of Somali Refugees and Asylum Seekers and States' Responses Thereto' (Neuchâtel, 2005: SFM).

27. This phenomenon is often referred to as 'chain migration'. For an overview of migration theories, see Douglas S. Massey et al., 'Theories of International Migration: A Review and Appraisal', *Population and Development Review*, 1993, 19/3: 431–66.

6. RETHINKING ASSISTANCE

1. Douglass C. North, *Institutions, Institutional Change and Economic Performance* (Cambridge, 1990: Cambridge University Press); Douglass C. North, 'The New Institutional Economics and Third World Development', in John Harriss, Janet Hunter, and Colin Lewis (eds.), *The New Institutional Economics and Third World Development* (London, 1995: Routledge), pp. 17–26.

2. Alexander Betts et al., *Refugee Economies: Forced Displacement and Development* (Oxford, 2017: Oxford University Press).

3. Betts et al., *Refugee Economies.*

4. See, for example, ILO, 'Impact of Syrian Refugees on the Labour Market', April 2015, http://www.ilo.org/beirut/publications/WCMS_364162/lang--en/index.htm.

5. Gordon Brown, 'The Syrian Refugee Crisis Calls for a New Marshall Plan', *Guardian*, 4 February 2016, https://www.theguardian.com/commentis-free/2016/feb/04/gordon-brown-syrian-refugee-crisis-marshall-plan.

6. Presentation by Wolfgang Müller, Managing Director of the Bundesagentur für Arbeit, St Anne's College, Oxford, 7 September 2016.

7. Joshua Hammer, *New York Review of Books*, LXIII/13 (August 2016): 58.

8. Richard Baldwin, *The Great Convergence: Information Technology and the New Globalization* (Cambridge, Mass., 2016: Harvard University Press).

9. See, for example, IRIN, 'Jordan Looks to Turn Refugee Crisis into Economic Boon', 21 March 2017, https://www.irinnews.org/feature/2017/03/21/jordan-looks-turn-refugee-crisis-economic-boon.

10. Dante Roscini, Eric Werker, and Han-koo Yeo, 'The Kaesong Industrial Complex (A)', Harvard Business School Case 710-022 (October 2009).

11. Charlie Thame, 'Ominous Signs for Migrant Workers in Thailand', *New Mandala*, 15 June 2014, http://www.newmandala.org/ominous-signs-for-migrant-workers-in-thailand.

12. The Baatan Refugee Camp, opened in 1980, to accommodate refugees from Vietnam, Laos and Cambodia, became the Bataan Technology Park in 2014, as part of the Morong Special Economic Zone, http://www.refugeecamps.net/BataanCamp.html.

7. RETHINKING POST-CONFLICT

1. See Paul Collier and M. Duponchel, 'The Economic Legacy of Civil War: Firm-Level Evidence from Sierra Leone', *Journal of Conflict Resolution*, 57/1 (2013), 65–88.

2. The World Bank, 'Syria's Economic Outlook – Spring 2016', http://www.worldbank.org/en/country/syria/publication/economic-outlook-spring-2016.

3. Government of Jordan 'white paper'. On file with authors.

4. BBC News, 'Jordan Minister: Syrian Refugees Stretching Economy', 10 August 2013, http://www.bbc.co.uk/news/world-middle-east-23631422.

5. Paul Collier and Anke Hoeffler, 'Aid, Policy and Growth in Post-Conflict Societies', *European Economic Review*, 48/5 (2004): 1125–45.

6. James Milner has highlighted the important and neglected relationship between refugees and peace-building. See James Milner, 'Refugees and the Peacebuilding Process', *New Issues in Refugee Research*, Working Paper No. 224 (Geneva, 2011: UNHCR). http://www.unhcr.org/research/working/4eb25c7f9/refugees-peacebuilding-process-james-milner.html.

7. Collier and Duponchel, 'Economic Legacy of Civil War'.

8. Alexander Betts and Will Jones, *Mobilising the Diaspora: How Refugees Challenge Authoritarianism* (Cambridge, 2016: Cambridge University Press), pp. 103–4

9. UNHCR, 'Slump Hurts Refugee Schools in Kurdistan Region of Iraq', 8 April 2016, http://www.unhcr.org/uk/news/latest/2016/4/57077c986/slump-hurts-refugee-schools-kurdistan-region-iraq.html.

10. The underlying figures from the census and the surveys are 3.6 per cent and 47 per cent. The figures in this section are from Daniel J. Clarke and Stefan Dercon, *Dull Disasters? How Planning Ahead Will Make a Difference* (Oxford, 2016: Oxford University Press).

11. The underlying figures are 13 per cent and 47 per cent.

12. The proportion of the highly educated in exodus declined over time, perhaps because so many had already left. The weak and changing data make estimation difficult, but the range is from a third to around a half of the entire stock of Syrian university graduates.

13. *New York Review of Books*, LXIII/13 (August 2016): 58.

14. Antonio Spilimbergo, 'Democracy and Foreign Education', *The American Economic Review*, 99/1 (2009): 528–43.

8. RETHINKING GOVERNANCE

1. *Guardian*, 'UN Agencies "Broke and Failing" in Face of Ever-Growing Refugee Crisis', 6 September 2015, https://www.theguardian.com/world/2015/sep/06/refugee-crisis-un-agencies-broke-failing.

2. Barbara Koremenos, Charles Lipson, and Duncan Snidal (eds.), *The Rational Design of International Institutions* (Cambridge, 2001: Cambridge University Press).

3. Martin Ruhs, *The Price of Rights: Regulating International Labor Migration* (Princeton, 2013: Princeton University Press).

4. See, for example, James Hathaway and R. Alexander Neve, 'Making International Refugee Law Relevant Again: A Proposal for Collectivized and Solution-Oriented Protection', *Harvard Human Rights Journal*, 10 (1997): 115–211, at p. 185; James Hathaway, 'Why Refugee Law

Still Matters', *Melbourne Journal of International Law*, 8/1 (2007): 89–103, at p. 101.

5. The five-year cut-off was originally proposed by James Hathaway.

6. The OECD and UNHCR have recently begun a collaboration to explore how alternative migration pathways, including work visas and family reunification, can complement existing solutions for refugees.

7. The penalties need to be token for two reasons: (i) if the penalties are high they will not be paid, which erodes compliance with other laws; (ii) if they are lowish but not clearly symbolic, they become misinterpreted as a price for an open choice and governments pay it.

8. See Steven Levitt and Stephen Dubner, *Freakanomics: A Rogue Economist Explores the Hidden Side of Everything* (New York, 2005: William Morrow).

9. Hathaway, 'Why Refugee Law Still Matters': 102.

10. Quoted in the *Financial Times*, 'EU Summit on Refugee Crisis Ends in Disarray', 19 February 2016, https://www.ft.com/content/93881f40-d725-11e5-829b-8564e7528e54.

11. Steve Krasner, *Sovereignty: Organized Hypocrisy* (Princeton, 1999: Princeton University Press).

12. Judith Kumin, 'Welcoming Engagement: How Private Sponsorship Can Strengthen Refugee Resettlement in the European Union' (Washington DC, 2015: MPI), http://www.migrationpolicy.org/research/welcoming-engagement-how-private-sponsorship-can-strengthen-refugee-resettlement-european.

13. See, for example, Alvin Roth, 'The Economics of Matching: Stability and Incentives', *Mathematics of Operations Research*, 7/4 (1982): 617–28.

14. Will Jones and Alex Teytelboym, 'Choice, Preferences and Priorities in a Matching System for Refugees', *Forced Migration Review*, 51 (2016): 80–82.

15. This is meant in the sense that it does not deliberately hire staff based on their political or economic training or expertise. For example, UNHCR employed its first professional economist in 2014.

16. Sergio Vieira de Mello went on to be UN High Commissioner for Human Rights; Leonardo Franco was Director of UNHCR's Division of International Protection; Kofi Annan became UN Secretary-General; Shashi Tharoor became UN Under-Secretary-General for Communications; Erika Feller became Assistant High Commissioner for Refugees; Irene Khan became Secretary-General of Amnesty International.

17. The Brookings–Bern Project was a collaboration between the Brookings Institute and the University of Bern that worked to develop 'soft law' Guiding Principles on Internal Displacement between 1994 and 1998. The Nansen Initiative was led by the governments of Norway and Switzerland and ran between 2012 and 2015 in order to engage in regional consultations and develop recommendations on the governance of disaster-induced displacement.

18. At the time of writing, the Global Compacts process is work in progress. The Refugee Compact will be led by UNHCR and is structured around a so-called Comprehensive Refugee Response Framework (CRRF). The framework aims to mobilize states, private actors, and civil society commitments to enhance operational responses in particular refugee situations. The Migration Compact negotiations will be led by Mexico and Switzerland, in collaboration with a number of UN agencies, and is likely to seek consensus around a number of ambiguous areas of global migration governance. The overall process may well offer a chance to advance a new business model for refugee and migration governance. But to achieve this the Compacts process will need to be transformative and go beyond mere ratification of the status quo.

9. BACK TO THE FUTURE

1. See Daniel J. Clarke and Stefan Dercon, *Dull Disasters? How Planning Ahead Will Make a Difference* (Oxford, 2016: Oxford University Press), for a general proposal on disaster insurance.

2. *Financial Times*, 'Dozens Killed in Ethiopia during Anti-Government Protests', 3 October 2016, https://www.ft.com/content/96e9600c-88b1-11e6-8cb7-e7ada1d123b1.

Index

ALLEN LANE
an imprint of
PENGUIN BOOKS

Also Published

Richard Vinen, *The Long '68: Radical Protest and Its Enemies*

Kishore Mahbubani, *Has the West Lost It?: A Provocation*

John Lewis Gaddis, *On Grand Strategy*

Richard Overy, *The Birth of the RAF, 1918: The World's First Air Force*

Francis Pryor, *Paths to the Past: Encounters with Britain's Hidden Landscapes*

Helen Castor, *Elizabeth I: A Study in Insecurity*

Ken Robinson and Lou Aronica, *You, Your Child and School*

Leonard Mlodinow, *Elastic: Flexible Thinking in a Constantly Changing World*

Nick Chater, *The Mind is Flat: The Illusion of Mental Depth and The Improvised Mind*

Michio Kaku, *The Future of Humanity: Terraforming Mars, Interstellar Travel, Immortality, and Our Destiny Beyond*

Thomas Asbridge, *Richard I: The Crusader King*

Richard Sennett, *Building and Dwelling: Ethics for the City*

Nassim Nicholas Taleb, *Skin in the Game: Hidden Asymmetries in Daily Life*

Steven Pinker, *Enlightenment Now: The Case for Reason, Science, Humanism and Progress*

Steve Coll, *Directorate S: The C.I.A. and America's Secret Wars in Afghanistan, 2001 - 2006*

Jordan B. Peterson, *12 Rules for Life: An Antidote to Chaos*

Bruno Maçães, *The Dawn of Eurasia: On the Trail of the New World Order*

Brock Bastian, *The Other Side of Happiness: Embracing a More Fearless Approach to Living*

Ryan Lavelle, *Cnut: The North Sea King*

Tim Blanning, *George I: The Lucky King*

Thomas Cogswell, *James I: The Phoenix King*

Pete Souza, *Obama, An Intimate Portrait: The Historic Presidency in Photographs*

Robert Dallek, *Franklin D. Roosevelt: A Political Life*

Norman Davies, *Beneath Another Sky: A Global Journey into History*

Ian Black, *Enemies and Neighbours: Arabs and Jews in Palestine and Israel, 1917-2017*

Martin Goodman, *A History of Judaism*

Shami Chakrabarti, *Of Women: In the 21st Century*

Stephen Kotkin, *Stalin, Vol. II: Waiting for Hitler, 1928-1941*

Lindsey Fitzharris, *The Butchering Art: Joseph Lister's Quest to Transform the Grisly World of Victorian Medicine*

Serhii Plokhy, *Lost Kingdom: A History of Russian Nationalism from Ivan the Great to Vladimir Putin*

Mark Mazower, *What You Did Not Tell: A Russian Past and the Journey Home*

Lawrence Freedman, *The Future of War: A History*

Niall Ferguson, *The Square and the Tower: Networks, Hierarchies and the Struggle for Global Power*

Matthew Walker, *Why We Sleep: The New Science of Sleep and Dreams*

Edward O. Wilson, *The Origins of Creativity*

John Bradshaw, *The Animals Among Us: The New Science of Anthropology*

David Cannadine, *Victorious Century: The United Kingdom, 1800-1906*

Leonard Susskind and Art Friedman, *Special Relativity and Classical Field Theory*

Maria Alyokhina, *Riot Days*

Oona A. Hathaway and Scott J. Shapiro, *The Internationalists: And Their Plan to Outlaw War*

Chris Renwick, *Bread for All: The Origins of the Welfare State*

Anne Applebaum, *Red Famine: Stalin's War on Ukraine*

Richard McGregor, *Asia's Reckoning: The Struggle for Global Dominance*

Chris Kraus, *After Kathy Acker: A Biography*

Clair Wills, *Lovers and Strangers: An Immigrant History of Post-War Britain*

Odd Arne Westad, *The Cold War: A World History*

Max Tegmark, *Life 3.0: Being Human in the Age of Artificial Intelligence*

Jonathan Losos, *Improbable Destinies: How Predictable is Evolution?*

Chris D. Thomas, *Inheritors of the Earth: How Nature Is Thriving in an Age of Extinction*

Chris Patten, *First Confession: A Sort of Memoir*

James Delbourgo, *Collecting the World: The Life and Curiosity of Hans Sloane*

Naomi Klein, *No Is Not Enough: Defeating the New Shock Politics*

Ulrich Raulff, *Farewell to the Horse: The Final Century of Our Relationship*

Slavoj Žižek, *The Courage of Hopelessness: Chronicles of a Year of Acting Dangerously*

Patricia Lockwood, *Priestdaddy: A Memoir*

Ian Johnson, *The Souls of China: The Return of Religion After Mao*

Stephen Alford, *London's Triumph: Merchant Adventurers and the Tudor City*

Hugo Mercier and Dan Sperber, *The Enigma of Reason: A New Theory of Human Understanding*

Stuart Hall, *Familiar Stranger: A Life Between Two Islands*

Allen Ginsberg, *The Best Minds of My Generation: A Literary History of the Beats*

Sayeeda Warsi, *The Enemy Within: A Tale of Muslim Britain*

Alexander Betts and Paul Collier, *Refuge: Transforming a Broken Refugee System*

Robert Bickers, *Out of China: How the Chinese Ended the Era of Western Domination*

Erica Benner, *Be Like the Fox: Machiavelli's Lifelong Quest for Freedom*

William D. Cohan, *Why Wall Street Matters*

David Horspool, *Oliver Cromwell: The Protector*

Daniel C. Dennett, *From Bacteria to Bach and Back: The Evolution of Minds*

Derek Thompson, *Hit Makers: How Things Become Popular*

Harriet Harman, *A Woman's Work*

Wendell Berry, *The World-Ending Fire: The Essential Wendell Berry*

Daniel Levin, *Nothing but a Circus: Misadventures among the Powerful*

Stephen Church, *Henry III: A Simple and God-Fearing King*

Pankaj Mishra, *Age of Anger: A History of the Present*

Graeme Wood, *The Way of the Strangers: Encounters with the Islamic State*

Michael Lewis, *The Undoing Project: A Friendship that Changed the World*

John Romer, *A History of Ancient Egypt, Volume 2: From the Great Pyramid to the Fall of the Middle Kingdom*

Andy King, *Edward I: A New King Arthur?*

Thomas L. Friedman, *Thank You for Being Late: An Optimist's Guide to Thriving in the Age of Accelerations*

John Edwards, *Mary I: The Daughter of Time*

Grayson Perry, *The Descent of Man*

Deyan Sudjic, *The Language of Cities*

Norman Ohler, *Blitzed: Drugs in Nazi Germany*

Carlo Rovelli, *Reality Is Not What It Seems: The Journey to Quantum Gravity*

Catherine Merridale, *Lenin on the Train*

Susan Greenfield, *A Day in the Life of the Brain: The Neuroscience of Consciousness from Dawn Till Dusk*

Christopher Given-Wilson, *Edward II: The Terrors of Kingship*

Emma Jane Kirby, *The Optician of Lampedusa*

Minoo Dinshaw, *Outlandish Knight: The Byzantine Life of Steven Runciman*

Candice Millard, *Hero of the Empire: The Making of Winston Churchill*